Diane;

Many thanks
for your support.
Best of luck to you
on your reading edge

Ron

Praise for
MANAGING AT THE LEADING EDGE

"Dr. Rose's new book, *Managing at the Leading Edge*, is an astute blueprint for any business leader keenly focused on transformational strategic leadership. The book is exceptionally well researched and insightfully instructive. From the beginning chapter, *Navigating,* to the concluding chapter, *Perseverance,* the chronology of the book was perfectly structured. In a business world that is increasingly complex and globally connected, the ability for leaders to operate with a heightened sense of strategic focus is essential. Dr. Rose's cogent analysis of strategic leadership is profoundly captured in this book."

—Sean N. Woodroffe, Senior Vice President and Chief People Officer, National Life Group

"Tom presents a thoughtful and well organized primer on how business leaders can successfully drive innovation and manage disruptive change. The challenges he discusses will be familiar to anyone in business, and the solutions he describes will be welcome insights to all of us who are seeking to improve our leadership."

—Ken McCullum, Vice President and Chief Actuary, Corporate Actuarial, The Principal Financial Group

"Today's business environment is one of constant change and headwinds within an increasingly competitive landscape. Tom Rose provides the map that modern leaders need to navigate successful outcomes for their organizations. Tom's book provides sage advice for new and experienced executives alike. His book is a timely reminder of the importance of ensuring that we strike the right balance between strategic thinking and the ability of senior leaders to effectively execute the desired strategy in a way that engages and empowers their teams. Tom has developed a leadership model for our times."

—Joanne Taylor, Executive General Manager Human Resources, Caltex Australia Petroleum PTY Ltd.

"Tom Rose's book quite rightly highlights how leadership performance can be fully optimized, specifically exploring how leaders should navigate and pilot their organization toward a culture of employee engagement, customer service orientation, and higher profitability. Not only does Tom guide the reader on what specific steps to take toward superior leadership, he offers specific and very actionable best practices in that regard. *Managing At The Leading Edge* is a really great read for both leadership and employees."

—Kevin Sheridan, internationally-recognized keynote speaker, *New York Times* bestselling author, and an authoritative voice on the topic of employee engagement

"Tom's new book describes leadership in nautical terms, as navigating, piloting, and managing the leading edge of the sail. The analogy fits. It parallels the highly dynamic environment where businesses compete today. And it's anchored in solid research and years of experience. Most importantly, it yields a wealth of tools, templates, and resources that readers can put to immediate use. This book is a keeper."

—David Maxfield, coauthor of three immediate *New York Times* bestsellers, *Crucial Accountability*, *Influencer*, and *Change Anything*

"Successful leaders drive business change by creating focus and driving agile responses to the challenges encountered in implementing strategic change. Today's highly rapidly evolving business context—both within and outside organizations—require leaders adopt what Rose describes as new ways of thinking and doing. *Managing at the Leading Edge* provides a new model for how two key leadership functions work together to drive results. It also provides tools and resources that leaders can use to implement successful change in the highly dynamic environments within which today's leaders make a difference. I recommend *Managing at the Leading Edge* as resource leaders can use to drive enduring business change."

—David House, Retired Group President of American Express

MANAGING AT THE LEADING EDGE

NAVIGATING AND PILOTING BUSINESS STRATEGY AT CRITICAL MOMENTS

TOM ROSE PhD

New York Chicago San Francisco Athens London Madrid
Mexico City Milan New Delhi Singapore Sydney Toronto

Copyright © 2017 by Tom Rose. All rights reserved. Printed in the United States of America. Except as permitted under the United States Copyright Act of 1976, no part of this publication may be reproduced or distributed in any form or by any means, or stored in a database or retrieval system, without the prior written permission of the publisher.

1 2 3 4 5 6 7 8 9   QFR   22 21 20 19 18 17

ISBN   978-1-259-86304-2
MHID   1-259-86304-2

e-ISBN   978-1-259-86305-9
e-MHID   1-259-86305-0

McGraw-Hill Education books are available at special quantity discounts to use as premiums and sales promotions or for use in corporate training programs. To contact a representative, please visit the Contact Us pages at www.mhprofessional.com.

*For my family . . . Fern, Max and Rebecca . . .
inspiration and reminder . . .
both the journey and the destination matter.*

Contents

ACKNOWLEDGMENTS   VII

INTRODUCTION   1

  1 NAVIGATING   15

  2 PILOTING   39

  3 WORKING AT THE LEADING EDGE: CONCEPTUAL AND ORGANIZATION SKILLS   69

  4 POINTS AT THE LEADING EDGE   91

  5 ACHIEVING CRITICAL SYNCHRONICITY   105

  6 CHANGE BLINDNESS   121

  7 THE RECOGNITION STAGE   143

  8 IMPORTANT MOMENTS IN CRITICAL REFLECTION   155

  9 COMMITMENT TO INITIATE   183

  10 PERSEVERANCE   211

NOTES   227

BIBLIOGRAPHY   233

INDEX   237

Acknowledgments

Publishing a book is a big task and requires the help and assistance of many people. I would like to take this opportunity to express my gratitude for their support.

I would first like to acknowledge and thank my family for inspiring and supporting me throughout the process of converting the idea for this book into the reality of the pages that follow. My wife, Fern, was a consistent source of support throughout the process. A person of insight and imagination, Fern helped me retain my focus on "true north" and stay the course. Her affirmations helped me plough through uncertain moments. I am grateful to my life's partner.

I would also like to thank my son, Max, for being a source of inspiration. His passionate commitment to his craft inspired me to do the same with this project. Max approaches musical innovation as problem solving. He experiments with persistence until he breaks through. Max also works in the wine industry. He understands the process through which the physical realities of vine, earth, rain, and time combine with the winemaker's art to produce something of quality.

My daughter, Becca, is a model of calm, organization, and humor under pressure. In her personal and professional lives, she uses her organizational skills, tenacity, and conscientiousness to turn jumbles of confusion into finished products of quality. Her example reminded me to keep going when things got difficult and to keep steady.

Ken Lizotte is my agent. A person of great experience, Ken shepherded me through the process of completing this book with a wise, encouraging, and steady hand. Ken Lizotte and Elena Petricone provided invaluable editing advice. Thanks also to Donya Dickerson of McGraw-Hill for her enthusiasm and encouragement.

I would also like to thank Graham Wright. Graham helped me with the statistical analysis of the research that is an indispensible foundation of this book. He was a valuable thought partner in the analysis of the data that is highlighted in the following pages.

My colleagues at AchieveForum were also very helpful. Russ Becker, president of AchieveForum, supported the administration of the survey research and sponsored the book within the company. I am grateful to Russ, Brian Hawthorne, and Mike Worth and their enthusiasm for using evidence-based insights to make companies and leaders better.

Karl Sparre, Ken McCullum, Julia Holloway, and Cathryn Klassen generously offered their feedback on early versions of the manuscript. These leaders model many of the behaviors described in this book. I am grateful for their help.

I would also like to thank the many other leaders with whom I have had the pleasure of working. These colleagues created moments of excellence from which I learned. My goal was to integrate the behavioral science of leadership with their examples into a blueprint for each of us, as individual leaders and members of teams, to utilize as an effective tool to achieve results that matter *and* have more fun doing it.

Introduction

> *Wind and waves are always on the*
> *side of the ablest navigator.*
> —Edmund Gibbon

We live in an exciting time of great change and opportunity. Technology, globalization, and demographic shifts provide new potential for personal and business success. Yet, research tells that only 30 percent of our attempts to implement change succeed amid the turbulence we encounter both within and outside today's organizations. We need new ways of thinking and doing if we are to turn unrealized potential reflected in the statistics we cited into performance. *We find inspiration for a new way of thinking and doing in an unusual place.*

Let us imagine that you are a ship's captain in the 1700s. Between you and the riches of discovery and trade lies a vast and dangerous ocean. You must make your way through changing currents and shifting winds, calm seas, and violent storms. To navigate successfully you must repeatedly and reliably plot your position against two directions: north-south and east-west. In other words, an accurate assessment of your latitude and longitude is required to merely stay on course.

Figuring out your latitude is easy. You use the stars. Polaris, better known as the North Star, is very close to true north and relatively stable in the night sky. By measuring the observed angle of your position to Polaris, you can easily determine your latitude. However, to establish your precise location, you also need to know how far east or west you are.

Determining longitude back in the eighteenth century was not so easy. Back then, sailors calculated longitude by using the moon's position in the night sky. By painstakingly measuring the angular distance between the moon and a star and then comparing this measurement to a book of lunar tables, sailors did their best to estimate accurately their longitude.

Unfortunately, this method was not as easy as it might sound, and so the result was often disastrous.

We can grasp a picture of how costly and even tragic the lack of reliable navigation methods could be in the story of the ship *Centurion* as described in the book *Longitude* by Dava Sobel. Under the command of Commodore George Anson, the *Centurion* set out from England for the South Pacific in 1740 with a crew of 400. Rounding treacherous Cape Horn in March of 1741, a severe storm blowing from the west assailed the *Centurion*. This storm punished the ship and its crew for 58 days.

By the time the storm had finally broken, the majority of the crew was suffering from scurvy, a disease that typically impacted marine voyages in those times. Drastic deficiency in vitamin C led to multiple symptoms including fatigue, open wounds, fever, neuropathy, and even death (from bleeding). Time lost to the storm had therefore proven deadly for the crew of the *Centurion*.

Commodore Anson knew he must find his way quickly to the closest source of food and water, Juan Fernandez Island. After sailing north for several days, the *Centurion* finally achieved the latitude of Juan Fernandez Island, but that now left Anson to figure out its longitude. In other words, should he turn left or right, head east or west? Using navigation aids on hand, Anson made the decision to turn west.

After four days at sea, Anson began to question his decision. Before long, his conviction weakened and he turned back toward the east. Two days later the crew sighted land!

Unfortunately this land was not Juan Fernandez Island but the barren, mountainous coast of Chile. Dismayed, Anson realized he had been within hours of his original island destination back when he made the fateful decision to turn around and reverse course toward the east. So now he corrected his course again, heading once more west where, after two more weeks of zigging and zagging, he could finally drop anchor at Juan Fernandez Island. In the course of all this, sadly, a sizable number of his crew had died.

Approximately 200 years ago when Nathaniel Bowditch, a shipping clerk in colonial Salem, Massachusetts, noticed the pattern of terrible losses of life and property at sea of the kind experienced by Anson. Bowditch set out to make things better, developing a new set of practices and tools that are still in use today: The American Practical Navigator.

Our current moment in history is an exciting one for leaders at any level. Epic shifts in the business global environment challenge leaders to set direction, build teams, and motivate people in more creative, efficient, and agile ways, much more so than has been needed in the past. To meet this challenge and avoid Anson's fate we must skillfully use navigational aids that meet the demands of the new business environment with confidence and discipline. From analyzing what those who are successfully meeting this challenge do, we have built these tools and describe them in this book.

- What are these aids and tools?
- What are the leadership skills needed to use them successfully?
- How do we build mastery of these capabilities?

These are the questions we address in this book. But first, let's begin with a story that describes the kind of navigational challenges we face today.

THEY CALL ME RAMBO!

A large healthcare provider wanted to expand service offerings to secure an advantage in an increasingly competitive market. But to afford this expansion, the executive team recognized that they would need to develop cost savings to generate the resources needed to invest in the newer services. Market data also told them that they had to simultaneously increase the quality of the services they already offered to achieve their growth goals. Shift investment priorities and strengthen quality at the same. Not an easy thing to do!

So the executive team commissioned a project to implement the needed changes. Later, with only weeks to go on the timeline, millions of dollars in costs still needed to be cut from the operating budget. The overall project was in danger of failing its first critical milestone.

To prevent this, Eric, a consultant with a reputation for energy and tenacity, was brought in to spearhead the project. With a kind of single-minded devotion that he had become known for, Eric began pushing his consulting team and client managers to uncover the remaining cost cuts, any way they could.

What Eric did not know, however, was that the goal of expanding services and implementing the required cost cutting represented highly charged political issues. In fact, these issues swirled at the center of contention around the organization's strategic direction, culture, and very future. The VP of Finance, for example, a veteran of previous political scuffles, had agreed to oversee the project as a favor to the organization's president despite the reservations he had about the project. Despite the VP of Finance's reservations, the president asked him to oversee the project. Over time, this VP began slowing the project work in order to create time for the organization's leadership to sort out their differences and build needed alignments in regard to the company's direction.

But the VP did not communicate his slowdown plans to Eric! So Eric came to the "logical" conclusion that the VP was harming the project by not holding teams accountable for performance goals and timelines. A person of conviction, Eric decided to directly resolve the situation by confronting the VP. During a one-on-one meeting, he bluntly laid out the problem. "As the chairman of the steering committee overseeing this project, you are not doing all you can to keep the project on track. You have to hold people to their obligations to the project. It's your responsibility as its leader."

Eric and the VP then exchanged a few "intense" words and the meeting ended. One week later Eric was shocked to learn that he had been fired from the project. The VP of finance had been infuriated that Eric would confront him this way and demanded that the president remove him. "We don't want 'Rambo' working here anymore."

The VP invoked the image of the fictional movie character of Rambo played by Sylvester Stallone to critique Eric's approach. In four movies Rambo comes in from the margin of society to restore justice as a one-man wrecking ball of special-forces combat skill. In using the image of Rambo, the VP sent the message that Eric's approach was creating too much collateral damage in frustrated people and strained relationships.

The expansion project went on without "Rambo," but in the end it only achieved a few of the outcomes that had initially inspired it. The leaders involved did not effectively work through the navigational issues it encountered.

All too many of us in business, and the nonprofit sector too, have found ourselves in Eric's shoes, tasked with keeping an important project on track while blind to the forces at play behind the scenes and/or all around us. Likewise, we've at times had to fill the VP's shoes as well, accountable for an initiative that is well intentioned yet lacks critical alignments among stakeholders.

This book focuses on addressing such challenges. Turning a strategic priority into concrete results is hard and tricky work. The moment that any of us begin implementing a change in what people are doing or how they do it, the dynamics of the situation we face push and pull at our understanding of the problem, the solutions we see as feasible, and the progress we make in achieving goals. Meetings often do not produce the hoped-for outcomes, colleagues resist plans, and solutions lose much of their potential to make things better.

Research sheds insight into the scope of this challenge. In 2010, researchers Davis, Frechette, and Boswell of Forum Corporation scanned results of large-scale strategic initiatives across several decades, finding that about 70 percent of organizations report abandoning strategic initiatives because of problems encountered during execution that could not be resolved.[1] More recently, McKinsey in a 2015 study observed that this pattern continues to persist.[2] Based on these studies and others (see Table I.1), we need a new way of thinking and doing to implement business change successfully.

While we must solve the problem of transforming strategic goals into results, we must also simultaneously meet the new challenges of today's business environment. A majority of executives anticipate disruptive changes in their marketplace—85 percent according to one study by Innosight in 2014.[3] In this study, executives report worrying that their leadership teams will be unable to meet this challenge. Industry reports from prominent consulting firms point to similar confidence gaps. In 2010, for example, Lepsinger found that 64 percent of executives worried that "execution gaps" standing in the way of achieving strategic goals will not be closed.[4] More recently, PwC.com likewise reported that upward of 70 percent of leaders fret that their organizational leaders fail to possess capabilities required to successfully drive initiatives designed to implement their most critical strategies.[5]

These worrisome statistics suggest we need to approach our strategic challenges differently. Not long ago, business commentators observed that the business environment within which we compete, serve customers, and innovate was changing radically. No longer paddling peacefully down a quiet stream with occasional turbulence, we now faced "permanent white water." And to stay with this kayaking theme, the environment has become more dynamic. We might say that yesterday's "Class 3 white water," medium waves with occasional hazards, seems to have upgraded itself to a Class 5, defined as "large waves, big hazards, continuous rapids."

Prescription? See our leadership task as maneuvering business change through and around obstacles in highly dynamic environments with agility. Precise maneuvering required!

In our work, we have encountered leaders that have shown the capability to lead change in today's business environment, and we have discovered a pattern that outlines how they manage to do it. These high-performing leaders implement certain practices and engage in certain behaviors that make a big difference. The patterns we discovered reflect special ways of thinking and doing that unlock unrecognized and untapped potential, and then convert this potential into effective action. To make it easy to understand and remember, and to apply these insights, we, of course, need a new leadership model.

OUR NAUTICAL MODEL

Models help us see things we tend to miss and recall and apply new ideas for how to achieve greater success. They simplify a critical activity we are trying to understand and incorporate mental images that help us focus on taking the best action for the circumstance we face. Here are a few leadership models currently in use today:

- **Leader as Coach.** Leaders expand individual skills and knowledge and help others solve problems like coaches on athletic teams.
- **Leader as Ambassador.** Leaders operate as emissaries that shape consensus among stakeholders from different disciplines or functions to create alignment and implement integrated plans.
- **Leader as Conductor.** Leaders function as conductors with visions of how to bring musical scores to life—outlining how the performances should look like (or *sound* like) and shaping what teams (sections of like instruments) each person (individual musician) needs to do to achieve the overall vision.
- **Leader as Transmission Belt.** Leaders convert strategy into action the way transmission belts convert the power of engines into forward movement of a vehicle's wheels.
- **Leader as Commander.** Leaders exercise command and control like military officers to ensure full execution of plans with the appropriate of amount of adapting, improvising, and overcoming obstacles.

The best of these models draw upon images from different areas of human performance, such as athletics, international relations, performing arts, or the military. These models help us frame problems in ways that help us see new options for action and identify what we can do differently to achieve a better result.

My colleagues and I have chosen a model different from these. We chose a performance environment that parallels what leaders encounter when achieving high performance in today's dynamic business environment. Several forces push and pull at people striving to achieve a goal that lies beyond their sight. Amid such challenges, hazards imperil the implementation of the plan and these must be negotiated with vigilance and agility. People must perform different but complementary functions in an integrated way and work *as one* if they are to prevail over daunting obstacles on their way to achieving their objective.

Our model builds on Bowditch's work we described earlier, featuring three powerful interconnected images from the world of high-performance nautical leadership: navigating, piloting, and what we call the leading edge and shows how to contribute one's success as a leader tasked with making successful business change. Let's take them one at a time:

1. **Navigating.** Many have invoked the idea of navigation to highlight what leaders do:
    - "What is our destination?"
    - "What's the plan for getting there?"
    - "How do we know where we are relative to our goal, and what reference points do we use to plot the most favorable path to our desired destination?"

    These are the questions skillful navigators keep top of mind and answer as they lead the way to the intended destination.

    But able navigation does not account for all of leadership effectiveness. A critical function of nautical leadership involves getting a vessel through the many hazards and time-compressed environment of the coastline passage, a very unique and important set of capabilities. Mariners use the "piloting" function in these situations This means making decisions with detailed knowledge of underwater obstacles, and the unique dynamics of tides, currents, and winds supported by acute situational awareness to achieve the final destination. Navigation brings the vessel to the coastline; piloting achieves the final destination.

2. **Piloting.** This function uses answers to these questions to achieve the final destination:
   - "What are the special dynamics of this coastline environment that we need to manage?"
   - "What are the hazards lurking below and around me, and how do we best negotiate them?"
   - "How do we deal with shifting tides and currents on the way to our final destination?"
   - "How do we maintain the vigilance on these challenges to ensure we make good decisions within tight time pressure?"

   The importance of piloting is underscored by two facts, one from the world of nautical leadership and the other from business. First, most nautical accidents occur within sight of the coastline. Second, analysis of failed strategic initiatives reveals that they are only declared failures *late in* the project implementation timeline. Skillful performance of the piloting function has an impactful and vital, though largely unrecognized, influence on successful initiatives. A key feature of our model is the attention it calls to how important it is that navigating and piloting functions work *together* to manage the business equivalent of the coastline passage.

3. **The leading edge.** A sail's or propeller's "leading edge" refers to its line of contact with the environment. Along the leading edge, a sail's job is to convert the push and pull of wind into forward thrust. Expert management of the position of the leading edge optimizes the forces in opposition to, and working with, the established direction. Sometimes the course zigs and zags and sometimes it is a straight line. Adjustments in the position of the leading edge optimize its ability to create momentum.

   In the context of business, our research points to the importance of successfully engaging the resistance of others (resistance showing itself as the most common response to change) at critical moments in driving business change. The leading edge focuses on how we convert the resistance we encounter from the people with whom we work into progress and forward momentum.

   We use these models to breakthrough the limitations in the ways we see and do leadership that scuttle the majority of initiatives we undertake. The approach we develop focuses our attention on the leadership functions that must be coordinated and performed well in achieving and maintaining direction and agile negotiation of the challenges that occur along the way.

Earlier we told the story of the VP of Finance versus Eric. If the VP had had a better sense of his destination, had he found a more efficient way to engage his colleagues and manage the leading edge with greater dexterity, he could have created greater value for his organization. As for Eric, he saw the way from "here to there" only as a straight line. He was not on the lookout for changing terrain below the surface—the unseen currents of resistance that had to be negotiated. Had the VP or Eric viewed his mission through the lens of our nautical model, each might have enjoyed a better outcome.

Beyond the skill of each leader in this situation, the system of leadership through which the contribution of both leaders was synchronized did not succeed. The leadership functions of navigating and piloting were not well coordinated. Interestingly, many of our clients have indicated to us that their organizations are frozen in the middle. Strategic priorities and initiatives get stuck at the cog and wheel connection between senior and middle-level leadership functions and here work loses traction. Our research indicates that success depends on each of us performing our function well and engaging others in the complementary function to make the whole work better than our individual parts. As we will illustrate in subsequent chapters, there are many ways to do this poorly and a few ways to do this well. Our task in this book is to show how navigation and piloting are best implemented at critical moments along the leading edge in a way that both gratifies and produces results.

The tragic tale of Commodore Anson and the *Centurion* that opened this Introduction shows how the lack of effective navigation and piloting, not at all unusual in that bygone era, led to the loss of too many lives, ships, and cargoes. Navigating and piloting the open ocean was a dangerous business in those times and luck seemed to play a bigger role than skill. Similarly, today, maneuvering important priorities through the dynamics of today's business environment often ends in far less success than we hoped—not in lives lost, thankfully, but in business outcomes that fail despite aspirations and plans that seemed right in the beginning and often most of the way along the journey.

But with proper navigation and piloting, such failures can be prevented and the chances for success enhanced. The purpose of this book is to teach business leaders how to avoid unwelcome scenarios by using easy-to-learn and easy-to-apply principles from high-performance seamanship so we prevail over the conditions that thrwart the mission-critical business change with which we are tasked.

OUR ANCHOR RESEARCH

This book is "anchored" in advice generated by a research study that we conducted in 2016. The study surveyed 1,200 middle- and senior level leaders on business performance, leadership practices, and leadership behavior, as well as key features of their work environments.

- We asked about 42 organizational practices associated with innovation, how people in organizations learn, customer focus, and patterns of consistent revenue and profit performance.
- Respondents rated over 40 business critical tasks that senior leaders and mid-level leaders perform in leading strategic initiatives and indicated how consistently their businesses had achieved revenue and profit goals, an important measure of organizational high performance.
- Finally, we asked respondents to identify how often 40 leadership behaviors occurred, and then related these results to ratings of leader effectiveness.

We also integrated insights from approximately 100 interviews of senior and middle-level leaders. The insights from these interviews not only shaped the advice presented in this book, they inspired the stories we use to illustrate the principles outlined in this book.

Our analysis of these data uncovered *patterns* of leadership behavior that reinforce our nautical model of high-performance leadership and illustrate how it can be enacted in the business world. We also outline tools that help take needed actions to achieve results in the evolving business environments within which we strive to make a difference that matters. The result is a blueprint for success that individual leaders and organizations can learn, adopt, employ, and enjoy (Figures I.1 and I.2).

THE OUTLINE OF THE BOOK

This book begins by looking at the leadership functions of navigating and piloting. We review the high-performance practices associated with these functions and the leadership skills through which they are enacted. We next introduce the concept of the leading edge. The book addresses the points along the leading edge through which resistance is developed into momentum. We then look at how the three functions of navigating, piloting, and management of the leading edge are synchronized within a system of high-performance leadership. The positive impact of a culture of customer-focused innovation on the optimal performance of the leadership system is also reviewed. In the final chapters each point along the leading edge is reviewed. The dynamics of change blindness, recognition, critical reflection, commitment, and perseverance are described, and the strategies we can use to address these dynamics are presented.

FIGURE I.1 Leadership by Design: System Focused by Purpose

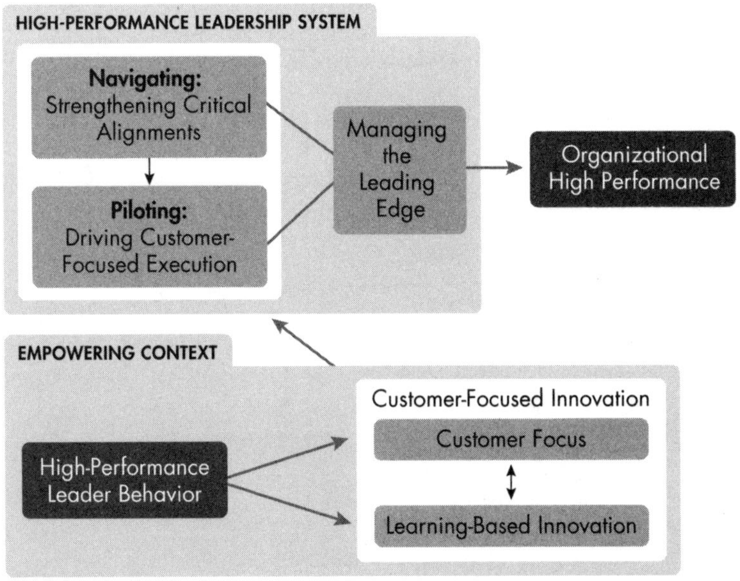

HIGH-PERFORMANCE LEADERSHIP SYSTEM

- **Navigating:** Strengthening Critical Alignments
- **Piloting:** Driving Customer-Focused Execution
- Managing the Leading Edge
- Organizational High Performance

EMPOWERING CONTEXT

- High-Performance Leader Behavior
- Customer-Focused Innovation
  - Customer Focus
  - Learning-Based Innovation

TABLE I.1 Recent Insights On Challenges Leaders Must Overcome In Implementing Strategic Change

Senior Leaders	• 42% of projects are well-aligned to organizational strategy • 53% of organizations react too slowly to environmental shifts or react quickly without aligning with strategy • 50% of strategic initiatives get the needed level of senior leader support • 60% percent of leaders see that initiatives struggle because of senior • leader coordination problems
Leadership System	• 80% of organizations lack effective system for implementing strategic change • 66% of leaders believe it is better to play it safe than striving for stretch goals • Minority of leaders are clear about their responsibilities in implementation of strategic initiatives • 50% of leaders struggle with accountability
Midlevel Leaders	• A minority of midlevel leaders consistently anticipate and avoid problems or resolve conflicts quickly and well (less than one third) • Majority of midlevel leaders resolve issues only after a significant delay (37%), try but fail to resolve them • 28% of field and line employees have information they need to make good bottom line decisions • 30% of midlevel leaders promote the adaptability needed to implement strategic initiatives

Sull, Homkes & Sull, 2015; Huy, Q., 2017; Economist - Intelligence Unit, 2013; Overfield, D. & Kaiser, R., 2012.

FIGURE I.2 Tailoring a Leadership System to Organization's Pursuit of High Performance

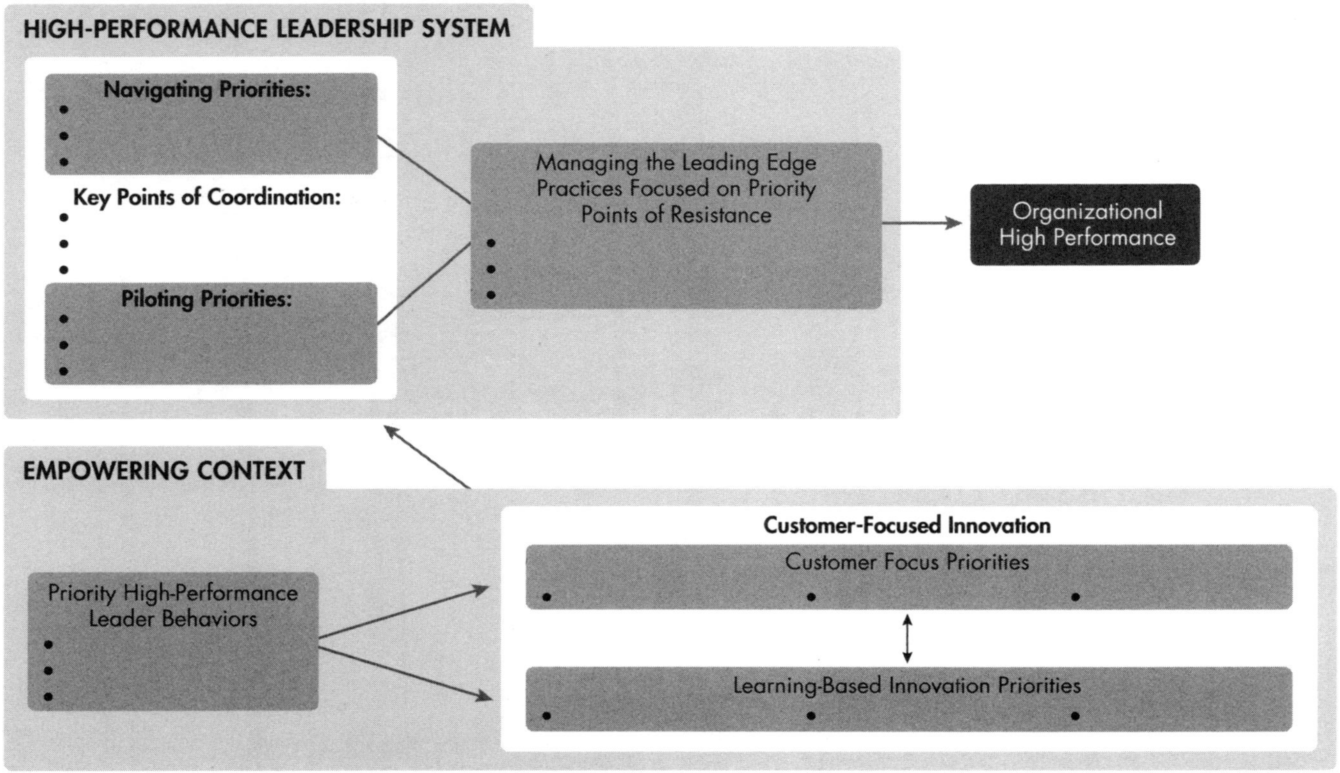

HIGH-PERFORMANCE LEADERSHIP SYSTEM

- Navigating Priorities:
  - • • •
- Key Points of Coordination:
  - • • • •
- Piloting Priorities:
  - • • • •

Managing the Leading Edge Practices Focused on Priority Points of Resistance
• • •

→ Organizational High Performance

EMPOWERING CONTEXT

Priority High-Performance Leader Behaviors
• • •

Customer-Focused Innovation

Customer Focus Priorities
• • •

↔

Learning-Based Innovation Priorities
• • •

Chapter 1

Navigating

*We cannot discover new oceans unless we have
the courage to lose sight of the shore.*
—ANDRE GIDE

Leaders inspire, focus, and enable people and teams to perform in ways that produce results that matter. Today's leaders must do so in a dynamic even turbulent context. Leaders who achieve meaningful outcomes in this environment constantly sense changes in their context and take action that successfully negotiates the challenges they encounter. This agile detect-and-act capability is performed through functions of organizational navigation and piloting.

In this chapter we turn to navigating, one of the two critical direction and decision-making functions leaders play. We will look at high-performance piloting, the other key leadership function, in the next chapter.

The challenge of navigating is dramatically captured by a single image displayed by the National Maritime Museum in Greenwich, England. Visitors to the museum are greeted by an image of the open ocean. You see a featureless expanse of water and, off in the distance, you see the line of a distant horizon. The image reinforces the aspiration, imagination, courage, and focus that define the work of navigation. Selecting a destination, setting a course, and crossing the broad expanse of the open ocean to achieve the coastline destination are its essential functions.

The image at Greenwich broadcasts a message: "Where am I? In the open ocean there are no landmarks!" You cannot peer over the side of the ship and see physical latitude and longitude lines marked out to guide you. Business leaders can certainly relate to the vast, sometimes intimidating distance between the start of a plan and the desired outcome. Once a leader sets out for the destination, staying on course is a persistent challenge as the environment—wind and wave—can easily push you off course.

At sea, navigation utilizes tools and instrumentation such as chart plotters, compasses, sextants, and chronometers to convert concepts like latitude and longitude into measures they use to stay on course. In business, engagement surveys, industry surveys, buyer preference research, customer satisfaction measures, lean/Six Sigma metrics and the like help the business navigator determine progress made on strategic priorities.

In Figure 1.1 we can see the parallels between navigating and piloting at sea and navigating and piloting in organizations. Let's begin with a quick reference guide of concepts and principles to keep in mind as we work through the chapter.

FIGURE 1.1 Reaching Your Destination: Parallels to Navigating at Sea

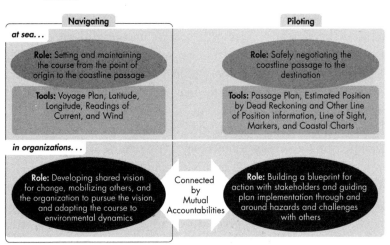

QUICK REFERENCE GUIDE

On what outcomes does successful organizational navigation focus?
Leaders engaged in navigation ensure that their people:

- Feel pulled to a shared vision of new benefits for customers, for the organization, and for the team that takes advantage of competitive opportunities and leverages internal strengths

- Make certain that the points of view of people in different disciplines and at different levels have been reflected in the plan that will be used to achieve the vision
- Believe that the plan stretches but does not excessively strain the organization to implement it
- Recognize that effective supports have been put in place to overcome the obstacles that may be encountered during implementation of the plan—especially involving communication and collaboration up and down and across the organization
- Trust that a climate of safety exists for the trial-and-error process of learning that will be needed to agilely solve the problems that will be encountered; that people can admit to the mistakes they make and be accountable for the results they take on
- Are invested in the plan as their plan so that they will push through the personal difficulties that they will encounter in making the plan a reality

With these outcomes above in mind, navigating is implemented in the steps outlined below.

PULL UP AND PULL ACROSS

In our research, we sought to uncover which of the more than 40 change leadership practices were associated with high organizational performance. We learned that the ability to bring people together distinguishes high-performance navigation. In organizations with a three-year pattern of achieving both revenue and profitability goals, senior leaders were primarily responsible for the following activities:

- Help stakeholders understand the strengths of the current operation to support long-range planning
- When developing plans for implementing strategic initiatives, get stakeholders to review potential implementation challenges and options for overcoming them
- Get stakeholders to ratify plans before they are implemented
- Regularly meet with senior stakeholders to get their insights on potential challenges to strategic initiatives

- Keep stakeholders updated on the progress of key initiatives

To excel at these tasks, leaders perform the organization navigation function with insight and knowledge of "boots on the ground" realities. To fulfill the obligations we found in our research, effective navigation relies on people doing skillful piloting for their knowledge. Organizational high performance requires synchronization of skillful navigation and skillful piloting, the critical foundations of high-performance leadership.

A CLOSER LOOK AT ORGANIZATIONAL NAVIGATION IN ACTION: THE STORY OF "MASTER AND COMMANDER"

A consumer products company faced a grim reality: its customers were expressing mountains of complaints, and its competition had seized the opportunity to crush the subject of our story's business. This was a hard realization to many in the company. A few years earlier, the company had been a top leader of its industry.

The board hired a new division leader, Sal, to get the business back on track. Sal quickly hired two new executives, and this leadership team took the reins of the troubled organization, hoping their efforts would lead to a big turnaround. Much like nautical navigators, Sal and the new executive team faced a lot of open water where anything could happen—without the benefit of easy landmarks.

As the new executive team entered the final stages of planning, Sal identified three key priorities. To get the business on the right course, he argued, they needed the right marketing strategies. To address this priority, Sal needed outside expertise—someone who had been down the path before and could help them think outside the box. He hired a consulting firm that had a reputation for helping other organizations successfully restage their brands. Having taken steps to clarify the approach to the turnaround, the senior leader turned to the executive team that would execute the plan, his second priority.

Sal built his team with a combination of new and former leaders, each of whom had special skills and abilities. However, Sal recognized that in assembling this team he had created a potential team management problem. He had a potent mix of strong personalities with firm convictions.

Sal knew that he had to focus this team with a clear and aggressive agenda. Without strong focus, he worried that members of the team would believe their own "BS" (expletive deleted!) and engage in unproductive clashes that would slow down the work. Once again, Sal determined that outside help would go a long way. He hired another consultant to keep communication channels open between members of the team and help facilitate team responses to the inevitable bumps and bounces ahead.

Meanwhile, the president's third priority was engaging the middle management team. But this too had a potential political obstacle: while many members of middle management were key to the successful implementation of the plan, these managers were also part of the "old guard." It was vital that this tier in the organization understood—and embraced—the change program, as they had to drive its execution.

Sal, the president, and other members of the executive leadership team selected a group of top middle managers from across the organization to help guide and oversee the implementation of the details of the plan. With this group, leadership outlined the competitive context, reviewed the strategy and plan, clarified expectations, and explained that they would hold people accountable. While intelligent mistakes were expected and plans would have to be readjusted, people would be expected to deliver.

The senior team held regular team progress report sessions, status updates, and problem-solving meetings. While a few people struggled to get in tune with the new program and exited the business, the senior team's commitment to the plan proved fruitful. Along the journey senior and mid-level leaders worked together to address differences in customer expectations, resolve tricky operational realities of the business that were beyond the sight of the executive team, and address misaligned business processes. Eighteen months later after hard work from a committed cadre of leaders across many parts of the organization, this organization reclaimed the mantle of market leader.

Navigation involves targeting a destination, plotting a course, and adjusting the course to address dynamic changes in the environment both internal and external so you can achieve the destination. The process begins with awareness of the competitive context within which a team is operating. This includes how customer needs are evolving—the ones customers can recognize and express as well as the ones they do not yet recognize.

Business navigation combines deep customer awareness with insight into the strategic moves that competitors are making and insight into how the capabilities of an organization can be used to create a competitive advantage. Strong analytical and conceptual skills, a broad array of work experience, an intuition about the influence that culture and behavior have in strategy implementation, and a deep knowledge of the mechanics of a business[1] equip navigators with the capabilities they need to develop and implement strategy.

People performing the navigation function also mobilize hearts and minds. By synthesizing a shared vision from the personal visions of team members, they build a view of the direction. They work with people across and up and down the organization to plot a course, initiate the plan, and guide its implementation. Frequent dialogue up and down and across the organization about the "what and why" of the strategy and the practice of candid evidence-based problem solving promotes the shared attitudes and values needed to achieve the coordinated and sustained effort that leads to success.[2]

The example of Sal demonstrates why navigating and piloting must both be effectively synchronized. Whereas organizational navigation bring initiatives to within sight of the "shoreline," organizational piloting leverages acute awareness of and agile maneurvering around and through hazards, and obstacles—adding value to the successful execution of strategy. These two functions are often not sufficiently coordinated, to the detriment of the success of strategic initiatives.

Alignment of stakeholders is a priority focus of navigation in high-performing organizations. In the dynamic environment of business organizations, successful navigation leverages inputs and integrates many inputs to achieve direction, set a course that can be achieved, and maneuver the open ocean challenges that occur. Five critical practices distinguish navigating in high-performing organizations in our research. Once again these include:

- Helping stakeholders understand the strengths of the current operation to support long-range planning

- Getting stakeholders to review potential implementation challenges and options for overcoming them when developing plans for implementing strategic initiatives
- Getting stakeholders to ratify plans before they are implemented
- Keeping stakeholders updated on the progress of key initiatives
- Getting key stakeholders to closely review progress on strategic initiatives to determine if changes are needed to keep things on track

THE CORE SKILLS OF ORGANIZATION NAVIGATING

Leaders rely on four fundamental change leadership capabilities that turn clarity into results. With the skillful application of these capabilities, leaders involve others in implementing change that matters.

The four skills are shown in Figure 1.2. We describe them below.

FIGURE 1.2 The Four Core Skills of Navigating

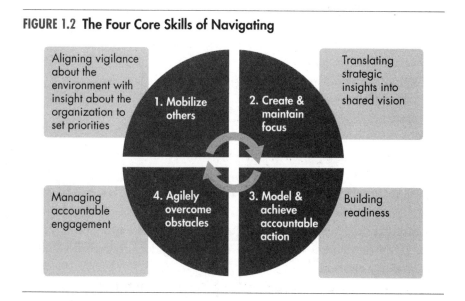

The core navigating skills are:

1. Aligning vigilance about the environment with insight about the organization to set priorities
2. Translating strategic insights into shared vision
3. Building readiness
4. Managing accountable engagement

Let's explore each of these in more detail.

CORE NAVIGATING SKILL 1

Maintaining vigilance on threats and opportunities in the external environment and aligning internal capabilities needed to achieve results that matter

Maintaining vigilance means keeping an eye on the various currents at work: What are your customers doing? What are your competitors doing? What are innovative companies in your field doing? Then, use the answers to inform and measure your own progress against strategic priorities. In *Execution: The Discipline of Getting Things Done*, authors Larry Bossidy and Ram Charan outline the main questions for leaders to ask:

- How am I doing vis-à-vis other companies?
- Have I made progress?
- Have I made more progress than my competitors?

These are simple questions. Yet, as this business executive and business school professor assert, answering these questions *candidly* is difficult if not rare. As Jack Welch, the venerated leader of GE, expressed it, determined commitment to "achievement-based candor" is a core value of effective organizations.

With a steady eye trained on the external environment, navigators plot a course that leverages an organization's strengths and minimizes its weaknesses. Once under way, effective navigators negotiate challenges to maintain their course.

The classic tool of SWOT (strengths, weaknesses, opportunities, and threats) focuses this critical inside-out and outside-in awareness (see

Table 1.1). As is true of all such tools, even one as well established and familiar as SWOT, it is not the tool but its application that is key. Too often biases in how we think limit the value people derive from this process. Biases in thinking and motivation constrain the critical thinking needed to make good strategic decisions.[3] As a result, effective leaders ensure two things are in place to cultivate the insights needed to make good decisions: a process and analytics. The process used is more critical than the analysis itself. Analysis plays a vital role as a powerful check on biases;[4] in other words, "What do the numbers say?"

TABLE 1.1 SWOT Framework

	PERSPECTIVE	
	EXTERNAL TO THE ORGANIZATION	WITHIN THE ORGANIZATION
Positive	Opportunities	Strengths
Negative	Threats	Weaknesses

Once the competitive situation is mapped, the next step is identifying how to take advantage of the situation. There are two questions to ask:

- Do we know what to do?
- Do we know how to do it?

Yes or no answers to these two questions create four types of strategic initiatives, as shown in Table 1.2.

TABLE 1.2 Four Types of Strategic Initiatives

		KNOW HOW TO DO IT	
		NO	YES
KNOW WHAT TO DO?	YES	Develop prototypes with go/no-go gates. Evaluate how the work is being done and make adjustments over time to increase success.	Leverage the competence and confidence of the team. Focus on executing on time and on budget.
	NO	Do small pilots. Evaluate their success and use lessons learned to implement new pilots. Actively engage internal stakeholders as ambiguity and uncertainty are high.	Stay in close touch with frontline staff, customers, and suppliers as you focus well-developed processes on new goals. Evaluate success for distinct and incremental phases of work, and make needed adjustments.

Once a set of strategies are developed into a crisp, easy to communicate and understand message, then leaders build an organization design to support the achievement of these changes and priorities.[5] Major points of organization design include:

- Structures that place power and authority in functions and roles, such as reporting relationships, roles and related responsibilities, and committees and task teams
- Processes used to coordinate and integrate decisions across and up and down the organization
- Rewards through which leaders reinforce alignment of the goals of the organization and people
- Culture shifts needed to support the priorities

Leaders ensure congruity between the different facets of their organization's design and its strategic direction. Figure 1.3 illustrates key points of alignment.

FIGURE 1.3 Key Points of Alignment

Strategy and culture top a hierarchy of linkages for two dimensions of vision—namely, "What are we going to do differently?" as well as "How?" Supporting these hierarchies are adjustments in enablers. There are four key enablers:

1. **Structure.** Structure places decision-making authority in the hands of roles. Structures define reporting relationships and outline the responsibilities that define the roles in the organization. It includes

who decides what and outlines shared responsibilities with other roles. Structure goes beyond job titles and includes informal structures like committees and special ad hoc work teams that leaders commission to coordinate and align work across organizational boundaries.
2. **Processes.** These are the sequences of activities through which a product or a service is created for an internal or external customer. A process puts information into the hands of people at each step in the process. At each step people add value to the information they receive and pass it on to others who do the same until an important outcome or result is achieved. Well-designed business processes help people create value.
3. **Systems.** Systems include the technologies that support the business processes in the organization.
4. **People Capabilities.** These are the alignment of mindsets and competencies (or the knowledge, skills, and abilities) of the people needed to achieve the goals and objectives associated with strategies.

Documenting changes with a simple framework like the one shown in Figure 1.4 helps clarify the changes that the leader needs to make in the organization to successfully execute the targeted change. Turning these "from-to" aspirations into plans for change is the next step.

FIGURE 1.4 Framework for Documenting Changes

	CHANGE LEVERS	FROM	TO
Strategy	• Priorities		
	• Tasks		
	• Actions		
Culture	• Values		
	• Practices		
	• Behavior		
Organization Design	• Structures		
	• Processes		
	• Systems		
	• People capabilities		

To convert a blueprint for change from paper to performance, leaders must ensure that key but hard-to-achieve conditions (as identified in the research) are present:

- **Collaboration between and among senior-level leaders.** One executive in a company describes the process of translating strategies into collaborative action as "weaving the fabric." Lack of collaboration across organizational boundaries is the key gap in driving strategic initiatives.[6] As Jim Collins, author of *Good to Great*, has said, success is 1 percent vision and 99 percent alignment. Senior-level leaders need to engineer collaboration, as their direct reports are mostly focused on their own responsibilities and pursue work that they can control.
- **Messaging occurs about the targeted change and how to achieve it in a way that resonates with different audiences within the organization.** Jack Welch recommended communicating often enough that you can be fairly accused of being "relentlessly boring." These communications work best when leaders articulate the tradeoffs that are made in pursuing a new direction. Here is a quick example. "We are going to work through the ups and downs of installing this new system so that we can better serve the needs of our customers as we expect them to develop in the near future." People are aware that change means exchanging one thing for another. Making this explicit helps people understand the change. Communications are quite effective when they are supported by good storytelling skills.
- **Dialogue about strategic goals and implementation plans happens up and down the leadership hierarchy so people are deeply engaged in how to achieve goals.** Most people embrace change when they have the opportunity to talk through what the change means and how challenges they anticipate will be overcome. High-performance leaders also invite resistance from others. This means surfacing concerns about goals or how they will be overcome. Questions like the following elicit productive resistance: "What holes do you see in our plan?" "What are we missing?" "What can we do to address these concerns?"
- **Deeper middle-level leader involvement throughout the course of a strategic initiative but most especially during implementation.**[7] As implementation gathers momentum, organizational pilots, often an organization's middle-level leaders, are critical to achieving the focus, aligning people, and clarifying and negotiating implementation

challenges that exist on the ground and are often beyond the sight of those who are implementing the navigation function
- **Agile and accountable problem-solving occurs.** Modeling agility and personal accountability encourages other leaders do as well and establishes a climate that encourages these behaviors up and down the organization.

Successful Navigator in Action: Eyes on the Horizon

To solidify what navigating effectively means, consider the following story.

Beth, a senior marketer in a U.S. business unit of a large global company, learned from her network of industry colleagues and well-respected salespeople that two of their top competitors were attracting customer mind and wallet share by implementing new customer programs and product innovations.

"OK," she wondered, "how big a deal is this really?" There was no arguing that revenue was persistently lagging behind budgeted sales and market share was slipping. But what was really going on? Sales defended their position and marketing defended theirs, and leaders on all sides could not build a critical mass of momentum on a solution. Making incremental changes wasn't making a difference that mattered.

Beth got her boss to agree that the organization hire a market research firm that had a compelling methodology for getting customers to clarify how they made purchase decisions. The first part of this process got customers to identify their buying criteria. Separately, it also got customers to share information about what they actually purchased. Analysis of what customers said and what they did were compared with another variable. Customers were asked to rate a range of companies based on both buying criteria and actual products purchased.

When the market research firm debriefed the organization on its findings, Beth's colleagues saw in objective terms what they had been afraid to or could not acknowledge to each other in the past. The survey research indicated that competitor sales and product innovations and their customer impacts were creating a real competitive advantage for the industry leaders. The reality of impact of these changes was something that Beth's organization had resisted until they saw the data.

In an act of some bravery, Beth also got her organization to fund the survey consultants to conduct a review the survey results with a broad cross-section of the organization. People knew where the organization was in comparison to competitors and what the issues were. There were some disquieting moments for some; this information was invaluable for developing an objective view of what Beth's team, as well as other departments, were doing well, what they were doing poorly, and what they needed to fix to win and keep more business.

Beth engaged teams to explore how they might leverage these insights during strategic planning exercises. Service, sales, and product development teams came up with ideas that addressed these challenges. The best ones were inserted into the agendas for product and service development.

Over the subsequent years the survey was continued. Over a couple of cycles of industry surveys, mind share and wallet share improved as Beth's firm implemented meaningful and evidence-based innovation.

Beth's insight that analytics were needed to break through definitions of what the problem was and how it could be fixed led to a more successful outcome. Analytics of data from customers ultimately broke through the limitations to practical problem solving that had deterred her organization from the customer-focused innovation needed to meet company goals.

CORE NAVIGATING SKILL 2

Translating strategic insights into shared vision

Vision is anchored in strategic insights. Developing shared vision is one of the most important functions navigators perform, but it is a persistently difficult thing to do for both executives and mid-level leaders.[8]

A shared vision that mobilizes hearts and minds is:

- Future-focused—contains an aspiration for results that matter
- Optimistic—grounded in a candid appraisal of the current state with a belief in new possibilities that people can work together to achieve
- Made up of ideas to which a wide audience can relate
- Concrete with milestones—people view the change road map as critical

Shared vision leadership often fails because people fail to adequately include the input of others.[9] Bringing together one's vision and the vision of others is challenging to do—especially if leaders have the organizational power to enforce their will. Our research indicates that high-performance leaders are focused and flexible enough to integrate the ideas of others. The best senior leaders exert restraint in using their power to force a personal point of view.

Effective navigations integrate three things, as shown in Figure 1.5. A framework like Table 1.3 can focus this effort. The idea is to synthesize a shared vision from one's views as a leader and the views of key stakeholders.

FIGURE 1.5 Three Points of Alignment

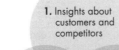

1. Insights about customers and competitors
2. Assessment of the capabilities of the organization
3. Shared vision about results that matter

TABLE 1.3 Framework for Synthesizing a Shared Vision

POINTS OF ALIGNMENT	PERSONAL VISION	KEY STAKEHOLDER VIEWS			SHARED VISION IDEAS
		GROUP 1	GROUP 2	GROUP 3	
Insights about competitors					
Assessment of the capabilities of the organization					
Shared vision about results that matter					

Once a broad shared vision is in place, the next step is to build commitment regarding how it is to be operationalized. This means cascading the vision to others and then using iterations of plans that will fulfill the shared vision to create top-to-bottom and horizontal alignments across team boundaries.

Successful Navigator in Action: Shared Vision

In an impressive instance of shared vision, a president took over an organization with the mission of turning around its business. In an act that reverberated throughout the organization, the new leader spent the better part of his first two months interviewing a broad cross section of managers in manufacturing settings, frontline service personnel, salespeople, and sales managers from across the globe.

When the president returned to the headquarters he brought leaders from all the organization's departments and divisions together. Informed by the various perspectives and points of view that he'd absorbed, the new leader wove together a new shared vision and articulated a new core set of aspirations.

Once he communicated this shared vision, the next step was to convert it into action. Here the head of the corporation contributed a key component, engaging the team with a remarkable act. He attended an onboarding session of a group of newly hired marketing managers. He outlined the vision of the business and then said, "I have no idea how we are going to achieve the vision." Then, after a pause he added, "but that is why you are here."

The audience left that meeting with a compelling call to action (and a bit of anxiety, too), for the mandate the CEO gave them was to make the vision a reality.

CORE NAVIGATING SKILL 3
Building readiness

It is obvious that people, teams, and organizations need the motivation and ability to implement change to be successful. An experienced senior HR leader observed that organizations rarely evaluate readiness, systematically close readiness gaps, or scale projects to meet the level of readiness that is on hand in the moment.

Limitations in readiness exist because senior leaders don't have the insight they require. Knowledge of the on-the-ground realities that are needed to make an informed, complete assessment lie with people who are close to the work—in other words, with people who are on the front lines. Senior-level leaders have to gather this insight.

However, when senior leaders ask others, they sometimes do not get candid appraisals. Fear of not being branded as someone lacking a "can do" attitude or fear of "being too negative" or even "clueless" constrains many from being candid with more senior-level leaders.

Taking time to learn about the perspectives of others can be frustrating for someone who wants to act with urgency. This insight however can be a quite powerful source of information in calibrating how business change is framed and communicated.

Table 1.4 outlines the conditions that need to be in place for a change attempt to be optimally successful. If sufficient readiness is not on hand, then the initiative should focus on closing the identified readiness gaps or the change should be scaled to the available level of readiness.

TABLE 1.4 Conditions for Successful Change

READINESS FACTOR

ORGANIZATION	
Perceived need	• People are uncomfortable with the status quo. • The problem to be solved is a high priority. • The perspective of leaders, technical experts, and end users shaped the definition of the need or the problem.
Perceived advantages	Supporters of the solution inside the organization will gain more than opponents inside the organization will lose.
Adequate resources	Adequate time, energy, and budget have been allocated to the change project.
Compatibility	Change requires that new practices be added to how work gets done but does not require radical change.
Clarity of the plan	• The plan for change can be simply communicated. • Assignments and schedule are clear. • The changes to work procedures are documented. • A process for evaluating progress and making course corrections based on feedback from customers and people involved in plan implementation is included in the plan.
SOLUTION	
Source	The solution reflects and is informed by ideas that have been tested successfully in similar types of organizations.
Evidence of success in other similar situations	People have seen evidence that the solution has been effective in similar organizations or similar situations.
Adaptability	The solution can be adjusted and tailored to local needs.

(continued)

TABLE 1.4 Conditions for Successful Change *(continued)*

READINESS FACTOR	
LEADER	
Credibility	The leader who is sponsoring the change is perceived to be an expert.
Commitment	The leader who is sponsoring the change is perceived to be committed to the values of the organization.
Customer focus	The change agent is focused on creating meaningful points of creative differentiation with customers.
PEOPLE	
Understanding of change	People involved in the change project: • Understand the need • Appreciate the benefits of the solution and any trade-off that the solution requires • Understand the criteria for determining success • Understand the plan to implement the solution
Motivation	• People perceive that change will create significant gains at moderate cost. • The solution will meet some needs of people across the organization—senior management, middle management, and staff. • People are not fatigued by other recent and large change initiatives.
Perceptions of support	• People perceive that they have access to key organizational supports (e.g., support of colleagues, training, hands-on technical support, advice, and coaches) that are needed to implement change successfully. • People feel that they can learn to perform against new expectations with tolerance for intelligent and well-intentioned mistakes along the way.
Change skills	Those who are involved have in the past demonstrated the capacity to absorb and exploit new ideas.
Technical ability	People close to the change are competent to implement its technical aspects.
Knowledge of how to use consultants	People involved have had positive experiences using consultants—internal or external—who are needed to support change initiatives.
Contingencies on hand	People see that some thought has been given to events that might push plans off course.
SCOPE	
Pace	Large amount of activity per week
Number of people involved	Moderate

TABLE 1.4 Conditions for Successful Change *(continued)*

	READINESS FACTOR
Length of focal projects that support change	Less than 9 months
Time to achieve some payback	Less than 18 months

Successful Navigating in Action: Readiness

We are on a mission. In the example we outlined previously, the leader of a large division of a consumer products company and two of his direct reports took the reins of a troubled organization months earlier.

The leader needed outside experts—someone who had been down the path before and could help them think out of the box. The leader hired a consulting firm that had a reputation for helping other organizations successfully restage their brands. Having taken steps to clarify the approach to the turnaround, the senior leader turned to the team that would execute the plan.

The leader rounded out his executive team with a combination of new and former employees, each of whom had special skills and abilities. However, he recognized a potent mix of strong personalities and deep convictions were focused on an aggressive agenda: a high-stakes combination. The senior leader hired a consultant to keep communication channels open between members of the team and help facilitate team responses to the inevitable bumps and bounces that lay ahead. Without the consultant, the strategy "would have failed . . . big time," as this leader said. He recognized that an effective executive team was a key condition of readiness that had to be established.

Finally, success required aligning senior and mid-level leaders. The leader established implementation reviews in which senior and mid-level leaders would work together to address the implementation realities they would encounter.

CORE NAVIGATING SKILL 4
Building a climate of accountable engagement

Accountability and engagement are linked. Research on organizational citizen behavior reveals that discretionary effort (answering the call of duty to achieve results on behalf of an organization) and accountability (honoring the commitments we make especially when difficult to do so) are highly correlated. Research also suggests that employee engagement tends to drop during periods of significant change[10] as does accountability, especially valuable to organizations when driving strategic change.[11] Interestingly, as a Harvard Business School study recently demonstrated, many organizations have a large accountability gap. One of every two leaders is terrible at accountability.[12]

Honoring personal commitments in words and action lies at the heart of integrity and an allied aspect of leadership performance: trust we inspire in others. Modeling accountability has a powerful influence on the accountable behavior of others. It enhances our ability as leaders to hold others accountable in a fair but firm manner, one of the critical functions of navigating.

We next focus our attention on two aspects of accountability within our concept of engaged accountability: (1) the reputation index and (2) accountability drivers.

The Reputation Index

Our reputation precedes us. It establishes a set of expectations that shape how others respond to what we say, and more important, it influences how much people invest in what we say.

A leader who follows through sets the stage for this practice in others. A handy way to remember our reputation for accountability is the following equation:

$$\frac{\text{Commitments Kept}}{\text{Commitments Made}} = \text{Reputation Index}$$

This simple equation captures a leader's reputation for following through. It reminds us to make commitments carefully, and to agree to what we have high confidence that we can execute. In the quest to be bold, many leaders overcommit. Later, when circumstances prevent them from following through, their reputation suffers, and their followers may find it more difficult to take the leader at his or her word.

Accountability

Accountable engagement is identified by five actions:

1. Acknowledging mistakes to advance problem solving
2. Advocating for shifts in policies or values that interfere with an organizational goal
3. Maintaining the pursuit of commitments even though personal and organizational challenges make it difficult
4. Directly renegotiating agreements made when conflicting priorities make this necessary
5. Assertively advocating for needed resources or abilities when an obligation cannot be fulfilled

These are the key behaviors of accountability.

Work Environment Drivers of Accountable Behavior

The work environment has a power influence on accountability. When people in an organization or a team perceive that these practices are in place, accountable behavior increases in frequency. We pair engagement with accountability to reinforce that the process of strengthening these practices involves dialogue among levels of leadership. Focus groups and surveys can help set priorities for which of these practices and behaviors must be strengthened and monitoring the impact of attempts to improve them over time.

1. Clarity of the expectation, commitment, or obligation
2. Seeing expectations, commitments, or obligations as appropriate to one's role or professional identity
3. Having control over the resources and abilities needed to fulfill an obligation
4. Seeing the person seeking a commitment as being driven by something broader than personal interest
5. Absence of fear that one will get punished or scapegoated for intelligent mistakes

FIGURE 1.6 Engaged Accountability

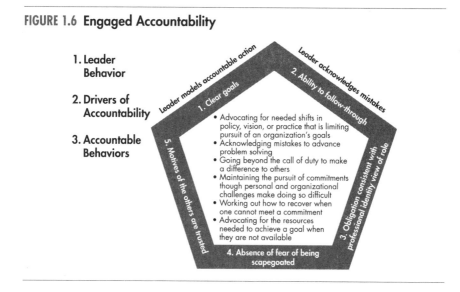

The extent to which a leadership team has created or is creating a context of accountable engagement can easily be determined by a variety of work environment assessment tools. Tools such as organizational surveys, focus groups, and the like can be used to document the presence or absence of key conditions and to address important gaps. The navigation task is to develop a context in which the drivers of accountability are present.

Successful Navigator in Action: Accountable Engagement

The buck stops . . . with us. A new leader of a start-up company faced the prospect of heading up a business that was being shopped by its owners, also known as the "mother ship," with employees that had been transferred from the "mother ship" to the start-up. The task of making a go of the new business was difficult and the future uncertain.

Given the precarious nature of the start-up, the leader made the challenges explicit and engaged the team on what was needed to meet the challenges in a set of town hall meetings. He also engaged the team in making sure the terms of engagement between employees and the company were clear. There was hope and candor. He promised to keep everyone updated on the status of the acquisition process. He also explained that he and the leadership team were going to try things. They would pull in the right people. If what they tried did not work, they would come clean. They would try something else.

A few senior people who did not agree with the new direction were encouraged to pursue greener pastures. Some moved on their own, but more than expected stayed. They felt that they were on a mission. Within a year the company launched its first new product.

One of the tougher accountability challenges is confronting direct reports, especially at more senior levels. The cost of replacing senior people is significant, and candid conversations are difficult for most. It can be easier to cope with behavior that does not support the direction of the company rather than address it directly. Executive coaches are used in some organizations to help achieve clarity between executives and their teams that is difficult otherwise.

ORGANIZATIONAL NAVIGATIONAL CHALLENGES TO OVERCOME

There are a few key challenges to overcome in navigation. Here is an outline of what to do to address some important ones:

- **Getting people to participate.** To engage fully in a participative process, four conditions need to be in place. People need to (1) trust the process, (2) view their input as voluntary, (3) experience the process of participating as rewarding, and (4) see their ideas as significantly affecting work products. These conditions overcome the cynicism that faces many change attempts.
- **Engineering the right balance between building ownership and being efficient.** Create boundaries within which good ideas can be developed and ensure that there is effective facilitation of these processes. Ensure that the idea space is broad enough so that people feel like there is sufficient freedom to develop good ideas.
- **Cascading commitment.** Four priorities serve as focus for cascading commitment. (1) Executive leadership is primarily involved in plotting strategy and culture shifts. (2) Operational leadership is primarily involved in building organizational structures, processes, and systems. (3) Middle management and supervision are primarily involved in team design, which includes how team roles are designed

and how roles work together to accomplish work. (4) Frontline staff is primarily involved in defining methods, resources, timing, and sequencing of activities to accomplish tasks.
- **Dealing with readiness gaps.** As plans for action are finalized, evaluate whether the readiness needed to proceed with confidence is on hand. If not, build a plan to fill readiness gaps. Pushing on without sufficient readiness is common but does not usually produce good outcomes.

A second set of behavior issues concerns behavior change imbedded in the solution itself and not just its implementation. The shift to a customer-focused organization illustrates this. This shift is enabled by changes in organizational structures, customer relationship management systems, and reporting systems.[13] Customer-focused organizations also require adoption of alternate management practices. These include:

- Facilitating the coordination between departments
- "Serving others" as a model for service excellence
- Promoting informal communication between people in departments
- Implementing flexible work structures
- Focusing on the well-being of employees
- Empowering employees
- Connecting employee work to actual customer outcomes
- Empowering teams to identify, develop, and implement solutions to service problems

This list emphasizes that when implementing a shift to customer-centric organizations, managers are altering how they approach work. Implementation of such changes is enabled by increased flexibility, versatility, and responsiveness. Increases in personal awareness and changes in communication, influence, and conflict management skills are required to make the transition to customer centricity work. These behavioral changes often do not receive the vigilance that they require. As we have learned, people tend to underestimate the difficulty of implementing a solution until difficulties are encountered during implementation.

Chapter 2

Piloting

It'll work, if God, wind, leads, ice, snow, and all the hells of this damned frozen land are willing.
—Matthew Henson, African American explorer and member of 1909 Peary expedition that was the first to reach the geographic North Pole

Piloting is one of the most important functions of high-performance leadership. Both business initiatives and nautical voyages involve high stakes: in both cases, it's not enough to navigate effectively. If the ship runs aground before reaching its destination, the voyage is considered a failure. A well-designed plan for business change that does not achieve its outcomes also fails. The leadership function of successful piloting uses detailed knowledge of the immediate environment—the dynamic forces at play and hidden hazards—and how to deftly negotiate them to achieve outcomes that matter.

A critical moment in the famous *Kon-Tiki* expedition gives us a window into the process in action. Thor Heyerdahl, an adventurer and anthropologist, had asserted that ancient South Americans had sailed 4,000 miles across the open ocean using primitive navigational strategies and boatbuilding techniques to reach and settle Polynesia.

Heyerdahl's critics refused to believe it, arguing that the distance and available raw materials were insurmountable obstacles to such a journey. Undaunted, Heyerdahl set out to prove it could be done. He fashioned a balsam raft that mimicked the sailing vessels of ancient coastal South America, dubbed the craft *Kon-Tiki*, and with a small crew set out for Polynesia. After the crew made several unsuccessful attempts to reach landfall, they searched for and selected their final approach. As Heyerdahl wrote of the adventure:

> The swell grew heavier and heavier, with deep troughs between the waves, and we felt the raft being swung up and down and up and down higher and higher. And the order was shouted: "Hold on!"[1]
>
> The sea tugged and pulled with all the force it could bring to bear... estimated the height of water was at twenty-five feet while the foaming crest passed by fifteen feet above the part of the glassy wall.[2]
>
> ... *Kon-Tiki* was being drawn out of the witches' caldron by the backwash, and a fresh sea came rolling over her. For the last time I bellowed, "Hang on!"[3]
>
> Everything above deck was smashed up, but the nine balsa logs were intact as ever. I shall never forget that wade across the reef toward the heavily palmed island.[4]

Navigating may have set the course, but as the 25-foot waves assaulted the *Kon-Tiki*, another skill set was required. As we can see, piloting presents leaders with the acute pressure of the immediate. The acute pressure of the immediate can certainly be felt when driving the execution of business initiatives. It's often as an initiative "sights land" that sudden, unanticipated factors are discovered as this work example:

> The timelines were aggressive. A lot of things had to come together. At the last minute we lost some people to illness, and we had to figure out how to cope. Overtime! Weekends! Some of our estimates were accurate; some were off. Some of the tasks took much longer than we planned and pressured subsequent work. The application we needed was ready at the last second. Testing had revealed some surprising problems. We got them fixed at the last second. We were ready, but with only minutes to spare.

Ambitious deadlines, underestimating the effort or testing required—these are the waves and swells that business leaders encounter at the coastline. Interestingly, it is here, near the comfort of land, where the most nautical mishaps occur.[5] In fact, groundings (where the bottom of the ship meets the seabed) account for about one-third of commercial ship accidents all over the world,[6] second in frequency to ship-on-ship collisions.[7] Failure to use the proper navigational aids that tell the seamen where they are relative to known hazards of the passage, to keep these aids calibrated, and to make decisions based on this information account for these nautical disasters. Paralleling the challenges of marine navigation, strategic initiatives in business run aground in the later stages of implementation,[8] a declaration that comes well after the actual failure is first recognized.

FIGURE 2.1 Reaching Your Destination: Parallels to Piloting at Sea

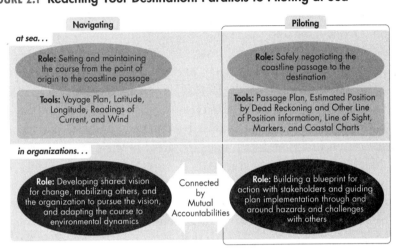

High-performance leadership is performed with great skill and implemented with well-engineered synchronization (Figure 2.1). This is not an accident. Focus and planning distinguish success from a crash. We see practices in those who race yachts to victory in this excerpt from Asian Yachting.com (emphasis mine):

> *People who do not win are unable to follow a plan*—because they do not establish one, because they make one inconsistent with their abilities, or because they become so preoccupied that they neglect it. *They shift rapidly from one concern to another*: Is the mainsail set right? Will the spinnaker go up cleanly? Will the boat on the lee bow force them about? Being so busy, they *miss the things that matter and so lose* and, being so busy, hardly notice that they are losing—until it is too late. In contrast, the *single-minded determination of the series winner . . . is consistent* because he is not bogged

down in a mire of doubt, indecision, and distraction. They do well in every race, in part because their *attention is constantly upon the things that matter*, in part because almost no one else's attention is.[9]

Like successful yacht racers, successful organizational pilots bring a sharp-eyed focus to the "things that matter," transforming strategic priorities into achievements and results. As they perform this vital function, organizational pilots resolve the tensions between the aspirations of strategy on the one hand and the realities on the ground on the other. Within the context of current systems, processes, and people, they balance the objectives of senior leaders, the goals of cross-functional teams, and goals of frontline personnel—which too often are not adequately synchronized.

Pilots use detailed knowledge of business processes, tasks, and the skill sets of the people involved[10]—knowledge that people who are performing the navigation function do not have by virtue of their distance from the "on the ground" realities that matter. To turn to nautical accidents once again, research demonstrates that lack of knowledge and use of real-time information about specific hazards like tides, currents, and underwater terrain as well as fatigue lead to piloting errors.[11]

Insightful executives recognize the vital function of organizational piloting. Rather than people who just do the mundane tasks of execution, pilots are vital partners to success. They realize that the quality of the strategy resides in execution. In the role through which the piloting function is most often performed, middle-level leaders address resistance, negotiate obstacles, and take advantage of opportunities as they arise.[12] This vital work makes strategy a reality.

At their best, pilots are masters of the "art of the possible." With insight the navigator does not have about the on-the-ground realities of people, processes, and systems, pilots make the critical difference in implementation of strategy. Their knowledge of important realities enhances their ability to make needed trade-offs and motivate people to do what is needed to achieve priorities. This means more than making simple sacrifices of one requirement for another—what some would say are "black and white" decisions. Often they are making sense of "gray."[13] On occasion, leaders in the role of pilot make trade-offs without senior leader knowledge of the grimy details.[14]

In this chapter, we outline the outcomes that drive successful piloting, the critical tasks through which piloting is implemented, and four skills upon which piloting success is based.

OUTCOMES ASSOCIATED WITH SUCCESSFUL PILOTING

To help pilots efficiently focus on optimizing their success at the leading edge, we outline the outcomes on which successful piloting is based below. These outcomes are the motivational states that effective leaders create in others when they are piloting. They are the starting point for building a plan to achieve an important goal.

Effective organizational piloting gets people to:

- Understand linkages between priorities, implementation plans, and the roles of teams and team members in making the plan a success
- Focus on solving problems that matter to customers or to people who engage customers at customer touch points
- See that important hopes, priorities, and concerns are reflected in the plan
- Are clear about what to do and how to do it—especially concerning the ways they need to collaborate with others to succeed
- Are encouraged by early wins and feel momentum developing for achieving goals
- Know the hazards that must be negotiated in implementing the plan and how such hazards are best negotiated
- See implementation challenges and difficulties as natural slips and lapses that one learns how to overcome rather than fatal flaws in the plan
- Feel encouraged to persevere in the face of difficulties or setbacks
- Understand the root causes of the factors that have pushed a plan off course and what to do to get back on track
- Perceive that the team, including senior leaders, are committed to learning from experience in better serving customer needs and working together to recover from slips in the plan or factors that drive it off course

In our research, middle-level leaders who often perform the piloting function are focused on these responsibilities in high-performing organizations:

1. Work with frontline staff and peers to figure out how to keep the initiative on track
2. Ensure that people have the skills needed to implement plans successfully
3. Participate in regular conversations with customers (including internal customers) to learn what we can do better
4. Reinforce people for exceeding customer expectations
5. Drive activities that close the gap between current and desired job behavior
6. Ensure that handoffs between teams occur effectively

The focus on solving customer problems, recognizing others for exceeding service expectations, aiding teams in figuring out how to implement change, and team handoffs distinguishes middle-level piloting in high-performing organizations. To succeed at these tasks, skillful piloting depends on strategic alignment of direction and enabling organizational capabilities for which the navigation function is responsible.

Interestingly, in our research we compare these results with organizations that do not have sustained track records of organizational success. We discovered no clear pattern of practices that account for suboptimal performance. As was true for senior-level leaders or navigators, there are lots of ways to not do it well, and a very few ways to excel.

FOUR CORE PILOTING SKILLS

Performing the piloting function successfully depends on proficient performance of four priority skills. In the previous chapter, we discussed such skills in relation to navigators. Next we explore critical skills tailored to pilots:

1. Focusing teams on the right work
2. Strategic thinking
3. Solving problems agilely
4. Exerting accountable influence

We address each of these in detail in the following sections.

Core Piloting Skill 1: Focusing Teams on the Right Work

Insights about effective project management[15] and research on the work of mid-level leaders[16] point to three work management priorities that are central to ensuring that teams are focused on the right work.

1. **Identifying the right goals.** In their piloting function, mid-level leaders stay informed on an ongoing basis about goals and actions, as well as the agendas of senior leaders. Mid-level leaders must also translate general priorities and directives into plans, defining goals, action steps, and the criteria that will be used to measure success.
2. **Optimizing resources.** Part of the detect-and-act function of piloting, mid-level leaders determine what resources are needed for what need and allocate the resources on hand to priorities. This includes working with other teams to ensure that the support needed from them will be and is being provided. Aligning resources also includes setting priorities for the pilot's team for responding to other teams.
3. **Clarifying what to do differently.** This includes clarifying how responsibilities need to shift to accommodate new work or priorities, and defining what adjustments in the handoffs between people in key roles must occur to succeed at new tasks.

We summarize the work management tools and resources of high-performance piloting at the end of this chapter.

A Pilot in Action: Passionate About the Plan

Viewing leaders who perform the piloting function successfully helps bring these practices to life. We have interviewed leaders about people they have known who have done this work with great skill. We begin with the skill of focus.

Dwight D. Eisenhower, U.S. President and Supreme Allied Commander in World War II, once said, "Plans are worthless, planning is everything." Bobby was a big fan of this quote. Bobby brought a lot of energy to what he called "working the plan." He had it on hand all the time. And he seemed oblivious to the annoyance people sometimes showed when he sat down with them, opened his laptop, and pulled up the plan. Early on he would kick out new versions of the plan right after meetings. Once there was buy-in and approval, his approach changed. When people suggested that additional tasks be added, he listened carefully and usually responded, "Sounds like a great idea. Let's do it next time. We've gotta get this done first." Bobby was like a missionary about it. He engaged senior people and staff the same way. He got stuff done.

Bobby's reputation for getting things done with a soft touch and firm hand made him one of the most widely sought-after project managers.

Core Piloting Skill 2: Strategic Thinking

Working across organizational boundaries to keep goals aligned, engaging others in anticipating future challenges, and deploying a broader perspective about the business are the key strategic thinking capabilities of the piloting function in organizations. Powering this capability is a deep knowledge about how the organization works to meet the needs of customers and make money.

A Pilot in Action: Thinking Strategically, Acting Locally

Louise was responsible for the financial analysis of one of the more complex divisions within a family of related businesses. Her company had adopted new financial reporting requirements to address regulatory pressures. As the regulatory requirements were new, many questions existed about how to satisfy them. Louise's team faced a jump in new and uncertain demands.

At the same time that analytics and reporting requirements increased, staffing levels decreased. In the past, new technical staff would regularly cycle on to Louise's team as they trained new talent in the basic technical and operational skills people needed to work in her division. Once trained, staff would move to other roles on other teams. Concerns about revenue prompted hiring freezes, so the flow of new talent decreased. Some staffing reductions had also been implemented. Unfortunately, many of Louise's team members had been trained and left for other divisions. Meanwhile, the more experienced talent was not anxious to join Louise's team given its work. Louise's challenge was to manage increasing but uncertain demands and uncertain supply.

Fortunately, Louise was a disciplined planner with strong operational acumen. She also had deep relationships with a broad cross-section of people and knew that the organization's culture would shape how this work would develop. Unafraid to consult others who were more senior in her discipline, she talked with senior leaders to learn which reporting priorities they defined as most important, and how they would use analytics in internal and regulatory reporting. For many of these conversations, she brought drafts of an approach she had been working through and used the reactions of her colleagues to tweak it.

Louise engaged two exceptionally gifted analysts who were interested in leadership roles to develop airtight procedures so that underexperienced team members could perform them competently. She won the support of a person in a systems group to build tools to streamline some of the work. She emphasized a strong focus on development across her team to focus reviews of work performed and how it could be improved. In the end, she prevailed and won wide recognition for her work.

Core Piloting Skill 3: Solving Problems Agilely

A vital complement to the focus and discipline of planning is agile problem solving. This includes mental agility and behavioral versatility.

Mental agility involves how one thinks. It includes tolerance for ambiguity, the ability to examine problems thoroughly, making connections between and extracting simple themes from complexity, and defining the core challenges to resolve. This capability is anchored in the ability to sense gaps and ideate alternatives. The ability to generate multiple creative options and then pick the combination of the most impactful and easy-to-implement option is a key part of agile thinking.[17]

At its best, agility also means recognizing the limitations of current mental models that people are using to define problems and construct solutions, and maintaining an openness to novelty. Successful pilots find a way of framing a stubborn or intractable problem in new ways that point to fresh solutions. By breaking through the old ways of defining problems, pilots are free to develop feasible and innovative responses to the dynamic and unfolding realities that occur at the point of implementation[18] where strategies ultimately succeed or fail.

Behavioral versatility refers to the capacity to deal with diverse people and difficult situations. This ability is one of the top leadership capabilities that define high-performance leadership. Verbal communication and listening skills are the important people skills that underlie behavioral versatility. These capabilities support the people performing the piloting function to have difficult conversations. When performance does not meet expectations, or surprises occur, expectations are reinforced, root causes explored, and agreements for getting the work on track finalized.

Behavioral versatility also includes the ability to adapt oneself and one's work plans to shifting circumstances and different personalities as well as promoting this capacity in others. We all need the comfort of stability and predictability. Framing how we adapt while preserving continuity is the art of this crucial capability. Advice from Peter Block, noted consultant and author of *Community: The Structure of Belonging*, calls our attention to the proper focus of agility. The challenge, Block argues, is "What can we create to overcome obstacles rather than struggling over what problems we cannot solve."[19]

Agility has the following components:

Flexible Thinking
- Translating broad goals into priorities that others can put into action
- Being aware of and evaluating changing circumstances, and discerning patterns that have implications for priorities and plans
- Examining problems thoroughly
- Differentiating symptoms from root causes of problems
- Making connections between facts and recognizing patterns
- Generating multiple creative options beyond the familiar
- Picking the solutions that are the optimal combination of being most impactful and easy to implement

Behavioral Versatility
- Blending work priorities with the needs and interests of team members
- Adapting one's work plans to these circumstances
- Getting others to increase their flexibility
- Helping others to adapt to shifting circumstances in a way that preserves alignment with broad goals

The mental abilities that underlie agile thinking can be developed. Insight into how others perceive us along these dimensions provided by multi-rater surveys and well-designed self-rating surveys can give us insights into how we can improve agile thinking.

Thinking flexibly is not enough. The ability to act flexibly is also critical. Behavioral versatility is critical in mobilizing the ability of others to adapt to shifting circumstances. Through our research we discovered that this ability is a top-rated leadership behavior. The mechanics of accountable influence focus on how to be flexible. The leading edge tool described in Chapter 3 focuses on how to fit behavior to the situational circumstances in which leaders find themselves as they drive the initiatives and priorities for which they are responsible.

Core Piloting Skill 4: Exerting Accountable Influence

The final of the four core piloting capabilities is exerting accountable influence. Accountable influence means getting others to alter their thinking, pursue different goals, or shift their behavior. By pairing accountability with influence, we highlight the importance of honoring one's commitment to others as a condition of high-impact influence. This skill requires maintaining strong relationships with key stakeholders. There are a few key categories of stakeholders that are especially important and we outline them below (Figure 2.2). Effective organizational piloting involves building relationships with these stakeholders to maintain the alignments of effort needed to achieve success in the bumpy road of change implementation.

FIGURE 2.2 Key Stakeholders

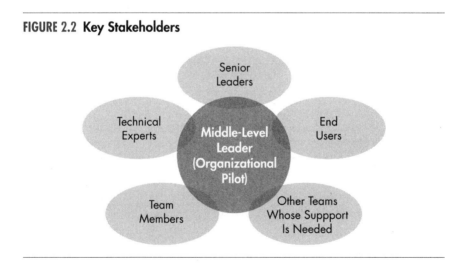

Accountable influence also involves modeling change one expects from others, and using influence strategies to drive results with others. This model is summarized in Figure 2.3.

Our model of accountable influence involves connecting, demonstrating, and influencing. Connecting leaders begins the process of building strong relationships, a pre-condition for effective influence. Demonstrating means modeling the behavior you expect from others, mobilizing the integrity and confidence needed to influence—in other words, to get others to do something differently. Finally, influence is the appropriate use of strategies that gets others to think and do differently.

FIGURE 2.3 Accountable Influence Model

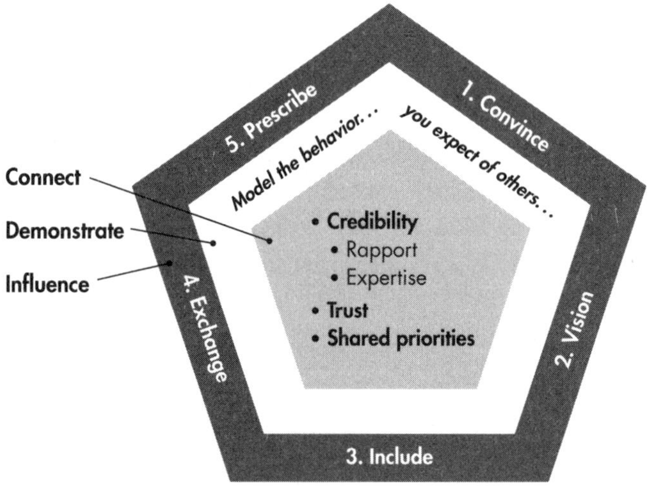

Connect
Demonstrate
Influence

- Credibility
  - Rapport
  - Expertise
- Trust
- Shared priorities

Model the behavior... you expect of others...

1. Convince
2. Vision
3. Include
4. Exchange
5. Prescribe

Connect

In the piloting function, leaders build relationships that are resilient to the stresses and strains that arise when working on challenging goals under pressure. Shared values, knowledge, and respect are the basis of strong relationships, and they are strengthened by frequent contact.

Strong relationships share the following characteristics:

- Credibility
- Trust
- Shared priorities

Table 2.1 is a useful tools for targeting "connecting" efforts.

TABLE 2.1 Network of Quality Relationships

KEY RELATIONSHIPS	CREDIBILITY	TRUST	SHARED PRIORITIES
Senior Leaders			
End Users			
Technical Experts			
Teams Whose Support Is Needed			
Team Members			

Demonstrate: Model the Behavior You Expect of Others

One of the most powerful practices of leaders at any level is that they model the behavior they ask of others. This practice lies at the heart of accountability. This practice also helps people decide what is important. Important things are what people will take personal risks to see through. Demonstration also means acknowledging mistakes and working with others to recover from a commitment we made when we have broken it.

Influence

With strong relationships and the power of modeling the behavior one expects of others, we now turn to influence. Influence means getting people to think and do differently without resorting to the use of power.[20] When an influence is used that fits the situation, a person in a piloting role moves people to accountable action. This includes describing the problem and identifying opportunities.

We have synthesized five main influence strategies from the research in Table 2.2.[21] They are listed in the order of how they are used to mobilize people to action from the beginning to the end of a strategic initiative. Accountability is increased when people feel that what they are signing up for is clear, that they have the skills and resources needed to follow through, that what is being asked of them is consistent with their role or professional identity, and that they are not fearful of making intelligent mistakes.[22]

TABLE 2.2 Five Influence Options

OPTIONS	DEFINITION	IMPACT CREATED	HOW IT WORKS	WHEN TO USE IT
1. Convince	Proposing an idea and offering data and reasoning that supports the proposal and is compelling to the stakeholder	Stakeholder recognizes that there is a compelling idea that will create benefits they recognize as important	The back and forth of evaluating proposals and the rationale upon which they are based, as well as making counterproposals, leads the target of influence to be convinced	Evidence and logic-based debate needed to mobilize minds to focus on an opportunity or problem
2. Share Vision	Using personal vision to trigger vision in others so that they help create an inspiring future	Stakeholders recognize common ground and are inspired by a shared vision for a big-picture outcome	Presenting personal vision galvanizes others to embrace vision, and knitting together a common vision from personal visions builds commitment to a big-picture outcome	When a task will require a compelling idea of the future to attract and sustain the motivation needed to maintain the pursuit of a long-term goal
3. Include	Building an idea for action that leverages the perspectives of others so that they see their ideas in the plans—especially concerning obstacles and how to overcome them	Stakeholder commitment to a plan to achieve an outcome	Getting others to disclose concerns and help develop ways of overcoming these concerns leads to commitment to action	When people will face several personal obstacles they must overcome to achieve a goal
4. Exchange	Clarifying needs and trading obligations to create a win-win agreement	Stakeholders have an agreement for how a conflict will be resolved	Clarifying needs and exploring alternatives for meeting needs leads to an agreement	A conflict exists for which rationale and data can be used to resolve the situation

TABLE 2.2 Five Influence Options *(continued)*

OPTIONS	DEFINITION	IMPACT CREATED	HOW IT WORKS	WHEN TO USE IT
5. Prescribe	Reinforcing expectations and applying contingencies to support compliance	A stakeholder complies with an expectation	Reiterating expectations and outlining positive and negative consequences encourages compliance	Stakeholders are not complying with a policy or standard

When significant organizational change is being implemented, upward influence is a vital priority. During these times, the majority of targets of influence are senior colleagues with whom one has to align priorities or plans.[23] Peers occupy second place in the list of common influence targets. Collaboration across an organization's boundaries with peers is an undermanaged success factor of strategy implementation.[24] Power relationships between peers are uncertain and competition for resources and promotions often strains collaboration between peers. Influencing skills are the means through which we overcome these challenges. Table 2.3 provides an influence strategy planning tool.

TABLE 2.3 Influence Strategy Planning Tool

1. Convince:

2. Share vision:

3. Include:

4. Exchange:

5. Prescribe:

A Pilot in Action: A Diplomat with Drive

"We were involved in a large project with a big IT element. The key to success early on was to get different departments and functional groups to buy in. [This was] not easy to do in our organization. Barb was able to come in and mold consensus out of a big and diverse group. She got people to share information, usually in one-on-one sessions. Barb kept people focused on what they had in common. When conflicts came up, she got people to focus on them directly. If she made a mistake, she was quick to admit. No one lost face when they made a mistake. People walked out of sessions with her believing they were going to get what they needed. That's pretty rare."

PILOTING FIELD BOOK

We conclude this chapter by outlining a set of tools to use in implementing effective piloting.

1. Translate Strategic Plans into Action

The starting point for the success of any initiative is goal alignment. Many in the role of organizational pilots begin with a disadvantage that they must remedy. Here are some facts from recent research[25] that reflects a perennial challenge of organizational change leadership that must be overcome. Only 55 percent of middle managers can name one of a company's five top priorities. While 90 percent say that executives communicate often enough, only 16 percent clearly understand the connection between the corporate priorities they serve. So, a common starting point for most pilots is creating clarity.

Clarity occurs when we can link our goals to strategic priorities. Figure 2.4 shows how. From the top to the bottom, broad priorities break down into smaller goals, into tasks, and these tasks into subtasks. This results in a hierarchy of work units in which the highest level of work sits at the top and the smallest units of work lie at the bottom (this is often called a work breakdown structure). By ensuring that each level below supports the work above, alignment is supported.

FIGURE 2.4 Hierarchy of Work Units

The next step is to translate this work into a project plan. At its simplest, this means the following:

- **Estimating how long it will take to complete each unit of work.**
- **Establishing dependencies.** Identify which units of work must be done before others begin. Some tasks must follow others, and some work can be done in parallel. Defining these relationships ensures that people are following the most efficient work plan and that serious disruptions will not occur because of poor planning.
- **Determining the resource requirements.** Identify what resources are needed and when they are needed to complete the work. This includes work that is required from other teams. Working with teams to ensure this alignment exists is an important piloting activity.

This work can be summarized in a simple project plan, shown in Table 2.4. People performing the piloting function use this information to socialize plans with others to refine and confirm alignment.

TABLE 2.4 Project Plan Framework

TASKS	SUBTASKS	DURATION	TIMING			
			WEEK 1	WEEK 2	WEEK 3	AND SO ON
Resources needed when						

2. Build Behavioral Momentum

Four practices build the momentum of people to sustain change projects. This momentum encompasses sustained effort and ongoing learning of how to overcome the problems that occur.

- **Expressing appreciation for progress made, celebrating small wins, and emphasizing the connection of small wins to the achievement of the end goal.** Making change is hard work. Expressing appreciation and gratitude for efforts made strengthens motivation. Many of us tend to overlook this important activity. Emphasizing progress that has been made toward milestones is also important; the closer we get to a goal, the more motivation builds.
- **Reinforcing positive expectations.** Communicating optimism about the plan for change and expressing confidence in the abilities of the people implementing it develops momentum. When we face difficulties in pursuing a goal, messages that the best is expected of a situation and that people have it in their power to succeed sustains the motivation to pursue challenging goals.

- **Emphasizing the benefits of change.** Regularly and repeatedly reinforcing the benefits of change helps maintain the sustained pursuit of a goal. When these benefits can be made personally relevant, they have even greater power to build momentum.
- **Reducing uncertainties.** Some important change efforts are ambiguous in nature. Broader changes like shifting the culture, promoting team effectiveness, and being more strategic, for example, can be difficult for people to grasp. Encouraging dialogue between people encourages the process, clarifying both the change and why it is important.

3. Monitor Performance Against Established Criteria and Expected Hazards to Detect Threats to the Plan

Effective piloting involves reviewing performance against preestablished success criteria. This helps us determine when we are on track and when we are not so the act part of the detect-and-act maneuvering can be accomplished.

During updates people must develop a plan for addressing emergent or actual critical deviations from the implementation plan. The challenge many encounter is that they allow updates to devolve into passive reviews of status reports in which simple descriptions of progress are given. Fear of discussing bad news or impatience with the process of creative problem solving prompts people to avoid the meaningful engagement of hazards or threats. If this happens, hazards and threats are unchecked and evolve into critical deviations that will compromise the project.

There are two steps to monitoring the progress of a solution:

Establish Success Criteria

Following are the typical criteria for each of the project variables at play in the implementation of a solution.

- **Quality of deliverables.** Reliability, maintainability, operability, flexibility, compliance, potency (ability of the deliverable to create the desired change)
- **Time.** On-time completion of project milestones and final project deliverables
- **Time.** On or under budget performance
- **Stakeholder satisfaction.** Extent to which the stakeholders are satisfied with the way change is being implemented

Monitor Performance Against Established Criteria

Being alert to how work is progressing against defined criteria helps pilots keep the work on track. King (1986) identifies critical deviations as being of strategic relevance, actionable, critical, and urgent. The following list defines these terms.

- **Strategic relevance.** The deviation threatens the long-term success of the project.
- **Actionable.** People can do something about the deviation.
- **Critical.** The deviation will have a serious negative impact on the deliverable.
- **Urgent.** Something must be done about a deviation immediately

There are two types of monitoring pilots use to detect critical deviations to the task variables, informal and formal. Informal monitoring involves being alert to evidence of potential threats as one listens to conversations among the people involved on a project or casually observes people working on project activities. The results of informal monitoring are used to identify a potential set of threats and then confirming the existence of such threats with formal monitoring information.

Formal monitoring means reviewing systematic reporting of project progress. There are five formal types of reports that are in common use.

1. **Time sheets.** Time sheets report the number of hours members of a team spend on the project.
2. **Budget reports.** These reports track progress on the project budget. The best of these reports lay out expected performance and contrast actual with expected performance, as well as featuring monthly projections of the total budget. These help the client and the consultant keep projects on track from a resource utilization point of view.
3. **Milestone charts.** A milestone chart lists project milestones and identifies the actual and planned time of completion. A milestone report lists the achievements that represent the milestones, the estimated date of completion, and actual performance. The comparison between actual with planned date of completion helps consultants and clients identify where special intervention may be necessary to keep the project on track. A sample milestone chart is presented in Table 2.5.

TABLE 2.5 Project Milestone Chart

MILESTONE	TARGET DATE	COMPLETION DATE

4. **Status reports.** A status report is a summary of progress since the last report. A status report includes the following elements: forecasts against the criteria for each variable (outcomes, schedule status, budget status, resource status); upcoming milestones; and potential threats to achieving the milestones. Status reports are often the most frequent means of communication between the participants in an implementation project.
5. **Progress reviews and senior management updates.** Pilots and navigators set aside meetings to formally review progress, monitor hazards, report threats to project deliverables and timelines, and develop and/or refine corrective measures. These sessions easily devolve into status reports. The point of these two meetings is problem solving. It generally helps to have reviewed some ideas for root causes and their potential remedies with meeting attendees before such meetings to streamline these sessions.

A summary of formal implementation plan monitoring and control methods is presented in Table 2.6.

TABLE 2.6 Formal Methods for Keeping a Plan on Track

MONITORING	PROBLEM-SOLVING CRITICAL DEVIATIONS
Time sheets	Progress reviews
Budget reports	Senior management updates
Milestone charts	
Status reports	
Progress reviews and senior management updates	

4. Identify and Address the Root Cause of Critical Deviations

This step involves reviewing the main issues that threaten the change project deliverables or timeline—called critical deviations—and uncovering the root causes of these deviations.

There is wisdom to be gleaned from the sea concerning the importance of the monitoring. Even experienced sailors make mistakes and have to recover. Consider the case of the *Torrey Canyon*, a cargo ship that ran aground while proceeding through the Sicily Islands and spilled 100,000 tons of oil. The *Torrey Canyon*'s grounding occurred on a crystal-clear day; stormy weather and low visibility were not problems. No, as Dr. Anita M. Rothblum of the U.S. Coast Guard Research and Development Center points out, the *Torrey Canyon*'s grounding can be attributed to other factors ... people factors:

> The *Torrey Canyon* was loaded with cargo and headed for its deep-water terminal in Wales. The shipping agent contacted the captain to warn him of decreasing tides at Milford Haven, the entrance to the terminal.
>
> The captain knew that if he didn't make the next high tide, he might have to wait as much as five days before the water depth would be sufficient for the ship to enter. This pressure to keep to schedule was exacerbated by a second factor: the captain's concern about his ship's appearance. He needed to transfer cargo in order to even out the ship's draft. He could have performed the transfer while underway, but that would have increased the probability that he might spill a little oil on the decks and come into port with a "sloppy" ship.
>
> The captain opted to rush to get past the Scillies and into Milford Haven in order to make the transfer, thus increasing the pressure to make good time. He decided, in order to save time, to go *through* the Scilly Islands, instead of *around* them as originally planned. He made this decision even though he did not have a copy of the *Channel Pilot* for that area, and even though he was not very familiar with the area.
>
> Human factors and equipment also conspired against the *Torrey Canyon*. The steering selector switch was in the wrong position: it had been left on autopilot. In this setting the steering selector unit did not give any indication of its setting at the helm. When

the captain ordered a turn into the western channel through the Scillies, the helmsman dutifully turned the wheel, but nothing happened.[26]

As this example illustrates, the majority of the off-track factors are people issues. Piloting is being vigilant about the people and team factors that can help or hurt an initiative.

The second task of managing critical deviations is to evaluate whether we have to recalibrate our plans. We determine the root causes that pushed us off course if this happened and determine how we get back on course. Sometimes we learn that our beliefs and assumptions have to be reset.

In evaluating progress of our plans, we often recognize results that are shy of our expectations or do not succeed, and we must adjust our plans to deal with these recognitions. The question we need to answer is: "Do I need to better execute what I planned?" or "Does my review of results suggest I need to revisit my assumptions that guided my plan and reformulate my plan?" Based on the answer, we plan the appropriate actions. Figure 2.5 captures the process of learning that is involved.

FIGURE 2.5 Process of Recalibrating Plans

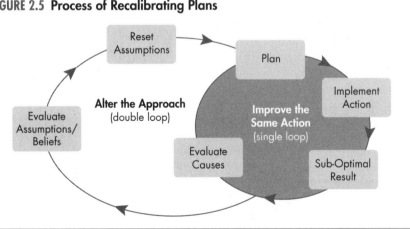

5. Develop the Strategy for Getting Back on Course

In this step, we confirm final action steps and specify a follow-up. This clarification gives particular emphasis to what the problem owner must do to resolve critical deviations. Having clear criteria can help us evaluate if we are making progress. As many of the deviations will likely be interpersonal, the success criteria will require some attention. Table 2.7 outlines some examples from the review of an initiative to improve safety performance in an organization.

TABLE 2.7 Examples of Action Steps and Success Criteria

Deviation: Injury rates spiked as managerial attention was diverted by a surge in production demands that strained management's problem-solving process.

ROOT CAUSES	PLAN TO ADDRESS THE CAUSES	SUCCESS CRITERIA
The initiative lost its high priority in the light of other urgent priorities with the facility manager and early successes had built a sense of overconfidence.	Clarify the set of priorities and ask questions to clarify what was making it difficult to maintain focus. Manager picked a strategy for calling attention to slip in focus and the importance of getting back on track.	The manager helped design a plan for bringing more personal attention to safe performance. The manager mentioned the slip in management commitment in his team meeting. Physical therapists reported that compliance with visits and treatment programs returned.
The manager did not have a way to model the priority that reflected his status.	Developed a managerial safe work methods audit tool that created a summary number that could be recorded and tracked with his direct report managers.	Manager conducted periodic safety audits and provided feedback to manager about his observations.

6. Build Enthusiasm for Maintaining the Course

Communicating the slip or deviation in the plan, emphasizing that such slips and lapses can be overcome, outlining the remedies that are being put in place, and expressing optimism for the success of the plan supports the motivation to continue. Socializing the revised plan so that key stakeholders are committed sets the stage for future success.

7. Maintaining Vigilance

Monitoring the success of the revised plan to make needed adjustments completes the seven steps through which successful piloting occurs.

THE SPECIAL CHALLENGE OF CHANGING BEHAVIOR

One of the special challenges of implementing a solution is implementing the behavior challenges associated with implementation. Driving behavior change is a common although not often recognized part of the process. Table 2.8 lists a summary of off-course factors encountered on a large business process redesign initiative.

TABLE 2.8 Off-Track Themes for Consulting Projects of a General Management Consulting Firm

CATEGORY	OFF-TRACK THEMES
Customer Issues (62% of off-track issues)	• Anger about being coerced into project work • Resistance to the implementation plan as too aggressive, too participative, or too analytical • Senior leaders have not assigned project work a high priority • Leaders do not have the needed project management, leadership, or conceptual/analytical skills • Conflicts among leaders slow down the project
Project Team Issues (26% of off-track issues)	• Staff not meeting expectations for their part of the work • Lack of agreement about approach to work slowing down work and threatening timelines • Lack of clear cascaded expectations leading to rework • Ineffective handoffs between staff cycling on and off project, creating slippage on plans

People problems represented 65 percent of off-course events, whereas technical issues represented 35 percent. These statistics led to the conclusion that piloting issues in this situation were largely people challenges. This list parallels factors identified by project management experts like John McManus and others who have documented common off-track factors encountered in implementing solutions to business problems. This work indicates that a majority of the events that threaten plans to implement technology, process, or other changes are people ones.

One of the realities that may emerge in the critical moments of piloting is that readiness needed to succeed does not exist. Lack of adequate preparation, changes in resources, a change in priorities, and other unexpected difficulties can weaken readiness, and the lack of readiness can push implementation off-track. There are two potential responses:

1. In the spirit of organizational learning, determine the root causes and develop a plan to address them.
2. Abandon the effort to solve the problem.

Response One

Reevaluating a plan change, its importance, and its feasibility can be quite embarrassing. People often feel incompetent, embarrassed, and demoralized in these circumstances. Our first goal in this situation is to maintain a sense of efficacy. This means being reminded of the best part of the people who are involved—the part that undertook the change while acknowledging limitations, normalizing the trial-and-error process of making change, and reinforcing beliefs in competence to make adjustments and sustain pursuit of the change goals.

The second goal of this stage is to evaluate whether we have to recalibrate our plans. We determine the root causes that pushed us off course "if this happened" and determine how we get back on course. Sometimes we learn that our beliefs and assumptions have to be reset. This means clarifying the vision for the solution, clarifying outcomes, and building commitment to outcomes and action plans.

Engaging us to persevere, to adjust, and to restart is an important obligation of the consultants or facilitators that we engage to facilitate change. In the example of the young management team that was presented earlier, the change agent asked the facility manager to apply the management skill he was applying to production problems in other aspects of facility operations.

Response Two

The other possible response we can make to the challenges of piloting is to abandon a change. We can decide that the problem is not worth the effort. When this happens, the goal is to encourage the people involved to make an appropriate assessment of the situation. This assessment should include the idea that the solution exceeds the current level of readiness. In this case, we can either scale back the solution to meet the readiness that exists, or we can enhance the readiness conditions. These tasks can become part of a new plan to make ourselves ready to pursue the initial goal, a plan we can pursue in the future with new insight and capabilities.

MOTIVATION CHALLENGES PILOTS FACE

This section offers solutions to some motivation challenges that pilots face.

Maintaining One's Own Motivation to Persist

A difficult challenge is maintaining one's motivation while you're piloting. One's esteem can be threatened when he or she is associated with a slip in the plan. To weather such assaults, many pilots construct peer-coaching networks to help them maintain their focus and solve problems in slip situations.

Maintaining the Courage to Engage Others About Their Role in a Slip in Commitment

When a slip in commitment occurs, a person with less power is engaging someone with more power about a deviation from expectations. The politics of accountability in organizations will lead the people to struggle with accountability and competence. The power difference and accountability dynamics involved in many situations complicate the task of working through a slip or critical deviation. When agreements exist for how people will work through these tough issues, they are more efficiently managed.

TABLE 2.9 Quick Reference Guide for Effective Piloting

STEPS	HOW THEY WORK
1. Translate strategic priorities into plans.	• Converting broad strategic goals into a set of sequenced tasks, subtasks, and milestones with a timeline and needed resources sets the stage for the clarity people need to execute successfully. • Collaborating with frontline staff and peers in functions whose support is needed to implement successfully develops a feasible plan in which people commit themselves. • Consulting with senior leaders and peer leaders helps secure the adjustments needed to launch the plan and the needed alignments. • Reconfiguring roles or how the handoffs operate between roles to support the new work and how it is best achieved.
2. Initiate action.	• Compelling messaging tailored to key audiences about the what, why, and how of the plan and a timetable for implementation cultivates a sense of mission and purpose as work begins.
3. Build behavioral momentum.	Four practices encourage the development of momentum in plan implementation: • Celebrating small wins and expressing gratitude and appreciation for efforts made • Reinforcing positive expectations • Emphasizing the benefits of change • Reducing uncertainties through dialogue with others
4. Monitor performance against established success criteria and identify challenges, assess hazards, and evaluate threats as well as develop preventive measures.	• Reviewing performance against preestablished success criteria and knowledge of hazards help us determine when we are on track and when we are not so we can make needed course corrections. • Accomplishing these tasks in progress reviews and management updates.
5. When plans go off track, assess the root causes of the deviations and slips to focus strategies for getting back on track.	• Mindfulness of the hazards of old attitudes, habits, and practices enhances strategies for negotiating the difficulties of driving change. • Use personal currency and relationships with senior colleagues to position challenges of the plan and its implementation to win support needed to operate with agility. • Leverage in-depth knowledge of operational details to win the support of junior colleagues.

TABLE 2.9 Quick Reference Guide for Effective Piloting *(continued)*

STEPS	HOW THEY WORK
6. Develop the strategy for getting back on track.	• By maintaining the tension between the initial plan and insight about the root causes of off-course factors and the engagement of others, a strategy is developed for getting the plan back on track.
7. Communicate to build enthusiasm for maintaining the course and implement the plan.	• Communicate the slips or deviations from the plan. • Emphasize that such slips and lapses can be overcome. • Outline the remedies that are being put in place. • Express optimism for the success of the plan and outline commitments to the end goal to help drive people forward to the performance improvement.
8. Maintain vigilance on what is working and not working and make adjustments.	• Staying focused on the progress people are making and adapting plans to maintain the course leads to success.

FIGURE 2.6 A Piloting Skill: Agile Problem Solving

Agile problem solving brings together four capabilities as depicted below:
- Three capabilities that support creative problem solving
  - Awareness of emerging threats to the plan
  - Organizational know how: how to make things happen in the organization
  - Agility in thinking and behavior
- The four steps of creative problem solving:

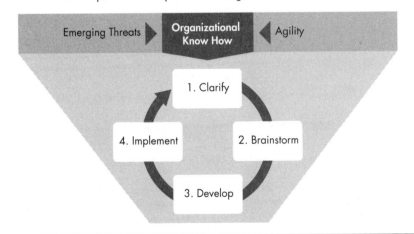

Chapter 3

Working at the Leading Edge: Conceptual and Organization Skills

The ultimate basis of success . . . is the skipper's decisive command of himself, his boat, and the situation.
—STUART H. WALKER

Earlier we outlined a model of leadership that draws on three powerful interconnected leadership functions we find in high-performance leadership: navigating, piloting, and managing the leading edge.

Our model captures what we have learned from studying high-performance leaders and organizations. It also organizes and clarifies patterns of thinking and doing that create results that matter. In the end, leadership is not only "what I do in the role I have," but "what I get others in complementary roles to do in order to achieve something great." In this chapter, we focus on managing the leading edge.

Along the line of the leading edge, goals, aspirations, and objectives make contact with the push and pull of the environment. In nautical terms, "leading edge" refers to the part of the sail that first contacts the wind. Just as the leading edge of a sail converts the push and pull of wind and wave into forward thrust, high-performing leaders take action at points along the leading edge that converts restraining and facilitative forces into progress. People performing in navigating and pilot functions productively address resistance, the most predictable response to change, as well as maneuver the ebbs and flows in the motivation and abilities of people whose support is required to execute business change—to drive results. The value of the detect-and-act functions of navigating and piloting is they focus on the need to adapt and improvise with focus. This is a critical success factor in driving the implementation of strategic initiatives.

There are four key elements involved in any strategic initiative.

1. Goals
2. The plan: tasks, schedule, and resources
3. Implementation launch
4. Progress reviews and senior management updates to make needed adjustments

Within each of these four steps, critical moments occur. There are several common critical moments. For example, a key stakeholder fails to follow through with an important action step. Progress stalls. In these critical moments, high-performing leaders productively engage the resistance they encounter and build the mindset and motivational momentum that brings people together in synchronized action.

WHAT WE CAN LEARN FROM HIGH PERFORMERS

In a survey of the attributes of high-performing mariners, Gary Jobson describes a few distinct characteristics that help them achieve their success. In his *Sailing World* summary, Jobson found two shared traits. High-performing sailors have been training (and competing) for a long time, and each of them is highly goal-oriented. A strong goal orientation seems to drive preparation—both physically and in the management of the boat—and persistence.

- **Boat preparation.** Jobson cites the example of Mike Martin, who won the 97-foot 505 Worlds in San Francisco Bay in 2010. But there is more. In 2000 he set out to do what no one in the class had ever done: win as both crew and skipper. Jobson relays Martin's description of preparation. "We did a massive amount of boat preparation," he adds. "The boat preparation paid off when we broke our rig and had a spare fully-tuned rig ready to go. We also had an on-the-water support boat that we shared with another team, stocked with lots of spare parts."
- **Physical preparation.** Jobson offers the example of David Loring, from Charleston, South Carolina, who raced in a specific class, the Sunfish

class, for 25 years. "I focused on training in the Bahamas for about nine months before the regatta to get used to sailing in those waves," says Loring. "Physical training is one of the most important aspects of being able to win a big regatta." Jobson emphasized Loring's belief that the key is understanding his strengths and weaknesses.

- **Persistence.** Finally, Jobson cites the example of George Szabo. Szabo honed his skills through 23 years of sailing in the San Diego area. From his first competitive event in 1986, at the age of 16, Szabo steadily ascended the class ranks. After many attempts and at the age of 39, he finally won his Star world title in 2009.

Preparation of how to apply the resources and tools needed to solve the problems and experience are key to success. In this chapter, we share a tool that we can use to manage the challenges at the leading edge. This tool reflects a powerful connection between two ideas that help us manage critical moments on strategic initiatives. Our model is based on the following formula:

Low Resistance = High Readiness

Resistance reflects a low level of change readiness. Conversely, a low level of resistance reflects a high level of readiness. So how does change readiness develop? It builds cumulatively across the four steps shown in Figure 3.1, each of them critical in developing the knowledge and motivation needed to drive effective change.

FIGURE 3.1 On the Leading Edge

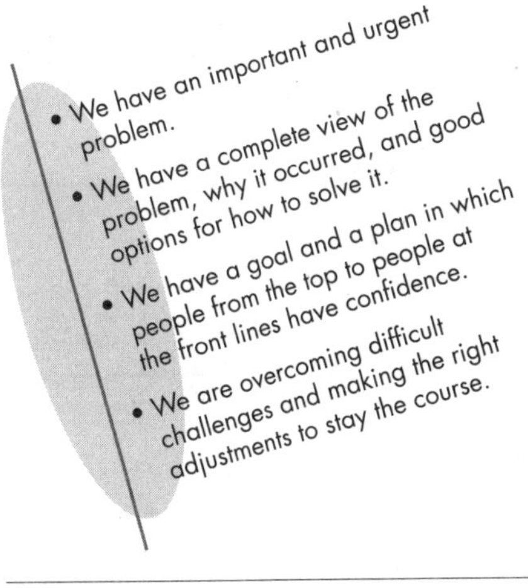

- We have an important and urgent problem.
- We have a complete view of the problem, why it occurred, and good options for how to solve it.
- We have a goal and a plan in which people from the top to people at the front lines have confidence.
- We are overcoming difficult challenges and making the right adjustments to stay the course.

Common Points of Resistance to Overcome

- "There is no problem." or "This is not an important problem."
- "This solution will not fix the problem."
- "The plan to implement the solution wont effectively install the solution."
- "We lack the ability to implement the plan successfully."
- "We will quit the plan when things get difficult."

There are four critical points along the leading edge. Our task is to cycle through these points with others in the sequence (Table 3.1). We cannot skip over any step, as each serves as a key building block for the subsequent one.

TABLE 3.1 Points on the Leading Edge

Key transition to the leading edge: Change blindness is blocking the recognition of an important and/or urgent problem.

POINTS ON THE LEADING EDGE	WHEN THIS POINT IS MISSING
1. We have an important and urgent problem to solve: Achieving Problem Recognition—breaking through change blindness	✓ People think that we are doing fine, that there is no problem. ✓ People believe that there is little support for working on a problem we have.
2. We have a complete view of the problem and good options for how to solve it: Promoting Critical Reflection	✓ We have many competing views of the problem that have not been addressed, or we have not framed the problem in a way that is compelling to a critical mass of stakeholders. ✓ We are jumping too quickly to implement a familiar, practical solution that will not close important performance gaps.
3. We have a goal and plan we believe in: Building Commitment to Initiate Action	✓ The solution won't work. ✓ The changes we have to make are too hard—we won't like the process. ✓ The effort we will have to exert is too great. ✓ We will not follow through—we lack alignment among key stakeholders on the plan. ✓ We have not clarified what success looks like—people are not striving for the same outcome. ✓ We lack the ability and resources to implement the plan successfully—people are not confident in the plan. ✓ We have not scoped out the challenges that lie ahead and how to respond to them—we will go off course—politics will prompt scapegoating and/or denials.
4. We are overcoming difficult challenges and making the right adjustments to stay on course: Motivating Agile Perseverance	✓ We are cutting too many corners—things will be different, not better. ✓ Scapegoating and denials are occurring.

At each of these four points, leaders have to organize both the work and the people needed to accomplish strategic priorities. At these moments, the pressure of getting on with it can prompt us to overlook actions that transform doubts and resistance into belief and commitment. For each point on the leading edge, there are actions that address these and in this chapter we outline them.

High-performance mariners position the sail to optimize thrust given the push and pull of the environment. High-performance leaders manage the psychological leading edge to develop the momentum to achieve results that matter.

A Brief Case

We begin with an example to illustrate what happens when we do not manage the leading edge properly. High Top Inc.'s goal was to integrate the customer service center groups of separate but related businesses within the company into one unit. Each service organization had different strengths and weaknesses, but as a group, the service centers were too costly. The business needed to reduce its costs, and more than half of its costs were associated with service operations. Senior leadership was committed to achieving significant cost savings; however, they also wanted to ensure that service levels were retained throughout the process of planning for and implementing the cost reduction.

Technology would be key to the solution, so High Top Inc.'s president assigned one of the company's top developers to the team working on the project. But more important than technology, the organizational design itself would have to be adjusted, particularly in its reporting structures.

The president of the firm asked Mary, the leader of one call center, and her peer leaders of the other service centers to build a business case for how the various centers would become one. As a team, this group was tasked to answer such questions as: (1) Who would run the new combined group? (2) What management structure should be adopted? What role would the other leaders play? (3) How would work processes be changed? (4) How would staff be developed to perform successfully in the new organization?

The president of the company believed that empowering the call center leaders with a broad mandate would produce a solution that the rest of the organization would support. With a "do your best" goal, the team set itself to the task.

While Mary had some misgivings about the feasibility of integrating the service groups, she was in the best position to pull the team together as the call center leader who had been in the organization the longest and an acknowledged expert on the design of service systems. Mary prided herself in being a team player, but she was sometimes perceived as a being a bit too direct, conservative, and control-oriented.

The other members of the team included Mark, who had recently joined the organization. Having led a larger service center operation for his previous employer, Mark was regarded as one of the new, hard-charging "high potentials" who would lead the organization into the future. Initially, Mark saw that a number of improvements could be made but was uncertain what the most important tasks were.

Jon was another member of the team. Jon had led of one of the service organizations for many years. He maintained strong relationships both within and outside the company. Though Jon possessed a deep knowledge about how the business worked, he preferred to avoid the limelight. Privately, Jon thought that the current system—where the customer service center groups operated as separate entities—worked well, even better than a combined service organization would. Different lines of business had different service requirements, and each required different service approaches. In other words, while Jon didn't vocally protest or try to interfere with the president's mandate, he wasn't inclined to push it forward either.

Mary and the team convened several times. Eventually, they reached an impasse. With vague goals, it was difficult to determine whether any idea the team developed was a good one or worth the effort. Team members naturally advocated for the practices of their own service organizations as possibilities for the new combined organization. Team discussions eventually devolved into squabbles about values, upon which the design of each leader's service organization was based; however, attempts to address values were constrained by differences in management style. The initiative stalled. Mary and the team felt defeated.

What happened? Mary and her peers set out with only a portion of the tools needed to solve problems successfully. Their tool kit was incomplete. The team had not advanced through the first two points along the leading edge:

- **We have an important and urgent problem.** The team had a general goal and one that did not connect to them personally. The president had tasked Mary and her peers with answering certain questions; however, that wasn't enough.

- **We have a complete view of the problem and good options for how to solve it.** The team saw parts of the problem and reviewed some options, but not well enough to proceed. Conversations devolved into squabbles where everyone was looking out for his or her own service organization rather than seeking a higher perspective or understanding.

WHY WE NEED A NEW TOOL

Let's begin with a description of how most of us organize work today. With some variation, most of us do the following to accomplish a result.

We plan the work:

- Define a goal to work toward in a measurable way such that we can determine if we have been successful
- Outline the tasks needed to achieve the goal
- Develop estimates for how long the tasks will take to complete
- Schedule tasks against a timetable so that the tasks that are building blocks for subsequent tasks are accomplished first
- Identify any special resources we need to accomplish the work

Then we implement our plan:

- Review progress against our plan
- Address tasks that have not been completed on time—especially those that are building-block tasks—and solve problems that prevent their completion
- Reset the plan if need be

Most of us will recognize these activities as the basic steps of work management. To make work management tools more complete and to improve our success rate, we need to expand our focus to include the ability and motivation of the people we work with. Our appreciation of the benefits of an enhanced tool kit deepens with explicit comparisons between the concepts of readiness that underlie effective management at the leading edge and the task management approach to make change happen.

HOW PROJECT MANAGEMENT DEVELOPED

Common project management practices are rooted in the same practices that engineers utilize in construction projects. When building a bridge, constructing a road, or developing an airplane, the problems faced by engineers are physical and interdependent. "How much time should we allot to excavating the rocky soil in light of our targeted completion date?" "A properly cured foundation is critical; what impact will an early freeze have on this process?" "How long after the foundation is poured can we begin assembling the girders?" "How do we redesign the skin covering the wing surface now that it has failed our stress tests?" "How much does this setback affect our original timeline?"

For the change projects most of us face in organizations today, the physical aspect of tasks (preparing a summary document, scheduling an important project meeting, testing a software application) is only a small part of the challenge. When people change what they do or how they do it, the ability or motivation of the person (or work group) to do the project task or use the outcomes of this work later on is vital. "How do we ensure follow-through among those who must implement the targeted change?" "How do we get these managers to feel confident enough in the project deliverables that they give their approval?" "How do we create alignment among constituencies whose goals are in conflict?"

For critical tasks, readiness for change is an important aspect that must be managed. People need to feel willing and able to do what is necessary. We need a way help us engage change readiness.

There are two main benefits to integrating the leading edge (readiness management) with organizing work.

1. Optimizing readiness is a superordinate purpose that keeps us focused on the motivation and ability to do the work and not just the work itself.
2. Readiness management emphasizes that motivation and ability develop in a sequence.

Superordinate Purpose

The superordinate purpose of managing the leading edge is that tasks should be explicitly designed to promote the development of the readiness conditions that accelerate change. A well-designed approach to implementing change with others outlines the work to do and mobilizes the ability and motivation of people to do it.

To fulfill this expanded purpose, the leading edge invites us to refine the requirements for successfully implementing business change. Clarifying scope is more than getting sign-off on a document. It is an opportunity to build a common vision of outcomes among multiple constituencies. A steering committee review is more than an update on status. This meeting is an opportunity to build motivation and confidence by recognizing and celebrating small wins. A progress review is more than a review of how we are doing against milestones. It is also an opportunity to alert a problem owner to potential threats to project outcomes and build commitment to potential responses.

By contrast, the project approach focuses on getting the deliverable completed on time by following the schedule and adhering to the budget. People problems are bothersome distractions that are to be managed on the side and with a big stick if necessary. Compliance with the plan is the focus. In the readiness perspective, building capacity to change, addressing readiness gaps, and promoting learning are primary focal points for leaders pursuing enduring performance improvement.

Typically, insufficient attention is given to whether the solution can be successfully implemented. The politics of maintaining stakeholder support is a priority only to the extent that it affects the production of the immediate deliverables. The basic perspective of the task approach is: "If people do what we tell them, they will fix the problem." "If they don't do what we tell them, they are either ignorant, crazy, or both." The common result of exclusively applying task management to business projects is the "credenza buster" phenomenon—on-time installation of software that no one uses; on-budget implementation of training that few apply to their day-to-day job performance; or on-spec operational improvement plans that management never implements, all of which are summarized in a big three-ring binder.

By contrast, the focus of the readiness perspective is on enduring performance improvement. Engagement and participation are used to clarify big-picture goals, to right-size actions to the level of motivation and ability that can be developed in the problem situation, and to develop the best means to achieve goals. Rather than letting resistance, the omnipresent feature of any significant change project, push the project focus to completing deliverables at the expense of genuine performance improvement, the personal and organizational issues that underlie resistance are sought out and addressed openly and directly. In this way, genuine progress toward meaningful performance is given the best chance for success.

Momentum Builds over Time

People and organizations develop motivation momentum over time. Psychology suggests that the idea of critical moments emphasizes two points: (1) the right timing and the right event must be synchronized to develop competence in a human system, and (2) the development of basic competence is vital to the development of later, more advanced levels of competencies.

Critical Moments

Psychologists have noticed that during the course of human development there are periods during which certain inputs from the external environment must occur if certain competencies are to develop efficiently. The acquisition of language skills is a good example. When the right environmental influences (hearing adults speak or seeing adults sign; being spoken to or being signed to) occur at the right time (early childhood), biological programming is activated, learning occurs rapidly, and a high level of proficiency is achieved. However, when this timing is disrupted, a skill may develop but not without a large investment in special remedial attention (special education activities, enrichment programs) and develops to a lower level of proficiency than is otherwise possible (limited understanding of grammar; lower verbal comprehension skills).

There are parallels in business change. In a change attempt, if insufficient effort is devoted to shaping consensus among a broad set of stakeholders right up front and early on, then commitment to the project will be difficult to achieve even with special remedial efforts (reengaging unsupportive stakeholders to build consensus after a project has begun). If a manager is contemplating expanding her managerial tool kit and insufficient time is devoted to how implementation challenges are addressed, then a change attempt goes off the rails.

The notion of critical moments also emphasizes fitting the right action with the right circumstance. Research suggests that watching video of adults speaking or signing does not have the same positive developmental impact on a child as being spoken or signed to in person. Similarly, on business change projects, the quality of input determines impact. Publishing a statement about deliverables does not have the same impact as engaging in dialogue with others about the scope and quality of deliverables and incorporating their feedback into a summary statement of deliverables. Critical moments underscore the fact that it is not just the quality of the timing but the quality of the input that must match the circumstance.

Finally, the notion of critical moments calls our attention to the fact that in a human system certain basic skills acquired early in development are building blocks for others that develop later. Interpersonal communication skills, for example, are a necessary building block for high-level conceptual thinking. When the development of a "building block" skill is disrupted, so is the development of other, more sophisticated skills whose development is dependent on that building block.

On change projects, early developments also serve as the foundation for subsequent ones. For example, a clear definition of the scope of the targeted business change is needed to develop initial estimates of the effort required to complete a project. When clear definitions are not present, initial estimates of the scope of work are widely off the mark, and a change initiative suffers. The critical moments of a business change project are satisfying the conditions of each of the four stages of readiness. These are summarized in Table 3.2.

TABLE 3.2 Leading Edge: Conditions for Each Stage of Readiness

POINTS ON THE LEADING EDGE	CONDITIONS RESULTING IN TRANSITION TO THE NEXT POINT
1. We have an important and urgent problem to solve. Achieving Problem Recognition—breaking through change blindness	• Recognizes that a problem exists • Sees that the problem has high priority • Feels the costs of allowing the problem to continue are too high to ignore • Perceives the benefits of making improvements can be achieved promptly • Feels that general approaches for solving problems are feasible

(continued)

TABLE 3.2 Leading Edge: Conditions for Each Stage of Readiness *(continued)*

POINTS ON THE LEADING EDGE	CONDITIONS RESULTING IN TRANSITION TO THE NEXT POINT
2. We have a complete view of the problem and good options for how solve it. Promoting Critical Reflection	*Perceives that the conditions of the previous readiness stages were met and . . .* • Separates the effects of the problem from its root causes • Sees the problem as a natural consequence of the history of the situation and the dynamics of the environment • Feels responsible for developing and implementing a solution to the problem • Recognizes past mistakes that bear on the problem situation but is not demoralized by them • Perceives options and choices that could be applied to the problem situation yet feels pressured to act by the situation • Has evaluated possible optional responses for solutions to the problem in terms of costs and benefits
3. We have a goal and plan we believe in. Building Commitment to Initiate Action	*Perceives that the conditions of the previous readiness stages were met and . . .* • Has defined which personal beliefs and values must be given greater emphasis and influence in decision making if the problem is to be solved • Sees that personal interests are reflected in the means that will be used to achieve the change goals • Sees how the components of the solution connect to the critical root causes • Perceives the personal benefits will exceed the costs of the change initiative • Believes that the risk of failure is low to moderate and the chances of success are high • Believes that triggers for old practices have been reduced or eliminated, or their influence reduced • Expects that a climate of safety and security will exist for the trial-and-error process of making the targeted change • Believes that adequate attention has been given to how persistent sources of resistance will be dealt with • Feels a sense of mission and purpose with others who are committed to implementing the targeted change • Believes that she or he possesses the knowledge and skill to make the desired change • Believes that people in key implementation roles have the knowledge and skill to implement the desired change • Believes that sufficient attention has been paid to how the change will be maintained over time

TABLE 3.2 Leading Edge: Conditions for Each Stage of Readiness *(continued)*

POINTS ON THE LEADING EDGE	CONDITIONS RESULTING IN TRANSITION TO THE NEXT POINT
4. We are overcoming difficult challenges and making the right adjustments to stay on course. Motivating Agile Perseverance	*Perceives that the conditions of the previous readiness stages were met and . . .* • Understands that a slip in commitment is a typical part of change • Has selected an approach for recovering from a slip situation • Perceives that the plan for recovering from a slip is feasible • Sees that a slip in commitment is incidental and not a character flaw or culture flaw

Addressing critical moments successfully calls for a focus on "soft issues" in organizational life. As a senior consultant once put it, soft issues (interpersonal and political dynamics) have hard impacts (time delays, scope creep, budget overruns). Readiness management integrates hard and soft issues, and thus its application puts a leader of change in greater control of the total project situation.

THE TOOL

In this section, the tools and procedures of managing the leading edge are outlined. These are: (1) conceptualizing the outcome, (2) organizing the action you will take, (3) implementing the plan, and (4) monitoring impact.

Step 1. Conceptualizing the Outcome

In conceptualizing the outcome, a leader identifies the point a person or group has progressed on along the leading edge. The physical form the change analysis takes is a hierarchy similar to a work breakdown structure, one of the tools of project management (see Figure 3.2). The targeted outcomes are located at top of the hierarchy. Actions that will contribute to the outcome appear in a series of subordinate tiers. Examples of hierarchies in project implementation and project monitoring/control situations are outlined in Figures 3.3 through 3.5.

FIGURE 3.2 Work Breakdown Structure

These figures also contrast the leading approach with a task approach. In the example outlined in Figure 3.3, stakeholder commitment to an action plan is the objective. The first level outcome is that stakeholders are committed to a solution to an important, high-priority performance problem. Each of these focuses attention and effort on important building blocks for commitment. First, the stakeholders (those who must live with the potential solution to a problem as well as senior management) must recognize they're focused on an important, high-priority performance problem. Second, the stakeholders must acknowledge that though there are multiple potential solutions to the problem, they must choose one, and that conflicts about the selected solution must be resolved. Third, stakeholders must confirm that the action plan is modified to reflect a critical mass of concerns and interests of stakeholders about implementation obstacles and how they can be addressed. Fourth, stakeholders must adjust detailed action plans so implementation success is deemed to be "highly likely."

FIGURE 3.3 Readiness Approach: Commitment to an Action Plan

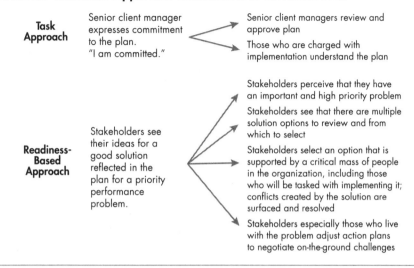

By contrast, the task approach focuses on task clarity (submit a plan with a request for approval) and speed of action (focus only on the senior leaders). While this approach is expedient, it limits the development of the readiness conditions associated with successful project implementation.

This example illustrates the sharp focus on the experience of the people with whom we work and not just the work itself that distinguishes the readiness perspective. Without such a focus, it is easy for leaders to become too task-focused and to lose sight of the need to promote a person's readiness for change. Readiness-focused planning maintains joint focus on the people and the work.

Step 2. Organizing the Work

The focus of organizing the work is figuring out what actions will satisfy critical and unfulfilled readinessconditions.

In Table 3.3, we continue build on the example we have been discussing and outline the actions that will support the targeted outcomes. For instance, a problem prioritization exercise is planned that features the use of the nominal group technique. This technique shapes consensus by systematically recording and then combining the problem importance ratings for multiple stakeholders.

Once the basic structure of a readiness intervention is developed, planning continues with the application of task management and project planning. Tasks are sequenced and scheduled, the resources allocated, the risks anticipated, and success criteria are established.

TABLE 3.3 An Illustration of Tasks Supporting Outcomes

We have a goal and a plan we believe in.

OUTCOME	ACTIONS
Stakeholders select a "best solution option" that reflects a critical mass of stakeholder needs, interests, and concerns; conflicts between stakeholders about the chosen solution options are surfaced and resolved.	In a group meeting, the group does the following: 1. Develops criteria for evaluating solutions (the performance improvement benefits exceed budgetary, political, and personal costs; risk of implementation is believed to be low to moderate; the solution is perceived as reasonable and compatible with the environment; support for the trial-and-error process associated with implementing the solution is perceived to exist) 2. Ranks evaluative criteria 3. Rates solution options against criteria 4. Selects best option based on criteria 5. Solicits important concerns about the chosen solution and achieves agreement regarding concerns.
Stakeholders adjust draft action plans so implementation success is perceived to be highly likely.	Select a cross-functional implementation team. Team develops a work breakdown structure for major tasks. In meeting, select smaller group to build conceptual work plan. Distribute conceptual work plan to team. In final group meeting, team ratifies conceptual work plan. Major tasks in conceptual work plan are assigned to appropriate stakeholder to develop into detailed work plans.

FIGURE 3.4 Readiness Approach: Resolving a Threat to a Project Deliverable

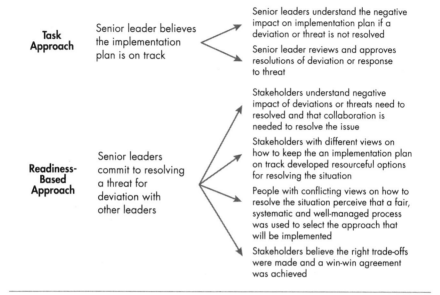

The links between outcomes, deliverables, and tasks that readiness-based project planning makes explicit are outlined in Figure 3.4. An illustration of readiness-based project planning that we have been discussing is presented in Table 3.4 for the situation summarized in Figure 3.3.

TABLE 3.4 Excerpt of Readiness-Based Project Plan for the Figure 3.3 Example

READINESS OUTCOMES	DELIVERABLE	TASK/SUBTASKS	START DATE	END DATE	RESPONSIBLE PERSON
Stakeholders are committed to a solution to a priority performance problem.	Stakeholders focused on an important problem.	Stakeholders ratify a summary of root cause analysis and problem rankings.	1. Stakeholders develop a set of potential problems following an analysis of the root causes of business performance issue.	3/5	3/5	Mary, Joe
		2. In a group meeting, stakeholders prioritize potential problems. • Develop a list of problems in consultation with stakeholders. • In a group meeting, post problems on a flipchart. • With stakeholder approval, combine repetitive statements into a single statement. • Stakeholders rank order problems. • Combine rankings to identify priority problem.	3/15	3/15	Mary
		3. Write summary document.	3/17	3/21	Jack
		4. Distribute document with request for approval.	3/22	3/22	Jack
		5. Secure outstanding stakeholder reactions.	3/26	3/26	Mary, Joe
	Stakeholders recognize that there are multiple, credible solution options for priority problem and that they must choose one.	A summary of potential solutions to priority problem is reviewed by stakeholders.	1. Appointed task team develops a couple of solution options for priority problem for stakeholder review.	3/29	4/09	Joe
		2. Team distributes summary document to stakeholders.	4/10	4/10	Joe
		3. Document is reviewed with stakeholders in one-on-one meetings.	4/11	4/15	Jack

Step 3. Implementing the Plan

Once the work is organized, then implementation takes place.

Step 4. Monitoring Impact

The primary questions that help guide effective monitoring impact are: Is there evidence that progress was made? and Is the person or persons behaving in a fashion consistent with what we expect? If progress has not been made, then the process draws the leader back to the conceptualizing phase. The leader uses the experience of the action the group took to clarify the readiness situation and reset their next steps. By maintaining a focus on the problem owner and adjusting accordingly, the leader has the best chance of creating high-value, high-impact outcomes.

FIGURE 3.5 Readiness-Based Work Planning

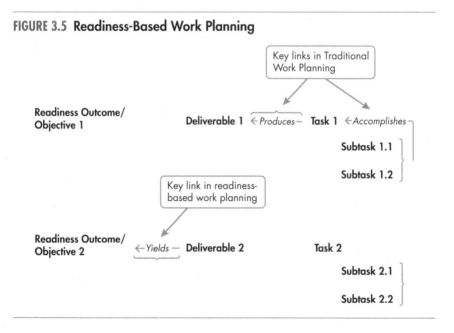

Figure 3.6 summarizes the challenge of positioning the leading edge across multiple constituencies successfully to create the momentum needed to implement change. The common challenge is one group is further along than another such that one is ready to act and the other is not. Figure 3.7 shows the process of building readiness among multiple

constituencies. Readiness begins with a few risk-takers who are sufficiently dissatisfied with the status quo that they are willing to suffer some inconveniences to make their vision of things come true. With smaller-scale pilots and limited experiments, this group provides the case for change and secures the support of others. A critical mass of support develops, and a bigger test of the idea is conducted. Finally, once the idea has a track record of success and people have seen others getting involved or supporting the concept, the majority of the organization gets onboard and supports the initiative. Over time a vision grows from initial concept to a viable alternative, and finally wins broad support.

FIGURE 3.6 A Common Readiness Problem: A Misalignment Between Management Tiers

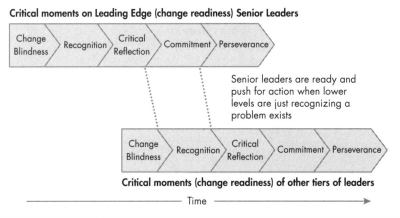

FIGURE 3.7 Building Readiness Among Multiple Constituencies

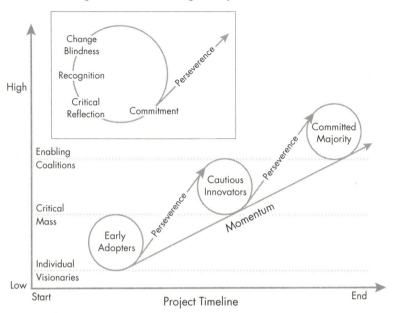

READINESS INVOLVES BOTH PROCESS AND CONTENT

The readiness-based approach to work management driving a strategy of change aligns tasks with motivation and ability to implement them successfully. A process focus includes clarifying the organizational decision-making or problem-solving processes that created the problem in the first place and what can be done to modify these processes.[1] This emphasis on motivation and ability, however, does not imply that the specific technical aspects of a particular change being pursued are unimportant (i.e., the correct network solution, the best marketing strategy for this business context, the best design for this business process). Both are necessary and indispensable if enduring solutions are to be developed.

Readiness-based task management empowers us with the processes that produce good ideas for ensuring we are doing the right things to support problem owners and implementing effective solutions to problems.

Chapter 4

Points at the Leading Edge

The ultimate basis of success ... is the skipper's decisive command of himself, his boat, and the situation.
—Stuart H. Walker

Driving change at the leading edge is a critical part of what defines great leadership. Resistance is the most common response to change, and how leaders negotiate points along the leading edge helps people overcome critical points of resistance. At the leading edge, we change five beliefs that inspire resistance.

- There is no problem
- We are solving the wrong problem
- The solution won't work
- People and teams do not have the capabilities they need to succeed
- Leaders will abandon or scale down the solution so that things will be different but not better.

The good news is that by working through five points of resistance along the leading edge we can overcome these beliefs and build the ability and motivation needed to make needed business change that sticks.

In this chapter we highlight the five transition points along the leading edge. These five points highlight the outcomes to focus on when converting resistance to momentum. We will explore each point and action we can take to transition through these points. At the end of this chapter, the reader will know the cycle through which leaders get people to believe change and have confidence that it can be achieved successfully.

THE STORY OF JOE

"Do you I think I screwed up on this one?" Joe asked a colleague. With an expression of candor we enter Joe's story and glimpse evidence of a practice that distinguished Joe's leadership of a big change.

We enter at a key moment in Joe's story, but his story does not begin here. The CEO had tasked Joe with implementing a large and difficult change to how it did business: the company was changing how it sold its products. Joe was a great candidate for this work. He had deep and broad business experience and was pace setting, resilient, and deeply results oriented.

To achieve its business goals in a more competitive environment, Joe's company needed to enter more complex strategic partnerships with its customers. Commitments to revenue and shelf space would be exchanged for such considerations as volume pricing and co-marketing agreements. In the past, the organization had used contract sales agencies to work with customers and sell its products. To power-steer these activities with greater control, however, relationship management would now be performed by a sales team of employees.

While anticipated benefits were large, the change in sales approach contained some risk. Long-term business relationships between sales agencies and customers were being disrupted; revenue was at stake. Some but not all of the people within the sales agencies would be retained as employees; some would lose their jobs. The leaders of several agencies—some who had been working with Joe's company from the beginning—would lose a large source of their revenue.

Not surprisingly given the scope of the change, there was a great deal of questioning and second-guessing as the launch date approached. Joe's leadership delayed implementation several times as the politics of this large and controversial change played out. Finally, the official start date was set and the plan was approved.

As Joe launched the project, things got off to a rapid start. He made a sequence of rapid-fire decisions. Communications, budget issues, people decisions, adjustments in implementation plan details . . . in the quest for speed, he was deciding them all. Unfortunately, while quick progress was being made, trouble began to brew. Joe's team was beginning to feel as though their leadership roles were shrinking and they were losing influence. "Why be proactive? The game plan is going to change anyway," one of Joe's team members disclosed. Another observed, "There are some issues out there. We expect that sales agencies would be upset ... but many customers are too. These guys have worked together a long time. I am hearing lots of complaints."

Still, despite some fits and starts, things were under way. Joe was at the first point along the leading edge. We call this Change Blindness. "Everything is "A-OK," was the mantra, but there was a problem and it was growing.

Then, as you might expect, Joe began to notice that things were not so OK. He observed that team members were deferring more and more decisions to him. He had a couple of difficult encounters with customers. The CEO began to express concerns. "Hey Joe, I am not sure we are on track." Joe had a conversation with one of his closest direct reports. Joe learned that people in his organization were expressing frustration with him.

"Whoa," thought Joe. Something was wrong. With this, Joe entered the second point along the leading edge, Recognition, and our story continues.

Joe wondered, "What is happening?" "What do I do about it?" Joe sought advice from the HR Business Partner (BP) assigned to him, someone he used as an internal coach. The BP suggested that she interview a few people on the team, and Joe agreed. The BP learned that, in the quest for speed, Joe had made himself the center of the initiative—he was control point—and that all important decisions, verdicts, and pronouncements were coming from him. Yet it was his sales managers who possessed the primary relationships with many key players in this drama. They saw the issues on the ground. They could deliver messages, surface local problems, and resolve emergent issues without them finding their way to the CEO. But they weren't involved. They felt disempowered, and the problems were getting bigger. They were frustrated. Sales results and their compensation were at stake.

"So, what can I do?" asked Joe. The BP gave Joe some options. Joe could acknowledge to his team that that he had made a mistake. He could disclose the motives that had driven him to make himself the center of the plan implementation. He could shed some light on the politics he was managing. Joe could make his expectations clearer for what successful implementation of the plan looked like. He could ask for input from the team on how he could balance his priorities on the one hand with the need to better leverage their involvement on the other. These were some of the options Joe considered as he made his way through the next point along the leading edge: critical reflection.

Joe decided to take action on some of the advice he had received from the BP. He picked the ideas he liked and tailored them to reflect his read on the situation. With this effort, Joe completed the Commitment stage and took action. He pulled his team together. He disclosed some of the directional shifts that he made and why. Joe emphasized that he needed the team to drive the change with him. He explained that he would reestablish a stable set of big-picture priorities with his team and establish a team implementation project status update conference call for reviewing progress and adjusting plans. Joe delegated tasks to his team with clearer boundaries and expectations. Joe also clarified his expectations of the team. He needed them to report to him concerns that "had legs"—namely concerns that heads of sales agencies or customers with strong relationships with the CEO would be brought to him.

The clock continued to tick on the implementation plan. A month later Joe had the BP do follow-up interviews. There had been progress. Joe's team reported that communication channels were working better. His team better understood the pressures Joe was facing. Managers felt better informed and more involved.

And yet, the team was not working in a completely aligned function. As the date for the cut-over to the internal new sales organization approached, agencies and customers escalated their pressure on company leadership. Some of the field managers were not upholding their commitment to help drive the change. To protect their relationships with customers, some were finding it convenient to side with customers against the leadership of the firm that was behind this difficult change. Joe learned that he could not count on everyone on the team. Some slips in momentum had occurred, and Joe had responded by acting with greater assertiveness and this was not working uniformly well. "There he goes again," some observed. Joe considered the personal feedback he received. With the BP's help, he thought through the root causes of the slips. It struck Joe that many of his managers had never experienced a change of this scale—one that changed the game in such a big way. "This is high stakes for everyone. I have to work with people through this."

Joe developed a plan for maintaining the course despite the obstacles he was facing and worked through the perseverance, the final point of transition along the leading edge. Once again, he pulled the team together.

He reiterated that he wanted to be kept apprised of key issues. "People out there are raising their concerns with you. They are also going directly above me. I am being asked to explain. I have to be able to respond. When something happens that could get escalated, you have to let me know. If an agency or customer has a concern, rather than side with them, say that you are bringing the issue up to us. We will do our best to find a way to work with their concerns. If groups of us need to meet with people, we will."

Joe then took the remarkable step of asking his team to hold him accountable for following through on his commitment to involve them in problem solving. Privately Joe also worked on a "pre-swoop" checklist. This was a short set of questions that prompted Joe to make sure he had fully leveraged his team before he intervened directly in a situation.

Joe also made it clear that it was the team's job to reinforce the plan. "If you want to be treated as managers, I have to be able to count on you. I get what's at stake. In the new organization, managers are people who can be counted on to get difficult tasks done." Joe also had a few difficult "expectations" conversations with people who were siding too closely with customers and sale agency leaders.

In the end, organizational change was successfully completed. As Joe recalibrated his leadership of this change, he progressed through points along the leading edge, from being unaware of the need to change to persevering through the more difficult but important changes he needed to make to achieve success.

POINTS ALONG THE LEADING EDGE: OPTIMIZING CHANGE READINESS

In his book *The 75 Greatest Management Decisions Ever Made*, Stuart Crainer observed, "Theories are neat, but reality is messy." Neat theories are like well-folded road maps. They are always on hand and available to be easily opened to help us through messy realities. They help us clarify our goals, anticipate contingencies, and evaluate options. Good theories help us plan a better course through the messy reality in front of us.

As a person (or team) progresses through each point in sequence along the leading edge, they gather the motivation, competence, and resources that are necessary to transition to the next stage, ultimately achieving the motivation and ability needed for sustained pursuit of change goals.

The Leading Edge model is summarized in Figure 4.1. In the following section we do a deeper dive into each stage.

FIGURE 4.1 Leading Edge Model

POINTS ON THE LEADING EDGE

Converting resistance into momentum proceeds through the five points of transition. At each point, there are actions we can take that ready people for transition to the next point in the process—bringing us ultimately to the implementation of change that sticks.

Point 1: Change Blindness

"We Are A-OK."

We begin before the process of problem solving begins. The central event that sets the process of change in motion is acknowledgment that a problem exists. In the space between not seeing a problem and acknowledging that a problem exists, there operates change blindness and the awareness blockers that limit problem recognition. A common phenomenon of human experience, change blindness is the failure to perceive what we see.

Our brains are built to process information in a way that promotes a sense of stability, of psychological safety and security, and bolster self-esteem. These are desirable aspects of psychological well-being and help insulate individuals and work groups from the negative effects of stress. Organizationally, this tendency helps maintain the web of assumptions and expectations that allow people to work together.

The conundrum of business change is that the mental activities that promote well-being and stability also thwart problem recognition. When the business context changes significantly, the current state becomes counterproductive. The personal and organizational quests for stability that serve a useful function in stable times become dysfunctional; they become sources of change blindness. In change blindness, people do not recognize that circumstances have altered and the time to adapt is now. While some individuals may suspect that a problem exists, they may also fear the implications of acknowledging that problem. Not wanting to be blamed as the "messenger" of bad news, or to be burdened with the task of solving tough problems, people may actively avoid or resist information that confirms a problem's existence.

In the case of Joe that we reviewed earlier, early progress on strategic initiatives and a decisive and pacesetting leadership style placed him at the center of the action and reduced his access to information, limiting his awareness of the trouble that was brewing.

Point 2: Recognition

"We Have an Urgent and Important Problem That Must Be Solved."

In Recognition, a threat pushes a problem into the awareness of people and work groups *and* people feel discomfort about it. In the story of Joe, the feedback he received indicated he wasn't supplying enough clarity to his leadership about priorities, and he was inadvertently usurping their ability to support the change he was driving. A highly achievement-oriented individual, this leader shifted his view of the role he was playing in his division's problems. He came to understand that he was part of a different problem than he initially thought, and that he needed to be part of a different solution.

Point 3: Critical Reflection

> "We Understand Our Problem and Why It Has Occurred and Have Some Options for What We Do About It."

In the Critical Reflection stage, people engage in critical reflection about the problem situation and its possible solutions. This reflection includes considering the problem from multiple perspectives, including those of other stakeholders or functional areas that might have a role in or be affected by the problem and one's personal responsibility for the problem situation. This reflection produces a more complete understanding of a problem situation. During the Critical Reflection, the problem comes to be seen as a web of root cause and effect relationships in which the relative influence of different root causes is defined and most important root causes are understood.

Critical Reflection also involves the search for the kinds of personal and organizational actions that can be taken to resolve the problem.

Psychologists tell us that people work through five questions when thinking about change:

1. What will it be like if we change?
2. How will we be better off?
3. Can we change?
4. Will it be worth it?
5. Can we trust the help on hand to get us there?

In the case of Joe, he got access to the help of an internal coach, the BP, who helped him clarify the specific implications of the feedback and to formulate some corrective actions. The insight the BP collected revealed that Joe's drive for success was undermining his ability to achieve it. Joe's high results orientation, high energy level, and commitment to engage the details were disempowering the leaders who wanted to help but were inhibited from lending the full weight of their support to the effort. The team needed different things from him: a stable set of goals, a set of accountabilities, and to be engaged when the decisions would impact their customers.

Joe faced a highly sensitive political situation. The stakes were high. Senior leadership was very concerned. Many customers went right to the

CEO when problems occurred. Joe needed his people to help him navigate change. There was a great temptation for sales managers to side with their customers, to join with them in blaming the corporate office. The team worked out a couple of options for how they communicated customer issues and how to reach out to them without further polarizing the situation into a "good guys versus bad guys" competition.

In the Critical Reflection stage, we appraise the costs and benefits of potential solutions and consider possible alternatives. Can I do this change? Will it be worth? For this process to work, outside perspectives help break through. Insiders can hold a vested interest in the existing process and the organization designed to support it. This is one of the reasons that the involvement of a coach is an indicator of high readiness for change.

When critical reflection is successful, people see their personal responsibility for the problem as well as possible solutions and options to choose from. Assumptions, values, and beliefs related to the problem situation and possible solutions are clarified and assessed for their validity both privately and with others. The bigger the change, the longer people engage in critical reflection and accomplish its critical tasks. Research tells us that big change requires more reflection than smaller change.

The challenge of Critical Reflection is resisting the pressure to define the problem and outline its solutions too quickly. The "get things done" stance, or what we call activity addiction, can prompt people to choose a problem statement and problem solutions that are convenient and immediately on hand. Unfortunately, these solutions do not likely address the more powerful root causes of the problem situation, and thus positive outcomes are short term or shallow at best.

Point 4: Commitment to Initiate Action

"We Have a Goal and a Plan We Believe In."

At the Commitment to Initiate Action point on the Leading Edge, motivation reaches the level necessary to drive action with great prospects for success. This motivation, while often intense, can only be maintained for a brief period. Researchers estimate that motivation to act endures from one to three months and on rare occasions persists for up to six months.[1]

The primary tasks of Commitment to Initiate Action are (1) clarifying a vision of a solution to a problem, (2) devising the plan with which the solution will be implemented, and (3) preparing for implementing the plan. Successful completion of these tasks resides in helping people develop visions of the desired outcomes and giving those who must implement a solution the opportunity to influence plans in a way that reflects their own personal needs and interests. Success at these tasks translates into personal commitments that are robust enough to weather the assaults any attempt at planned change encounters.

In Joe's case, he had internalized the feedback he had received about the unintended impact his approach to driving the project had created for the team. His engagement with his team would need to involve an exchange of commitments. Joe also needed something from his team. He needed an early heads-up from the field so he could be prepared for calls about the more contentious issues that would end up on the CEO's desk.

Joe talked with his team. Issues were placed on the table and commitments were exchanged. A plan was developed. The plan began.

Point 5: Perseverance

> "We Have Some Difficult Challenges to Overcome and Are Making the Right Adjustments to Stay the Course."

While a well-developed plan helps keep a solution on course, encountering off-course threats to solutions is typical. Commitment often slips multiple times before success and long-lasting behavioral changes are achieved. In James O. Prochaska and Carlo C. DiClemente's *The Transtheoretical Approach: Crossing Traditional Boundaries of Therapy*, and the large amount of research this work inspired, the researchers have found that individual clients generally lapse or slip up to three times before they maintain a desired behavior change. An important implication of this observation is that ongoing monitoring and adjustment during the implementation phase of a change project is indispensable to success. To maintain the pursuit of business change, the the change plan is often modified to deal with changed circumstances—without sacrificing the spirit of the initiative.

Even though significant progress is being made and the prospects for success are good in the Perseverance stage, people can still experience this stage as a bit uncomfortable. As someone cryptically observed, "Change sucks."

What lies behind this reaction? In part, people quickly come to realize the interdependence of organizational and personal change. While making organizational change is challenging in its own right, it also involves making adjustments to oneself. Personal practices must be altered. Greater emphasis must be given to previously under-emphasized work values. Often power must be shared or realigned to accomplish an important result.

Back to Joe. During a check-in with Joe's team, the BP re-interviewed the team about the project and how critical leadership functions were being performed. Joe had made progress. The plan for driving the change had stabilized. It was clear what the plan was and what the timeline was. Communication between Joe's field managers and Joe had improved. However, there was more progress to make. Joe was still making more decisions and directing more action than he needed to. Joe had to develop a "pre-swoop" checklist to help him achieve the needed restraint.

We often fail to give maintenance of behavioral momentum sufficient importance. Designing and developing solutions consume most of the resources available to solve a problem. Feeling pressure to solve problems fast, we allow ourselves to act as if solving problems were always a simple, linear process. We fail to recognize that slips and lapses in Commitment are common and weaken momentum and that managing this messy reality is part of the formula for success. We don't set aside appropriate resources to address the important work in implementation. Inevitably, problems occur, and slips and lapses in Commitment weaken momentum. Effective leaders keep an ear to the ground for concerns that will trigger a slip or lapse in Commitment. Worries about having the skills and resources needed for success are common triggers as are worries about whether people will stay the course or withdraw from active participation in making a change a reality. Learning what events trigger slips in commitment and disarming these triggers is an important step. An ongoing focus on maintaining or restoring Commitment is a key success factor of change initiatives.

SPECIAL TOPICS

Having laid out how readiness develops through the five points along the leading edge, we overcome three challenges to promoting effective action.

Are We Really Ready?

As we complete the work of the Commitment stage, an assessment of pre-action readiness is a wise investment. As one experienced chief human resources officer observed, organizations rarely give attention to this activity. Assessing readiness often reveals gaps that need closing. When gaps are uncovered, we face two choices. We can adjust the plan to reflect the readiness we can muster in the short term. Alternatively, we can postpone the pursuit of change until we are ready. Failure is likely if the goal is too big or resources are not in adequate supply.

What happens when we are not ready and change fails? When change attempts fail, people tend to overattribute failure to personal shortcomings ("I was not committed enough, I cannot make this change," etc.) or find blame in others (they were not capable of doing this work). Yet, the common problem we often face is that the goal was too big given the level of readiness. Attributions of personal failure demoralize and limit the prospect that change will be undertaken in the future. Cynicism that we can make things better is the unfortunate consequence of failed change attempts.

Synchronizing Across Multiple Levels

Building the critical mass of change readiness needed to propel successful change often requires that we synchronize the readiness process of several types of stakeholders, from early adopters, to the cautious innovators, and finally to a committed majority.

One of the special challenges of business change is synchronizing the evolution of readiness across people with different orientations to change as shown in Chapter 3. The people who first recognize the problem may be quite far along the readiness process before others first recognize the problem.

Another aspect of this challenge is aligning readiness between organizational levels as we also showed in Chapter 3. Synchronizing between levels is one of the big challenges of organizational change. Recognizing this gap is the starting point for addressing it. Cascading information about the problem and then boundaries within which an effective solution would be developed help achieve alignment, especially when it corresponds to the injunction expressed by a successful consultant. Vision is top-down and implementation is bottom-up.

Lapses or Slips in Commitment

The primary consequence of achieving commitment is action. A planned, intentional effort to change begins. However, once action has been initiated, the factors that maintained the problem, such as personal anxieties and organizational resistance, can reassert themselves and weaken conviction. Often, it is only when change is imminent that personal and organizational defenses reveal their formidable power. When these defenses prevail, the results are backsliding or a lapse in the effort to pursue the change (Figure 4.2).

FIGURE 4.2 A Slip or Lapse

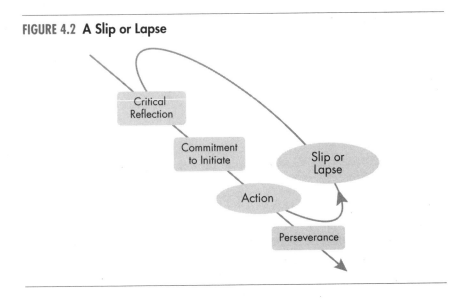

A slip or lapse involves abandoning a change attempt once it has been initiated and reverting to pre–change attempt status. Interestingly, slips and lapses are common outcomes to any change attempt.[2] Often, it is only after taking action that we can appreciate the adjustments in personal or organizational work practices that a given change will require. Making important business change is a process of continuous improvement. The process is best understood and trial and error learning occurs as people figure out how to achieve new goals or achieve existing goals in new ways. When people attempt organizational change, they engage in a process of trial and error as they figure out how to achieve new goals or work at old goals in new ways.

If missteps occur and are followed by punishing consequences or, on a larger scale, if politics deprive a change initiative of its support, then the pursuit of change loses momentum. Knowing that this is likely disposes us to embrace these moments as opportunities for learning and not frustration. In short, we return to Critical Reflection and move forward with a better and more refined plan for implementing change that will work and stick.

FIGURE 4.3 Planning Guide for Managing the Leading Edge

	POINTS ON THE LEADING EDGE	WHAT ACTIONS COULD PROPEL US TO THE NEXT POINT ON THE LEADING EDGE?
An important unrecognized change has occurred but... →	**1. We are OK.** *(Change Blindness)*	
	Transitioning to Recognition	Steps to promote Recognition • • •
	2. We have an important and urgent problem. *(Recognition)*	
	Transitioning to Critical Reflection	Steps to promote Critical Reflection • • •
→	**3. We have a complete view of the problem, why it occurred and good options for how to solve it.** *(Critical Reflection)*	
	Transitioning to Commitment	Steps to promote Commitment • • •
	4. We have a goal and a plan in which people from the top to the front lines have confidence. *(Commitment)*	
There is a slip in commitment and momentum stalled	Transitioning to Perseverance	Steps to Launch Strategic Initiative • • •
↑	**5. We have some difficult challenges to overcome and are making the right adjustments to stay the course.** *(Perseverance)*	
There is a slip in commitment and momentum stalled		Steps to Accelerate Initiative • • •

Chapter 5

Achieving Critical Synchronicity

Interdependence is essential for the running of any vessel.
—M. G. Sherar

Previously we outlined a new, evidence-based approach to high-performance leadership. Our model integrates three functions: navigating, piloting, and managing at the leading edge. This system draws upon the foundation of talent and culture that Steve Jobs saw as the key to greatness. Jobs said, "Over a period of time, you realize that building a very strong company and a very strong foundation of talent and culture in a company is essential to making great products." The leadership system we are implementing is a blueprint for focusing talent and building a culture of high-performance leadership.

When this system operates effectively, it helps unfreeze the middle of organizations by synchronizing the efforts of senior and mid-level leaders to drive results. In so doing, a system of leadership breaks through a common frustration many observe in organizations—an observation crisply summarized by this statement from an executive who engaged his team in the task of achieving high performance: "We are frozen in the middle and . . . stuck at both ends."

In this chapter we review tips for leadership effectiveness we developed from our research about the links between what leaders do and the context within which they do it. We pull a silver thread through three leadership variables: organizational practices, leadership functions, and leadership behaviors that we uncovered in our research. This research featured surveys of 1,200 first, middle, and senior leaders and related their observations of leadership activities and behaviors to ratings of individual and organizational high performance. By the end of this chapter, we provide a set of evidence-based prescriptions for leadership and organizational effectiveness.

ACHIEVING CRITICAL SYNCHRONICITY

A leadership system focused with purpose and powered by mastery

We present our research-based model in Figure 5.1. In the following pages we review each part and emphasize the vital role it plays in high performance.

FIGURE 5.1 A System Powered with Purpose—Focused with Mastery

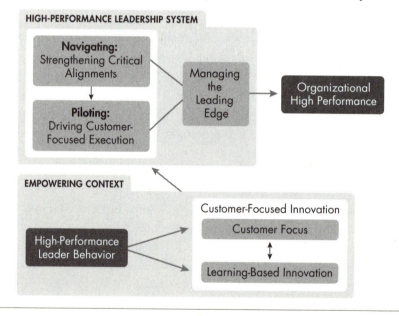

Our model is comprised of two elements. The first element is the high-performance leadership system we outlined earlier.

- Leadership system
  - Expert piloting
  - Expert navigating
  - Effective management of the leading edge

The second element is the empowering context. This context consists of a concentration on customer-focused innovation and high-performance leadership behavior.

- Empowering context
    - High-performance leadership behavior
    - Customer-focused innovation
        - Customer focus
        - Learning-based innovation

The arrows in our model convey the direction of influence that each part exerts on the other parts of model. To provide guidance about how to turn the model into practice, our research isolated the critical difference-makers for each element.

THE LEADERSHIP SYSTEM

In our study, we provided a list of activities to our leader participants and asked them to consider each within the context of implementing strategic initiatives. We then asked them to categorize each activity into one of three buckets:

- Primarily middle leader
- Primarily senior-level leader
- Shared

In high-performing organizations, we found that a few key responsibilities resided with middle-level leaders in the role of pilots, and others resided with senior-level leaders in the role of navigators. We show these linkages in Figure 5.2. We detail the elements of these functions in Table 5.1. When people who occupy these roles focus on these responsibilities, high performance occurs. The shared accountabilities are many, and are summarized below.

FIGURE 5.2 Responsibilities for Navigating and Piloting

Expert Navigating
Pulling up and pulling across critical stakeholders
Achieve mission-critical alignments that empower

Expert Piloting
Driving customer-focused execution
Solve customer problems, develops skills, and motivate people to implement targeted changes

TABLE 5.1 Piloting and Navigating Functions

HIGH-PERFORMANCE PILOTING FUNCTIONS DRIVING CUSTOMER-FOCUSED EXECUTION		HIGH-PERFORMANCE NAVIGATING FUNCTIONS PULLING UP AND PULLING ACROSS (TO ALIGN ACROSS ORGANIZATIONAL BOUNDARIES)
Works with frontline staff and peers to figure out how to keep the initiative on track.		Helps stakeholders understand the strengths of the current operation to support long-range planning.
Ensures that people have the skills needed to implement plans successfully.		When developing plans for implementing strategic initiatives, gets stakeholders to review potential implementation challenges, and options for overcoming them.
Participates in regular conversations with customers to learn what we can do better.	**SHARED FUNCTIONS**	Gets stakeholders to ratify plans before they are implemented.
Recognizes people for exceeding customer expectations.		Keeps stakeholders updated on the progress of key initiatives.
Drives activities that close the gap between current and desired job behavior.		Helps stakeholders understand the strengths of the current operation to support long-range planning.
Ensures that handoffs between teams occur effectively.		When developing plans for implementing strategic initiatives, gets stakeholders to review potential implementation challenges and options for overcoming them.

When people in navigating and piloting roles focus on the critical tasks associated with their function, they advance their organizations toward high performance. Our research also uncovered that people in both roles must coordinate their effort to achieve shared accountabilities.

The most important shared accountabilities are summarized here.

- Works across team boundaries to build plans that have the support of key teams
- Ensures that people have the resources to implement plans successfully
- Keeps action plans for implementing on strategic initiatives on track
- Ensures that there is adequate time to implement the plans successfully
- Determines how to implement priorities using detailed knowledge of strengths of the team and existing business processes

A high-performance leadership system occurs when senior and mid-level leaders perform the accountabilities of their roles with discipline and collaborate effectively to accomplish shared responsibilities. Understanding common miscues in how navigating and piloting functions are synchronized helps keep important initiatives on track. We present the common miscues in Figure 5.3. A few well-implemented organizational mechanisms, described in Figure 5.4, limit the likelihood that these miscues will occur.

FIGURE 5.3 Miscues Between Navigating and Piloting Functions

NAVIGATING PRACTICES THAT LIMIT SUCCESS	PILOTING PRACTICES THAT LIMIT SUCCESS

• Failing to engaging insights gathered from customers about how well you are meeting their needs, diverse perspectives of the business from different points along the value chain, and dissenting opinions from people within the organization when framing strategic priorities
• Giving insufficient attention to clarifying how people have to work differently to achieve results and then monitoring and problem solving gaps in implementing new ways of working
• Failing to model change that others are asked to adopt—not inviting constructive resistance to improve plans
• Approving the plan without engaging people from across the organization—risking success because real-world issues are not openly discussed and resolved and insufficient resources will be deployed to important hazards and gaps
• Failing to stay close to reviews of the progress of strategic initiatives—risking successful adaptation of plan to events that are pushing plans off course
• Swooping in to micromanage implementation
  • Decreases the accountability felt by others—and limits proactivity from others
  • Lack of access to detailed knowledge of the real situations will result in poor decisions
• Forcing ahead with the current plan because you do not want to acknowledge you over-overcommitted
  • Triggers others to sugar-coat the truth
• Dismissing the concerns raised by those performing piloting functions about the plan as a lack of team play, imagination, resourcefulness, or commitment to results
  • Triggers "malicious compliance" and gamesmanship in others
• Avoiding tough conversations with leaders about the collaboration issues that stall strategic initiatives
• Encourages a climate of victim blaming and scapegoating that suppresses achievement-based candor
	• Failing to proactively support senior leaders with insights about customer problems, organizational performance gaps, and ways of closing them—risks that real problems are missed
	• Avoiding opportunities to be constructively resistant—prevents the organization from having the ability to calibrate plans to problems
	• Failing to invite constructive resistance from team members to get issues and how they are overcome on the team
	• Failing to give adequate attention to resourcing project with needed people and schedules
	• Not focusing on helping team members think resourcefully about the resources that they have on hand to meet goals
	• Failing to model change that others are asked to adopt—not inviting constructive resistance to improve plans
	• Not staying alert to hazards and problems and engaging people about them early—allows issues to become bigger and harder to resolve
	• Conducting progress reviews and updates without first identifying options for how to problem solve addressing key threats
	• Avoiding difficult but necessary conversations needed to keep the initiative on track
	• Avoiding giving bad news because of the fear of the personal risks involved—compromising personal integrity and ultimately one's reputation
	• Feeling so driven to surface an urgent problem that you fail to identify what can be done to address it—stalls problem solving
	• Driving others to implement a poor plan because you are overcommitted
	• Limits your credibility and triggers lack of candor in others

FIGURE 5.4 Now Navigator and Pilots Synchronize

MUTUAL ACCOUNTABILITIES	HOW THEY ARE FULFILLED
1. Create and maintain a shared sense of mission and purpose about how customers needs will be better and more completely served than competitors, reflecting views of senior leaders, mid-level leaders, and first line staff and insights about customers 2. Bring together vision and reality with a set of priorities that address gaps that senior leaders, middle-level leaders, and first line staff see that must be closed to achieve mission and purpose 3. Clarify the measures that will tell us that we have been successful 4. Develop commitment to a plan that closes people, process, and system gaps, and define new "ways of working" that define how people work together differently to achieve the mission critical priorities 5. Implement a launch plan that reinforces the vision and gives people the opportunity to express concerns about real-world obstacles and ideate how to overcome them 6. Address issues and hazards that could push the initiatives off course and outline options for how senior leaders, middle level leaders, and first line leaders and their staff will work together to overcome them 7. Clarify and reinforce what is working and not working in and their causes during open evidence-based reviews of progress; forecast emerging threats and how they might be addressed 8. Adapt the plan to immediate problems and lessons learned with the active involvement of both leaders and those in implementation of plans	Strategy development processes that use insights from across organizational boundaries, levels of leadership, and external data sources to shape strategies Goal setting, scheduling, and resources planning sessions that synchronize across organizational boundaries and between levels of leadership Clarification of leadership functions, roles, and feedback loops that will support risk detection, and problem solving based on lessons-learned from debriefs of miscalculations, mistakes, and experience Communication planning sessions that work out how the needs and concerns of different levels of leadership will be addressed in messaging Cascaded Project Kick-offs Progress Reviews that include senior and middle level leadership supported by open and evidence-based documentation of successes, obstacles, and agile problem-solving about how they can be overcome Recognition of successes in early stages that build momentum

Synchronized and expert performance of the piloting and navigating functions contribute to high performance. Through effective management of the leading edge, leaders performing navigating or piloting functions convert resistance into momentum. They lead people through four points along the leading edge that culminate in high performance. We depicted this in the model in Figure 5.5. As pilot and navigator focus on fulfilling their key responsibilities, they drive performance that matters.

FIGURE 5.5 Managing the Leading Edge

- We have an important and urgent problem. (Recognition)
- We have a complete view of the problem, why it occurred, and good options for how to solve it. (Critical Reflection)
- We have a goal and a plan in which people from the top to people at the front lines have confidence. (Commitment)
- We are overcoming difficult challenges and making the right adjustments to stay the course. (Perseverance)

As is true for any system, the whole is more than the sum of the parts. Unless each part operates effectively and in a synchronized fashion, the whole cannot perform optimally. Like the well-documented relationships among a high-performing jet crew such as those captured in the movie *Sully*, each member must do his or her job well and each has a responsibility to help the crew perform well as a unit. The management of handoffs and transitions from one role on the crew to the other is key. If these transitions are managed poorly, failure results. Our research tells us that when mid-level and senior leaders do their jobs well and are effectively synchronized, high performance results. There is more. We also discovered that this system works best when it functions within a work environment that provides purpose and supports the right behaviors. Both mid-level and senior leaders are responsible for building and maintaining this context of purpose and excellence.

EMPOWERING CONTEXT

Focused with purpose and powered by high-performance leadership behavior

High-performance organizations are distinguished by a work environment of commitments about customer-focused innovation and leader behavior that drive success. We explore each of these next.

Customer-Focused Innovation

Customer-focused innovation is driven by two elements: customer focus and learning-based innovation. Innovation management is a difficult-to-learn leadership competency,[1] and many leaders struggle to figure out how to do it well. Imposing some order on the messiness of the innovation process is challenging. By focusing on some key factors, productive innovation can occur with more reliability. Here we outline our success formula.

Customer Focus × Learning-Based Innovation = Customer-Focused Innovation

In high-performance organizations, two features of the environment work together to drive productive innovation. These features are not just "nice to haves." When these elements are not present, performance is lackluster at best. Let's look separately at each component.

Customer Focus

In our research, we asked participants to rate a variety of practices they observed in their organization. We then related these responses to participant responses to revenue and profit performance achieved over consistent years. We excerpt the following practices from our analysis.

Key Customer-Focus Practices
- Gather information from multiple sources to understand customer needs
- Work closely with customers to clarify their expectations for service and quality
- Focus teams on developing ideas for meeting customer needs better than competitors do
- Focus planning on exceeding customer expectations
- Focus teams on developing ideas for closing service and quality gaps
- Work with customers to improve ease of doing business
- Closely monitor performance against customer expectations
- Respond quickly to customer concerns
- Take risks to solve customer problems in new ways

These customer-focus practices predict organizational high performance. While at first blush they look fairly straightforward—common, even—it is remarkable how infrequently people witness these activities in practice.

Approximately 50 percent of our sample saw these practices as relatively infrequent.

Customer focus creates the fuel for productive innovation. It provides answers to questions like:

- What problems do customers have?
- What do they expect?

The task of gathering customer insight sometimes is not so easy. People in organizations sometimes believe they know what customers need and want. The sources of data are limited. "What did sales say?" or "What do our internal experts believe?" While such insights are important, they are incomplete.

Best practices in customer-focused innovation involve reviewing metrics and statistical analysis on data collected from multiple sources about customers' evolving needs. Casting a broader net of diverse perspectives is a vital check on the biases present in most organizations. The standard of utilizing evidence-based insights may seem to be a level of precision that does not require emphasis but it does. Often such data are needed to break through the biases in thinking and doing that limit genuine customer-focused innovation.

To limit the impact of thinking and doing biases, effective leaders ensure two things are place to cultivate the candid insights needed to make good decisions: good process and good analytics. The process used is more critical than the analysis itself. Analysis provides a powerful check on biases.[2]

To overcome the bigger challenge of biases that people usually bring to decision making, high-performance practices involve a couple of important tasks.

- Incorporating all perspectives, even those that may contradict senior leadership: perceptions of frontline staff and operations personnel in daily contact with customers, insights from formal surveys of customers, etc.
- Exploring uncertainties: acknowledging the limits of the information on hand and how lack of information can be addressed
- Ensuring that the people who participate in these discussions do so based on skill and experience rather than seniority or job title:

integrating the viewpoints of organizational pilots who serve in key implementation roles

An effective decision-making process leverages the perspectives of others. To realize these benefits, effective leaders build these processes on a foundation of trust. This foundation helps people incorporate diverse perspectives into an integrated and holistic view of the external environment and internal capabilities. When trust is present, creative abrasion (a culture where ideas are productively challenged)[3] can take place. An example of effective creative abrasion would be a team where people critique and debate each other's ideas, not each other as people. Such freedom and safety enables teams to take input and bring about better ideas.

Analytics are the second bias-busting action we can take to help people break through the tendency to ignore evidence that contradicts assumptions. Evidence-based decision-making limits the negative impact of bias. Measurement is a vital discipline to adopt to weaken bias. The discipline of regularly measuring and reviewing data about the customer experience and the employee experience of a team's customer focus strengthens the feedback loops needed to achieve customer focus.

Such research uncovers blind spots. In one organization, for example, a survey revealed that while senior most leaders gave a particular practice a high rating, the remainder of the organization reported levels of customer focus that trailed far behind an industry benchmark—over two standard deviations, in fact.

However, customer focus is not sufficient. Customer focus fuels the second and indispensable component of customer-focused innovation: learning-based innovation. With deep customer insight as input, the throughput of innovation processes transforms this insight into the output of innovative products and services that make a difference to customers.

Customer Insight → Learning-Based Innovation → Productive Innovation

Learning-Based Innovation

Learning-based information involves a candid appraisal of the gaps between desired high-performance practices and the reality of today, an assessment of the root causes of those gaps, and ideas for how they can be best closed. In our research we found these practices to have the greatest influence on high performance.

Top Learning-Based Innovation Practices
- Begin solving problems with a clear definition of the problem
- Evaluate gaps between current and desired performance to focus improvement.
- Involve teams using lessons learned to improve performance
- Work across team boundaries to clarify root causes of performance gaps
- Involve people with regular customer contact in developing ideas
- Thoroughly review ideas with people who have multiple perspectives
- Include those who will implement decisions in developing ideas
- Contribute ideas regardless of management level
- Brainstorm multiple ideas for solving a problem before picking the best one
- Develop clear plans for implementing innovative ideas

As we discussed in connection to customer focus, these are commonsense and straightforward practices. With a sharp focus on what matters, organizations efficiently convert insight about customers and knowledge of organization performance gaps into solutions. As Jack Welch, the venerated former CEO of General Electric, has said: "An organization's ability to learn, and translate that learning into action rapidly, is the ultimate competitive advantage."

Our research revealed that most organizations have significant gaps to close before claiming the title of high performance. The practices of customer-focused innovation are not commonplace. Only 17 percent of the organizations in our sample exhibited these practices. Organizations and teams that have not yet achieved high performance often try to innovate before they've truly understood their gaps and blind spots in providing solutions that customers need. To help leaders set the agenda—to figure out where we are so we can lay in a course to start—we provide the diagnostic tool in Table 5.2. As we have outlined before, surveying one's organization is a great place to begin on defining and then closing mission-critical gaps.

TABLE 5.2 Customer-Focused Innovation

CUSTOMER FOCUS		LEARNING-BASED INNOVATION	
		LOW	**HIGH**
	HIGH	Highly Customer Reactive	High Performance
	LOW	Lower Performing	Highly Innovative Without Focus

Having located our teams in this matrix, we can develop the plan to close our most outstanding gaps. Customer interviews, focus groups, and surveys provide part of the answer. Work environment surveys and focus groups that capture "how we do things around here" provide another. Shared perceptions have a large influence on the leadership practices and behaviors that people exhibit. They are the social glue about "what matters most" that holds people together when differences in individual goals, urgent problems, or varying perspectives of different functions or disciplines threaten to pull people apart. Researchers have documented that perceptions of the work environment have a powerful impact on what people do, including leadership skills on which leaders focus.

Some organizations have documented the kind of work environment they wish to create to achieve their goals and communicate this information broadly. A couple of organizations we have worked with call this "ways of working." Measures can be developed for reporting on progress and evaluating the impact of solutions designed to close important and persistent gaps in achieving a new plateau of success.

High-Performance Leader Behaviors

We have also learned that several leadership behaviors are key to enabling the context of a high-performance business. These behaviors distinguish high-performance leaders regardless of management level; that is, they describe high performance at the first-level, middle-level, senior level, and executive high-performance leadership. We highlight the top ten on the following page.

Key Leader Behaviors
- Leverages current skills and abilities of team members
- Is consistent in words and action
- Helps people figure out how to optimize resources and time
- Models the highest ethical standards
- Recognizes others for progress made
- Models personal accountability
- Gets people to think about problems in new ways
- Helps people develop solutions for problems
- Adapts plans with input from others
- Motivates team members to give extra effort

Our research tells us that these behaviors make the engine of customer-focused innovation happen; and they also power the piloting and navigating functions.

All of us have some of these practices in our repertoire. Almost none of us have all of them. So, how do we ensure that we have full complement? Self-rating surveys and multi-rater surveys help us compare our perceptions to the perceptions of the others with whom we work—peers, senior colleagues, and junior colleagues. We can also ask others to tell us what we could do more of or less of to have greater impact. Noted Executive Coach Marshall Goldsmith calls this powerful practice feedforward. The insights we generate from these comparisons helps build the versatility we need to fulfill the call to action that most of us feel: how can I "do great"? By setting goals to increase the frequency with which we engage in underutilized behavior, building a plan of sequential steps, and working this plan, we progress toward our goals.

Pulling It Together

We have laid out the components of high-performance leadership: both the leadership system and how to focus it with purpose. Through what we call Critical Synchronicity, we can help organizations achieve results that matter.

Achieving Critical Synchronicity
- Leaders performing the navigating function empower high performance by pulling up and pulling across leaders and teams to achieve mission critical alignments.
- Leaders performing the piloting function drive customer-focused execution.
- Leaders convert resistance into momentum at four points along the leading edge.
- Leaders fuel the innovation engine with customer insight and the practices of learning-based innovation.
- High-performance leadership behaviors power leadership functions.

Our next five chapters are devoted to the five points of transition through which resistance transforms into momentum.

Chapter 6

Change Blindness

Those unaware are unaware of being unaware.
—E. Cioran

We continue our exploration of business change by reviewing a dramatic moment in history: the market meltdown of 2008. Postmortems of the "Great Recession" revealed that the sharp economic downturn in the late 2000s through the early 2010s was far from unforeseen. Managers in the companies at the center of the crisis saw plenty of signs that danger lay ahead. Within Lehman Brothers, for example, people in risk management roles had noted that the firm was deepening investments in mortgage-backed securities and that the scope of these investments violated Lehman's own risk management standards. Lehman Brothers' risk managers repeatedly engaged senior leaders about the firm's overexposure through e-mails and in meetings. At the same time, some outside industry analysts publicly questioned the soundness of these investment vehicles.

Leadership ignored these warnings. The potential for large financial rewards was irresistible. There were revenue to grow and big bargains to leverage. To silence internal concerns about the path they were on, leadership demoted the senior risk manager that had issued the warnings and banished her from meetings and communications. She left the organization not long after.

Unfortunately, leaders later learned that the bargains they saw were not the result of a temporary dip that could be exploited but the beginning of a wholesale collapse. The bankruptcy of a once-proud institution was the result of an inability to see a problem.

At first blush, the willful ignorance of Lehman Brothers' leadership seems a remarkable thing. Yet Lehman Brothers is far from the first organization to ignore what seems obvious to everyone else—and pay dearly for it.

How can we explain this? How can people not "see" the problems before them? It turns out though that "not seeing" a problem is not an uncommon part of the human experience. We turn to the concept of change blindness to understand the phenomenon, outline the awareness blockers that produce it, and lay out what we can do to limit its impact.

CHANGE BLINDNESS

Psychologists who study human perception have given the term "change blindness" to the failure to *perceive* what we *see*. The following example gives a clear view of change blindness in action in our day-to-day life.

> On a Friday morning a police officer pulled over an SUV because he noticed that an infant was not sitting in an active restraint car seat. The police officer turned on his flashers and directed the driver to pull the car over to the side of the road. As was customary, he parked his patrol car behind the other vehicle so that a portion of the police car was sitting on the shoulder and a portion in the traffic lane. The officer walked up to the SUV, spoke with the driver and retrieved his license and registration, and returned to his vehicle. The officer's lights were still flashing. Moments later, a courier truck driver plowed his truck into the back of the police car.

Let's highlight the facts. The collision occurred with the officer's car in plain view, with lights flashing, and in the direct path of the courier truck. There should have been enough time for the courier to avoid a collision. When asked why he had not noticed the officer's car, the driver of the courier truck stared back in disbelief and said that he must have been "distracted."

A remarkable event? No. Nearly half of all traffic accidents are thought to occur when a driver's attention is diverted by one aspect of the visual environment while failing to apprehend a big change in another. Magicians entertain audiences by exploiting this phenomenon in sleight-of-hand tricks.

Designed for survival, we humans are hardwired with biases in the way we process information, store it, and retrieve it. Here are a few pieces of research that highlight these biases:

- We prefer to focus on pieces of information that we would prefer to be true over information we do not like.[1]
- We are motivated more to avoid failure than achieve success.[2]
- We are more likely to remember our successes than failures.[3]
- We tend to misinterpret information that does not reflect our preferences.[4]

Generally, such human biases in perception serve us. They give us confidence in our understanding of the world, as well as in our ability to cope effectively with its challenges. If our brains attempted to take note of every change and every new event, we would soon be overwhelmed and paralyzed. But these "helpful" biases also constrain our ability to recognize new problems and see ourselves in that new context. At Lehman Brothers, a variety of factors played into the organization's crisis: a single-minded focus on a goal, the past momentum in the mortgage-backed investments market, the allure of compelling compensation packages, and the prerogative of being "in charge" blinded leaders to the obvious change in front of them.

In this chapter we deepen our understanding of the organizational conditions that give rise to change blindness. We will call these awareness blockers, and they include:

1. Curtains over the Johari window
2. Courage killers
3. Activity addiction
4. Accountability suppressors

Before explaining these blockers, how they function, and what we do about them, in Table 6.1 we present a quick reference list of actions to take to overcome change blindness.

TABLE 6.1 Quick Reference for Overcoming Change Blindness

BREAKING THROUGH CHANGE BLINDNESS TO ACHIEVE PROBLEM RECOGNITION

GOAL	ACTION
Overcome awareness blockers	
Pull back the curtains on the Johari window	Gather data with interviews, organizational surveys, multi-rater surveys, customer focus groups, and surveys that examine performance from multiple lenses to illuminate blind spots. Recall that people cannot recognize their own blind spots without help.
Overcome the courage killers	Achieve clarity and match people to the work. Clarify "ways of working" that establish practices such as acting with courage, standing alone to champion an important change, and being persistent, which are all desired behaviors when implemented with respect for colleagues.
Defeat activity addiction	Ensure that people are doing the right thing. High achievers want to get going—to get into action. Guard against the tendency to get going without first doing the necessary and occasionally frustrating work of aligning with others—more than just the boss—on what is important. Do not let the urgent overwhelm the important. Link goals to customer outcomes with clear explicit linkages and have them publicly reviewed by people with differing perspectives. Anchor initiatives to customer data to complement the internal beliefs people hold about what the customer wants and needs.
Weaken accountability suppressors	See that people have a stable and focused set of prioritized goals, that what is asked of them lies within their view of how they contribute, and that they have the skills and resources to implement them.

We highlight the activities that leaders can take to break through change blindness in Table 6.2.

TABLE 6.2 Activities that Promote Transition to Problem Recognition

Frame frustrations into a coherent picture of cause and effect relationships that others in your situation have experienced.	Provide articles from trade journals, industry reports, benchmarks studies, and research reports from prominent consulting firms or industry associations that link root to problems and frustrations that people in your organization are expressing.
Outline solutions that others have implemented to address problems like yours.	Provide access to consultants, the types of literature outlined above, and conversations and site visits with organizations that have solved the problem you face to acquaint people with what the solutions are like.
Show how other organizations like yours implemented the solution, answering the question: "What is it like to make this change?"	Provide descriptions of how the change was implemented and outline the key success factors that made solutions successful.

THE CAUSES OF CHANGE BLINDNESS AND WHAT TO DO ABOUT THEM

Having provided an overview of actions, we now turn to taking a deeper look at the causes of change blindness and the actions we can take to address them. There are four primary awareness blockers that contribute to change blindness.

Curtains over the Johari Window

George was a prominent leader in a division of a global enterprise who aspired to rise once more within the company. Executives were impressed by George's capacity as a leader. He had very high standards for his work and exhibited a strong executive presence. George was regarded as accomplished, tough, no-nonsense, and decisive.

Then there was this: "You are not a candidate for the position." These shocking words reverberated in George's mind has he slowly walked back to his office. He had spent a career preparing himself for the position that he had just been denied. "What happened?" he asked himself. "What went wrong?"

George had enormous pride in his capability to achieve results. When he talked about his career, one got the sense that he felt he was person of special abilities—almost entitled. He'd spent a career developing his reputation as being results-oriented and possessing special expertise. He carefully selected work at which he could succeed and aggressively marketed his successes to other leaders within the business.

But, there was more to George's career strategy. He devoted himself to building close relationships with powerful people. He cultivated the interests of senior people and used this common ground to reinforce close work relationships. He actively courted powerful peers, gathered their views of what they felt about the status of key initiatives, and then selectively shared this information with executives. George career management strategy was successful; his stock was on the rise.

George's organization then entered a period of great turmoil. To drive operational efficiencies in a context of acute market pressures, leadership gave the corporate office more control over divisional operations. George's division was impacted. Strategy and policy moved from the divisions to the corporate office. Then, there were layoffs within George's division and on his team. George suddenly found himself engaged in power struggles with peers in the corporate office about differences in strategy, priorities, and resources.

Perceiving himself to be more politically savvy and accomplished than others, George set about vigorously driving his agenda. In private conversations with superiors, George criticized colleagues whose views differed from his. He revealed disclosures that his peers had shared with him in confidence. Such information was welcomed by the superiors; intel about what people thought was a precious commodity given the turbulence in the organization.

As one would expect, staff reductions produced a spike in problems—even in George's organization. Anxious to make it clear that the problems were not his fault, George found scapegoats among his direct reports to blame. But people talk. Over time George's political behavior came to be known by others who grew to resent him and made their resentments known.

When a couple of George's senior sponsors left the organization, George thought his fortunes had changed. A role that George coveted and had spent his career preparing for opened up.

Unexpectedly, however, the leadership informed him, "You are not a candidate for the position." Unfortunately, the cumulative impact of strained relationships and his reputation for backbiting had scuttled George's prospects for promotion. Yet George was dumbfounded. He had the right answers, had delivered results, and had been politically astute. However, George did not see his blind spot. A deep sense of entitlement and feeling more deserving than others blinded him to the negative consequences of his political maneuverings. The expert politician was undone in by his own politics.

From the outside, it seems obvious: *of course* behaviors such as leaking confidential information and throwing direct reports under the bus would alienate George's colleagues and threaten his ambitions. How can we understand George's situation?

Psychologists Joe Luft and Harry Ingham formulated a simple and popular framework for understanding self-awareness. This framework is created by the intersection of two dimensions: (1) aspects of ourselves that we see and (2) aspects of ourselves that others see. This framework is called the Johari window (reflecting the first names of our two psychologists, Joe and Harry). The Johari window is presented in Table 6.3.

TABLE 6.3 The Johari Window

		SEEN BY OTHERS	
		YES	NO
KNOWN TO SELF	YES	Public Face	Hidden Self
	NO	Blind Spot	Unknown

The quadrant of particular interest to us is that one created by the intersection of (1) what others see and (2) what we do *not* see. This region is called a blind spot. The special challenge of blind spots is that they obscure our view of a part of ourselves that others can see. Like a blind spot in a rearview mirror, we can be told that they exist and stare in their direction, but we cannot see what resides in this space.

The special challenge of blind spots is that people tend to believe that they are above average on the trait that sits in a blind spot. Any of us who have seen TV shows such as *American Idol* will have witnessed many unfortunate examples—some of them quite extreme—of people who consider themselves to be much more skilled than they actually are.

Psychologists Justin Kruger and David Dunning documented this phenomenon in a variety of traits including humor, grammar, and logic.[5]

As George's story illustrates, the Johari window has significant influence in limiting recognition of problems in the workplace. In the case of George, others saw but he did not see that his political skills came at the price of eroding support from peers—support he didn't think he needed.

What to Do About Blind Spots?

The good news is that we can pull back the curtain on the Johari window. Getting insights from others is a great help. We can ask the people with whom we work for their views. Observations from bosses, peers, and junior colleagues collected in interviews or on surveys (often called 360-degree surveys) can also bring blind spots into view. Similar methods like organizational surveys, customer interviews and focus groups, and evaluations from outside experts are among the actions one can take to pull the curtains back on the Johari window. Comparing what we think is true with what others tell us through their eyes illuminates blind spots. Gathering and reviewing the data takes an act of courage, but those who commit to developing their own self-awareness are better empowered to achieve business results that matter.

We get others to help us limit the negative impact of a blind spot. One can assign others to tasks for which they may be more capable and that lie in our own blind spot. A leader who may not be especially creative and who is relatively blind about what it takes to drive the innovation process, for example, may assign innovation to someone on the team who has this capability.

Research also suggests other remedies for blind spots. Training to improve a "blind spot" skill sharpens one's understanding of his or her lack of ability in that skill. We can also simply ask people for their advice on what to do to enhance our impact. Marshall Goldsmith, a prominent executive coach and author of several books, has called this practice feedforward. Although blind spots are persistent, progress can be made in promoting recognition of them and limiting their impact by learning how to address them.

Courage Killers

The story of Beth, a senior leader of a manufacturing unit, illustrates the power of courage killers. Beth saw herself as a great manager and builder of teams. While Beth was capable and friendly, she was also wary of risking anything that might negatively affect her reputation as a team player.

At one point in her organization's history, Beth was given some aggressive business goals to achieve, and cost cutting was involved. Beth's team warned her that these goals could not be achieved without serious risks to quality. If staffing was to be reduced, Beth's team argued, then adjustments ought to be made to their production targets. The group could not succeed at doing more with less. Less was too little.

However, Beth's need to please leadership steered her away from engaging her boss or internal customers, like the sales organization, about the implications of budget cuts or the need to adjust service standards. Beth knew that the business was under pressure as revenue had slipped over the two previous quarters. In the end, Beth kept her team's objections to herself and made the budget cuts. Quality problems spiked, and customer complaints increased to the point that Beth's reputation with her boss was tarnished.

Later, formal feedback on a team survey suggested that Beth's team's morale had deteriorated, and that members had lost some confidence in her ability to fight for them and for quality. Beth was mystified by what she should do with this feedback. "What did the team expect? That I risk my job? I happen to work well with others on the teams I am on!"

On occasion, the problems that push at us require courage. Courage Killers prevent us from recognizing these problems. For many of us courage is understood to be deciding "what hill to die on"—or career suicide, as others would call it.

The work of a colleague, Cliff Bolster, helps us understand what courageous acts at work are and how to behave in a prudently courageous way. Bolster asserts that what makes an act or decision courageous is that it contains the risk of personal harm. In organizations, harm means the loss of one's job, an eminent promotion, or the favor of leadership, and blame for organizational troubles. While courage involves personal risks, it is not foolhardy. Bolster's research suggests that the ultimate risk, losing one's job, is *not* common when problem or solution advocacy is done in a respectful way. If respect is absent and advocacy is done in a way that makes people feel stupid, out of control, or incompetent, then yes, an agent of change will likely face the most-feared punishment. Skillful influence reduces the chances that career suicide will be the result of acting with courage. These abilities can be developed with commitment, training, and practice.

Acting with courage does mean acting in ways that are contrary to the typical and slightly tongue-in cheek recipe for career success that emerges from research on career advancement:[6]

1. Avoid confrontation.
2. Do not ask your boss to champion unpopular positions.
3. Always agree with your boss.
4. Concentrate on presentation skills and looking good in meetings with superiors.
5. Demonstrate an intense desire to win career advancement and best your peers.

Doing well (that is, career advancement) and doing right (being effective) are different things. These dual priorities are in constant tension. People tend to favor one side over the other. The most able leaders do both, balancing what's best for their careers and what's best for the organization.

One important source of courage killers is compensation. Three compensation-based awareness blockers are being overextended on personal finances, poor person-job fit, and greed.

Overextended Personal Finances

The president of a prominent consumer products business observed that many performance problems endured by organizations are traceable to people living beyond their means. Seduced by the prospect of bigger houses, more lavish vacations, the acquisition of a summer house, better cars, and/or the latest in home theaters, managers spend to the limit of their income. Constrained by their financial situations and in desperate need of compensation corresponding with the next promotion, managers become more protective of the status quo and conservative in their decision making. In addition, they become less focused on team contributions and more focused on their own contributions. But a highly cautious disposition and a preoccupation with personal contributions aren't managerial traits conducive to sustained focus on important business problems.

Poor Person-Job Fit

Many people pursue bigger jobs to achieve greater compensation. Bigger jobs are bigger because of the addition of people management responsibilities and their larger scope. Success in these roles is dependent on the ability to build and implement vision with others, coach performance in subordinates, and remove obstacles to team performance. Many people have not developed these skills at the levels needed to succeed in bigger jobs, and problems occur.

Unfortunately, managers sometimes move people into bigger positions on the strength of a person's ability to get things done as an individual contributor—because they have a high level of technical skill and/or have achieved results within the context of familiar strategies. These capabilities alone are not associated with success in a bigger role.

To address this common misalignment, some forward-thinking organizations create dual career paths—one for people managers and another for exceptional technical managers. This gives top technical leaders the opportunity to contribute in ways that bring greater value to the organization while providing a path for increasing their income potential.

Greed

The lure of lucrative bonuses and long-term incentives drive some people to pursue goals that are not achievable without unwanted compromises—compromises that can have serious consequences in the long term. Harkening back to the Lehman Brothers example, the pursuit of business growth supported by ample bonuses blinded leaders to the perils around them.

Activity Addiction

Jim led a sales team, and sales were off. Jim quickly prescribed sales training for his team to address the problem. Sales reps had to get better at dealing with customer objections. Privately sales reps believed that neither product pricing nor product features were competitive. Indeed, some reps were quietly but actively searching for employment elsewhere. One of the top reps, in fact, left the company for a competitor. Jim understood the complaints were driving talent away, and there was little he could do about them. But he was action-oriented . . . and he reasoned that training couldn't hurt. Except that it did. His team of reps resented the oversimplification of their obstacles that was inadvertently conveyed by the training program he arranged. A couple of months after the training, sales results revealed that the situation had not improved much.

People succeed in organizations because they get things done. Sometimes, however, getting things done is overdone. While a strong focus on implementation is desirable, the other aspects of problem solving are equally vital to secure long-term solutions.

When a strong achievement orientation combines with a single-minded focus on implementation, a problem-solving bias takes root that, if taken too far, becomes activity addiction. Activity addiction prompts people to focus on problem symptoms that are immediate and can be addressed with conventional means. The humorous phrase "ready, fire, aim" nicely encapsulates this practice. This bias is also commonly associated with three related biases that can limit the success of a change project. The authors of Strategic Speed: Mobilize People, Accelerate Execution[7] identify these biases as:

1. Trying to do everything faster
2. Stoking the boiler by assigning more people or budget to tasks
3. Cutting corners by eliminating steps in the process

Activity addiction blocks awareness of problems that require deeper clarification or new or unfamiliar remedies. Failure to break through activity addiction means we have the experience of solving the same problems over and over again. Creating organizational disciplines that encourage underutilized aspects of problem solving provide potent remedies to activity addiction. Formal product development processes, project management structures, and organizational prioritization processes help contain activity addiction by focusing people on all four parts of the problem-solving process: clarification, ideation, development, and finally implementation.

Accountability Suppressors

"If they would only step up to the plate and make it happen." This is a common lament one hears in organizations—from both sides of the management divide. Senior managers wish that middle-level leaders would act with greater accountability, and middle-level leaders wish this of their more senior colleagues as well. What do both sides want? People are looking for someone to admit the well-intentioned mistakes people make, claim ownership of a problem, and influence stakeholders in the organization to implement a solution that gets things back on track. What's getting in the way of claiming such ownership? We present the impediments to accountability: accountability blockers.

AchieveForum,[8] the writers of *The Oz Principle*—Roger Conners, Tom Smith, and Craig Hickman—and others have outlined common accountability blockers that limit awareness of problems. Listed below are the key blockers.

It's Not My Job

As Conners, Smith, and Hickman observe, this blocker is inspired by the desire to avoid taking on additional effort without additional reward. This is reinforced by the precision with which organizations create job descriptions as well as the effort some organizations invest in developing clear boundaries concerning who can make what decisions. While job descriptions and decision-making boundaries make work management more efficient, the organizations that implement these practices do not intend people to limit their contribution to problem solving in the narrow ways that these structures can elicit if taken to extremes.

"This is not what I do." A recent AchieveForum POV explained that people are not inclined to assume responsibilities for tasks that do not fit their understanding of their role or their identity as professionals.

Here is an example that illustrates the challenge. In a leadership development program being implemented in a pharmaceutical firm that was devoted to building the important skills of cross-boundary collaboration, participants described the process of influence as "manipulation" and their worse image of "used car salesmanship" (with all due respect to those who perform this function with skill and integrity). Active advocacy was not seen as a legitimate expectation of their role as managers of technical areas. "The facts and the science speak for themselves," they argued. While credible information is undoubtedly necessary for good decisions, advocacy and alignment were also needed. To address the concerns about advocacy, these leaders were helped to see how one could use advocacy with a technical perspective through reviews of examples of high-performing technical managers in their organization doing just that.

Wait and See

"Wait and see" is a posture that people adopt believing that either a problem will be solved by someone else or the problem situation will change. As either of these possibilities happen often enough, people are reinforced to wait and see. In a few organizations people have expressed that "wait and see" is actually an important rule of the road. In hyperreactive organizations, for instance, waiting until you are asked to do something—at least three times, one manager said—is a good way of saving yourself from wasted effort.

Cover Your Tail
This accountability blocker involves steering clear of problem situations for fear of being blamed for the problem or a failed solution. As most of us have learned, there can be a lot of missteps in implementing business change. Protecting oneself from the scapegoating that often occurs when something goes wrong is common.

It's Not Clear Enough; I'm Confused
The internal logic of this blocker is that people cannot assume accountability for defining a problem or a solution if they do not completely understand it. Related to the confusion blocker is the appeal for direction: "Tell me what to do." This passive posture is reinforced by the common managerial practice of telling people exactly what to do when problem situations occur. This way I limit my accountability. This posture contrasts with the alternative accountable response: "Here is what I am going to do. What advice do you have for how I proceed?"

Our Number 1 Is Their Number 10—Uh-oh!
In our research and that of others on accountability, the topic of clarity surfaces as a persistent theme. While it is often true that the measures of success are unclear, the larger priority is the overwhelming set of goals people have.

A business unit of a large organization identified a new product as mission critical. The launch of the product was priority number 1. Leaders focused resources, developed plans, and implementation began. One quarter into the implementation of the project, the project leader who was driving the implementation of the plan uncovered a startling fact. The group that had to do the financial engineering to make the product work did not have this project as its top priority. In fact, the project was number 10 on their list. In both the words and in the facial expressions of the project team a collective "Oh no!" went out. Leaders had not worked sufficiently to pull across organizational boundaries to resolve the equation that number 1 does not equal number 10. The problem was quickly escalated with a plan to address it. Candidly, this recovery had benefit of the unrelenting focus of the head of the business, who was, to say the very least, "none too pleased" with the situation. The good news is the product was successfully developed and implemented with strong impacts on the company's bottom line and in the bonus checks of employees.

In the absence of goal clarity, people have to figure out what to do and what to ignore when they encounter colliding priorities. As the famous business consultant Jim Collins has said, success is 10 percent vision and 90 percent alignment.

HOW DO THESE BLINDERS DEVELOP?

There are three main ways blinders develop: the way rewards are distributed, how goals are set, and prerogative gone too far.

How Rewards Are Distributed

First, the distribution of rewards in organizations fosters the development of accountability blockers. It is often said that success has many authors. Organizations support this by dividing rewards of a big success among many people. Because the rewards are divided among many, for any single individual, they are relatively small in scope. By contrast, the penalties of failure are often attached to a single or a very small number of scapegoats, and thus, for that individual or individuals, can be quite large. The perceived imbalance between the distribution and scope of rewards and punishment discourages accountability.

How Goals Are Set

The authors of *The Oz Principle* assert that the second source of accountability blockers is a powerful negative circular process that develops among people in organizations. The cycle begins harmlessly enough: senior management does what it is supposed to do and issues goals and objectives. However, the beginning of the problem lies in the quality with which this process happens. Speed kills. Involving people close to the problem—when people in navigating roles fail to involve those in piloting roles, for example—about the implementation approach is perceived to take too much time in the time-compressed environment of most organizations, so more senior leaders decide to make the key implementation decisions rather than delegate them. As Mark Samuel observed, managers often adopt the unfortunate posture of: "We have studied the problem thoroughly, developed an in-depth plan, and now *you* are empowered to implement it."[9] As a colleague once noted, the better course is to understand that, "vision is a top-down process and implementation is a bottom-up one." A better process is to clarify the vision, engage people close the work to build a plan to get there, and align top, middle, and front line on the final plan.

Prerogative Gone Too Far

Managers are often attracted to the familiar details of doing the work of direct reports rather than the more unfamiliar and ambiguous elements of developing strategy, creating alignment among senior stakeholders, building organizations, and working with others to keep initiatives on track. The result is that management often makes decisions about implementation that people closest to the work ought to be making. Because senior managers are removed from the immediate task environment, they often lack the detailed knowledge needed to drive implementation successfully.

Because the plans are flawed, problems emerge, and plans falter early in implementation. This causes a chain reaction. When leaders learn of implementation problems, they begin asserting greater control over the work to power-steer remedies. While well intentioned, these efforts can backfire. The proactivity of middle-level leaders weakens when upper-level managers countermand lower-level decisions. This pattern continues until people at lower levels in the organization gradually come to expect that goals will change and direction will come from above. Empowerment weakens. Sensing (or fearing) a lack of urgency, senior managers assert even more control over the problem-solving process, and lower-level managers begin to abandon proactivity altogether.

As problems mount and progress slows, the "blame game" develops. In this game, searching for scapegoats, covering one's tail, and adopting a wait-and-see posture take precedence over problem solving. An attack-defend spiral develops and ultimately freezes people in their tracks. "Was it your fault?" "Not my fault!" "Was it yours?" "Hey, handling this is not in my job description." And so it goes, until avoiding blame and steering clear of problems becomes the primary objective.

What is the antidote to the blame game? Clearly aligned goals and plans both up and down and across work teams. This will ensure that goals and plans are well developed. The challenge here is that goals were not well developed in the first place. Optimally, goals must be developed across team and organizational boundaries to address the interdependencies between teams (recall the 1 does not equal 10 problem identified earlier). However, this takes time and sometimes conflict management skills. People too often perceive that time is in short supply and are anxious about conflict management. "Wouldn't it just be easier and faster to jump in and micromanage?" many managers reason with themselves. Driven by the desire to exert personal control (which, in the moment, can seem even more important than pursuing the organization's best interests), goal quality suffers. We outline some remedies to this pattern in future chapters. As we have said, the implementation of strategic priorities falters when people in navigating roles engage in piloting and when people in piloting roles do not perform their accountabilities effectively.

HOW DO WE BREAK THROUGH CHANGE BLINDNESS?

There are several actions that break through change blindness.

Use Information to Set the Stage for Problem Recognition

People usually encounter the symptoms of a problem well before they register a coherent picture of causes and effects that require an integrated solution. A troublesome set of reports from the customer service department regarding customer complaints, the failure of new product launch to produce expected revenue, and the loss of a couple of key salespeople can frustrate the managers of the service, product development, and sales departments.

To set the stage for problem recognition, one can help frame various frustrations people feel about their progress on goals and priorities into a coherent view of cause and effect relationships. The frustrations of our service, product development, and sales managers may reflect that their business is no longer aligned with its market. When this process is evidence-based and addresses the fears of those involved, problems are more likely to be recognized.

Trade journal articles, benchmarks studies, and research reports from prominent consulting firms can help. How-to, advice, and in-depth explorations of problem topics faced by others in their industry give people credible frameworks for understanding issues and what to do about them. Such literature can offer an encouraging balm to dissatisfied workers: capable people and organizations encounter problems like yours all the time, and in most cases these problems are solvable without heroic levels of commitment or outrageously good luck. This can prompt effective reflection. When a threat pushes a problem front and center, previous exposure to cause and effect models reduces the time needed to crystallize a problem statement that compels action. This practice is far more easy to do in a work environment of learning-based innovation. This environment is described in the next section.

Detect and Solve Smaller Problems Before They Become Bigger Ones

The knowledge that change blindness and awareness blockers are common prompts us to do all we can to ensure that the environments within which we work have the ability to openly and directly detect and solve emergent or smaller problems before they become big ones. The detect and act practices of organizational navigation and organizational piloting help train our attention in these capabilities. Building this kind of work environment means developing a culture that is disposed to search for emergent problems, pulls people together to understand them from multiple perspectives, admits mistakes, identifies root causes, and encourages experimentation with solutions. There are many well-developed disciplines that organizations use to promote these conditions (Lean/Six Sigma disciplines, for example). Systematic cross-functional goal development involving multiple levels of management as proposed by Larry Bossidy and Ram Charan in the 2002 book *Execution* offers a powerful means of limiting the presence and pernicious impact of change blindness as well of the blockers that prevent people from "seeing" the problem before it's too late.

To help the reader focus on critical gaps that are closed when organizations build cultures that limit change blindness, Table 6.4 outlines common culture gaps as well as actions that can be taken to address them.

TABLE 6.4 Developing a Work Environment That Supports the Early Detection and Solution of Problems

POTENTIAL OPPORTUNITY FOR IMPROVEMENT	ACTION STEP
Management of mistakes: Does the work environment allow people to openly discuss the mistakes they have made? Are intelligent mistakes seen as part of the natural process of striving for new goals and new ways of doing things? Is the pressure to act or to avoid embarrassment overwhelming the need to develop sound plans?	Establish norms of open acknowledgment of mistakes among the leadership team as part of a candid approach to keeping initiatives on track. As a manager, acknowledge mistakes to direct reports and openly discuss remedies. Promote open and honest participation by having leaders model this activity with their direct reports. In one-on-one management updates, ask direct reports to talk about upcoming challenges and how they are being addressed.
Openness: Do people openly discuss the problems they see, their root causes, and potential responses of addressing root causes before finalizing action plans?	Implement a public problem-solving process, during which root causes and their potential remedies are identified from the point of view of various stakeholders. Lead a process during which the highest impact and most doable options are selected from a range of options. Periodically meet with the subordinates of direct reports to learn how progress is being made.
Alignment of stretch goals: Do goals represent a stretch for people, the organization, and systems—or are they bound to strain them? Are goals aligned up and down and across the organization?	Engage people in developing stretch goals by cascading goals. Define measures for performance that meets expectations and performance that exceeds expectations. Calibrate goals between organizational levels and across organizational boundaries. Ask people to surface implementation challenges and engage leadership, stakeholders, and those in implementation roles to develop potential responses to implementation challenges before finalizing goals.
Appropriate use of incentives: Are the incentives that are tied to goals driving people to reach too far? Are incentives blinding people to the implementation obstacles, or prompting people to minimize them?	Ensure that incentives are not so large that they encourage people to overlook important risks.

(continued)

TABLE 6.4 Developing a Work Environment That Supports the Early Detection and Solution of Problems *(continued)*

POTENTIAL OPPORTUNITY FOR IMPROVEMENT	ACTION STEP
Challenging the status quo: Are people rewarded for openly but respectfully challenging the status quo?	Establish process improvement disciplines that invite people to critique the way decisions are made, evaluate the way work is accomplished, and recommend improvements. Publicly reinforce direct but respectful challenging of the status quo. Ensure that this process occurs within the leadership team. Use executive consultants to facilitate this process if managing egos is a significant challenge.
Candor about skill gaps: Do people in key positions have the interpersonal and leadership skills needed to lead people? Can people talk openly about skill gaps?	Review the competencies and technical skills needed to achieve new goals. Be wary of the tendency to underestimate the scope of skill gaps. Clarify competency gaps and develop means of coping with them with temporary staffing, contractors, or consultants.
Insight into blind spots: Do people know their blind spots and have mechanisms in place to limit their impact?	Implement 360-degree surveys, engagement surveys, team climate surveys, and customer surveys processes to clarify blind spots and develop ways of coping with them. Arrange training on topics identified as blind spots.
Links between activity and outcomes: When problem solving, do people relate potential solutions to the ultimate goals?	Require that people explicitly link activities to outcomes to limit the danger of "activity over results."

Shifting culture toward the practices described in Table 6.4 requires focus and imagination. One technology organization developed a "12-step program" to address its "activity addiction." Modeled on the idea of 12-step programs that people use to gain control of addictive behavior, managers openly discuss how difficult it is to resist speedy implementation of easy solutions that address symptoms and not root causes of problems. In this organization, leaders established a context within which people do not have to engage in remarkable acts of courage in order to put problems openly on the table for examination and effective problem solving.

TACTICS IN THE CHANGE BLINDNESS STAGE THAT LEAD TO THE NEXT READINESS STAGE: RECOGNITION

Even when the problem owner does not yet recognize that a problem exists, change agents help set the stage for progress. They can help by breaking through awareness blockers and educating people about links between symptoms, problems, the root causes, and solutions. Expert sources like trade journal articles, benchmarks studies, business publications, and research reports from prominent consulting firms can help support a case for business change. These sources can assuage anxieties by reminding people that organizations like ours have encountered this problem—and more important, organizations like ours have surmounted the problem with the right remedies.

Minimizing change blindness involves increasing an organization's ability to openly recognize problems for what they are: a natural and common part of success. Problem solving, acknowledging mistakes, learning from them, and figuring how to avoid them in the future are part of what makes high-performance organizations succeed.

SUMMARY

As E. Cioran observed, people are unaware of being unaware. There are personal and organizational factors that keep important problems from penetrating our consciousness. Wisdom about what promotes change blindness helps the able leader—either functioning as a navigator or pilot—engage the leading edge of business change by helping colleagues transition from being unaware to recognizing a problem that matters, the first critical point along the leading edge.

Chapter 7

The Recognition Stage

The common problem, yours, mine, everyone's is ... finding first what may be, then to make it fair up to our means.
—Robert Browning

The story of the *Emma Maersk* and crew illustrate able problem recognition. On the evening of February 1, 2013, the container ship loaded with 14,000 containers of cargo suffered a devastating mechanical failure just as it initiated its passage into the Suez Canal. The main engine room flooded and caused the loss of several of the ship's systems. The good news is that despite a series of unfortunate events, the crew contained the emergency situation and brought the ship alongside at the Suez Canal Container Terminal without personal injury or negative impact to the environment. The crew accomplished this despite a remarkable series of events:

- Several severe technical breakdowns including propulsion, electric power, steerage, and maneuverability
- Continuous inflow of water into the ship
- Lines from one of tugs that came to the aid of the vessel broke several times
- A ship carrying explosive natural gas was nearby
- Four inexperienced cadets were on their first voyage

One sequence of actions among many taken by the chief officer and the crew illustrates problem recognition in action.

At 2141 hours, shortly after the pilot's arrival on the bridge, a fire alarm sounded. The chief officer heard the fire alarm when he was in his cabin and hurried to the ship control center. Immediately after, three bilge alarms sounded. On his way, he noticed that all fire doors had closed. Once he arrived at the control center, he discovered that the crew had assembled according to the fire procedure. Once there, the chief officer concluded that somebody was fighting a fire in the shaft tunnel and needed assistance. He assigned another officer to take over and hurried to the shaft tunnel to investigate the fire alarm.

The chief then learned that were problems with the communications to the bridge, a vital link in communications about the scope and nature of the problem and what to do about it. As a result, he placed himself at the bottom of the emergency exit shaft where he knew the VHF connection to the bridge was better and acted as a liaison link between the engineers in the shaft tunnel and the master on the deck. In a sequence of other decisions, the chief maintained his vigilance over another emerging threat. He closely monitored the state of the ship's deteriorating navigation system. Before it failed he accelerated the ship to reach safety.[1]

Problem recognition begins when a threat breaks through the awareness blockers we described in the previous chapter. This requires multiple inputs that signal we are encountering a threat that will require a nonroutine response.

Let's drill into the process of recognition by surveying the types of threats that we face at work (all of which, thankfully, are rarely life threatening). Author Edgar H. Schein identifies five main types of work threats in *The Corporate Culture Survival Guide* (1999):

- **Economic threat:** If change is not made, you will lose money, lose important business, or lose a driver of your business success (cost, quality, etc.).
- **Political threat:** If change is not made, some powerful entity will gain some advantage over you.
- **Technological threat:** If change is not made, you will be obsolete.
- **Moral threat:** If change is not made, you will be seen as socially irresponsible.
- **Internal threat:** If change is not made, you will not achieve important goals you have.[2]

A threat of one of these types metamorphoses into recognition of a problem when we answer several questions positively.

FIVE QUESTIONS THAT BUILD RECOGNITION IN SOLUTIONS

People tend to recognize problems for which they see feasible solutions. These questions include:

1. What will it be like if we change?
2. How will we be better off?
3. Can we change?
4. Will it be worth it?
5. Can we trust the help on hand to get us there?

When we can give positive answers to these questions, we mobilize ourselves to pursue a solution to a problem.[3] Recognition occurs. Let's flesh out these questions in a little more detail.

What Will It Be Like If We Change?

To pursue a solution to a problem, we need to believe that we will like inhabiting the future it will create. Sometimes people can take this too far, constructing exaggerated views of change as though it will open a path to a nirvana of perfect bliss: "Finally, everyone will get it, start doing their jobs, and stop driving me crazy!" Or people may exaggerate the downside. "This will be awful. I will have to do all this warm and fuzzy team-player stuff that is not me." An early task of the Recognition stage is developing an image of change that is energizing, credible, and realistic.

How Will We Be Better Off?

To take on a problem, we need to believe that the solution will make things better. While this observation seems obvious, in real life it's not always so straightforward.

For instance, consider a smoker who wants to quit. We all know that giving up smoking creates benefits. A smoke-free life means achieving important improvements in health. Respiratory and cardiovascular problems decrease and the prospect for a longer and higher quality of life increase. There are other benefits, too, including better relationships with nonsmokers who worry about the health impact of secondhand smoke as well as the cost savings associated with not having to regularly purchase cigarettes.

Smoking, however, also produces important benefits that must be addressed. For many smokers, smoking is a source of stress relief, an aid to concentration, and a weight control strategy. Giving up smoking therefore can mean the untantalizing prospects of being stressed-out, performing below personal standards, and becoming overweight. Who would sign up for that?

To help smokers quit, smoking cessation experts recognize that they must help their clients shape a vision of change that defines, assigns value to, and focuses on the new benefits they will experience once they free themselves of the smoking habit but also reflect how they will cope with the lost benefits of smoking.

Can We Change?

To recognize a problem, we need confidence in our competence to implement change. Following are questions that require positive and thoughtful answers in order to mobilize higher levels of readiness.

- **Capacity to learn.** Can we learn to do the new behaviors or practices required by a solution?
- **Support.** Will we have access to the supporting resources that are needed to make the change work?
- **Technical know-how.** Do we have the needed technical skills, and if not, will we have access to them?
- **Stakeholder alignment.** Is there alignment among and between powerful constituencies?

If people do not see these dimensions of readiness in place, a change initiative may proceed, but many will not be optimistic about its prospects. "Things will be different, but not better."

Will It Be Worth It?

To pursue a problem, we need to believe that benefits of the change are clear, tangible, and immediate. A quick appraisal of these benefits must exceed the costs of the change, including the time and effort that will be devoted to pursuing change, the uncomfortable process of disrupting the status quo, doing the trial-and-error learning that comes with implementing most change efforts, and the difficulty of implementing the technical aspects of the change successfully (a new process, system, or procedures). Our goal as leaders, either as change agents or change facilitators, is to work with others to develop a balance sheet on which the benefits are greater than the needed investments and likely costs.

Can We Trust the Help We Have on Hand to Get Us There?

Confidence in leadership and access to needed tools and resources are important sources of trust in needed help. Trust in the change methodology or the "black box," as Dormant (1986) terms it, is important too. It is influenced by a grasp of the methodology and the capacity to exercise control over the change process once it begins.

The presence of a change facilitator is a key readiness condition when the change is big or complicated. When a person evaluates a change facilitator as a potential partner in the change process, the person who owns the problem determines whether the person (or people) who will help and their prescription for change can be trusted.

HOW TO SUPPORT POSITIVE ANSWERS TO RECOGNITION QUESTIONS

Having worked through the five questions, let's turn to how we can support positive answers.

What Will It Be Like If We Change?

> **Action: Outline positive views of what it will be like to live with the solution.**

An early task of Recognition is developing an image of change that is energizing, realistic, and acceptable.[4] Documentation of a solution, the results it produces, and illustrations of how people make a solution work all help people build a positive answer to this question. Arranging for or providing testimonials from others or case examples are also helpful tactics.

Here is an example from the world of career transition support. Networking with others is the most effective solution to finding a new role if you have lost your former one.[5] Networking is not a natural activity for many people. Career consultants often help clients develop a day-to-day picture of what effective networking looks like by exploring what kinds of tips and actions have worked for other job seekers. This picture includes the number of new contacts to make and the number of meetings with contacts to target each week. The content of networking events is demystified with sample agendas and draft language to use in e-mails and in meetings. Career transition coaches help people strengthen résumés and LinkedIn profiles. Participants in career transition programs are also often connected to people who have successfully found new employment to build confidence that networking leads to jobs. With a combination of time-tested templates, new disciplines that can be learned with practice, and support from others who have been successful, the threat of not having a job is transformed into the problem of finding a good role through the networking solution.

How Will We Be Better Off?

> **Action: Outline positive outcomes by relating the solution to satisfying the needs and interests of key stakeholders.**

A commonsense starting point for any change effort is a vision of how things will be better. Clarifying the vision of the outcomes to be achieved is a key step that answers this question in a positive way. What will customers say differently once the solution is implemented? What specific improvements will appear in the measures used to determine success? Clarifying outcomes that capture how we will be better off addresses this important core readiness question.

Sharing the positive outcomes experienced by others who have faced similar situations is a common starting point for shaping outcomes. The main message of this type of communication is that others like you have implemented successful solutions like the one that is being considered. In addition, using questioning and active listening skills with stakeholders enables one to gather data about concerns and needs. This information makes it possible to make connections between felt needs and a solution: "This solution will meet your need for X."

Two categories of needs are particularly important: organizational needs and personal ones. Keeping one's eye trained on both is the key to shaping a compelling vision of the outcomes of a solution.

Organizational needs are the formal requirements for a business change project. They can include concerns such as improving efficiency, effectiveness, quality, and customer satisfaction. Usually organizational needs are easier to identify than personal ones. Organizational needs, however, tend to vary across end users, technical experts, and the people who control budgets. One requirement for success is finding a way to integrate these perspectives.

Personal needs are often hidden but quite potent. Within this category are psychological and social motives[6] such as enhancing one's reputation with a boss, correcting a personal oversight perceived by one's boss, building status among peers, and retaining control. As change agents and facilitators, we tend to do a good job assessing organizational needs but often overlook personal needs. Yet, in the end, personal needs often prove to have as great or even greater influence on whether a decision to proceed with a solution will be achieved or not.

A consultant was working in client organization that had a reputation as having a highly political work environment. To assess the political dimensions of a potential project, the consultant asked a client manager questions about personal needs (e.g., "What would make this project a big success for you?"). The manager responded that he had been assigned this project as a final step to an imminent promotion. He explained that he wanted to steer clear of elevating big issues "onto the management team's radar screen." Such issues could entangle him in an intractable problem and delay his promotion. This manager's objective for the project was to complete a safe, noncontroversial intervention that could be completed quickly and be perceived as successful. This manager's personal need was greater than the organizational one. The consultant responded by narrowing the scope of the project, documenting issues that would be addressed by a later problem-solving activity. The consultant also outlined recommended actions to take once the documentation of issues was completed. In this way, the consultant maintained momentum and set up future and more potent actions to fix the problem.

Can We Change?

> Action: Assess ability.

Here too personal and organizational needs must be considered in order to assess the ability to change.

Assessing Ability for Personal Change

Our ability to make personal change is influenced by one's view that a solution is a reasonable stretch over what a person can do now, whether the person has been able to make similar types of change in the past, and whether the social world around the person will support his or her pursuit of change.

Assessing Ability to Change in Organizations

To assess ability to change adequately in organizations, experts recommend prioritizing an explicit assessment of readiness for change.

This assessment involves two basic questions: (1) Is the change clear? (2) Are the critical enablers in place to convert clarity into results? Is it clear? Have we cascaded strategy to tasks and actions? When there is a shift in *how* results are to be achieved, has the shift in values, practices, and behavior been cascaded? Are the key enablers in place? Making focused adjustments in enablers is often needed. Making an appraisal that big shifts in organizational structures, processes, systems, and people are needed makes the change much bigger. It is more difficult for people to recognize big problems.

Will It Be Worth It?

> Action: Emphasizing benefits to key constituencies and building confidence that the problem owners can implement the change.

A consultant was part of a large consulting firm. The firm engaged in process-redesign projects that generally persisted over nine months and required a large financial investment from its clients. From the early moments of the consulting project, the senior client leader and the consultant agreed that they would visit client stakeholders on a weekly basis to reinforce the value of the outcomes from the project overall and to emphasize how the project had contributed that week to satisfying the varying needs of the client's stakeholders. While financial results were important to all client leaders, there were a variety of other priorities across the client personnel involved in the project. One manager, for instance, wanted the project to save enough resources so that investments could be made in business development priorities (the budget for which could not be secured given the organization's current run rate). The opportunity to do this work was an important entry the manager wanted to make on his résumé. For another manager, current business processes needed to be redesigned to resolve the customer problems that impaired customer satisfaction and made her work life difficult. For another manager, the project represented an opportunity to better align goals across several departments. He was investing too much time in meetings trying to resolve squabbles among peers—time that could be better applied to more important tasks.

By relating the project to progress on these differing priorities, the consultant and the senior leader with whom she was working increased the perceived value of the project. They strengthened confidence in the project by reinforcing staff accomplishments each week and positioned these accomplishments as building blocks for the work that was ahead.

Can We Trust Those Helping Us to Solve the Problem?

Action: Build trust over time.

People with a problem must trust in those who would help them. Significant business change entails risk: risk of the change itself and risk in using someone to help. Trust grows over time. It is personal, involves both rational and emotional elements, and is the product of the relationship dynamics that evolve between people over time.[7] It ultimately reflects the belief that a person has positive goals and a positive approach in how he or she works with others to achieve them. It also reflects the belief that what a person says and does is consistent and this alignment of word and deed is consistent over time.

Just as trust develops with positive experiences over time, the scope of change that people are willing to undertake grows. Consequently, people tend to do more modestly scoped projects early on and larger projects with highly trusted people at later stages in the relationship.

The Problem of Negative Past Experiences

When we orient others to how we plan to implement change, negative past experiences with similar initiatives may interfere. As most change initiatives do not achieve their stated goals, people tend to be privately if not publicly skeptical. If people see that the change process contains the elements they found unattractive in a previous work, they may rankle and overtly resist the methodology, or passively disengage. If preliminary assessment reveals a previous bad experience with a similar change approach, we must separate past methods from the current ones we are proposing.

Helping People Have Vision

Early in the process people in a problem situation try to clarify for themselves a picture of what the future will be like if the targeted changes are made. A compelling picture is exciting and energizing as well as credible and tangible. Giving clear descriptions of the new business results that could be achieved, referring to improvements in what customers, financial analysts, suppliers, and employees would notice if they made the change, and highlighting how people can work together differently if the change is made help make these changes compelling. While these activities are easy to express, the pressure to get to the solution can push people past this important step.

Refraining from Overselling Benefits

Overselling the benefits of the targeted change is one of the major causes of project failures in organizations.[8] While overselling can lead to short-term approval of a change initiative, it can also lead to significant failures once a change project has begun and the reality of what is possible becomes clear.

A FINAL NOTE

In the end, author Jeffrey A. Kottler reminds us to keep these things in mind when engaging the resistance in our effort and converting it into momentum.

- Keep a sense of humor.
- Do not retaliate.
- Clarify roles and ground rules.
- Stay flexible.
- Be pragmatic
- Use self-disclosure.
- Confront.
- Be patient.
- Reframe the meaning of resistance.
- Be compassionate.

When all else fails, let go. When nothing else can be done, let go of the fantasy of omnipotence.

The following two tables highlight the change readiness conditions to achieve in recognition and the actions to take that lead us to critical reflection, the next critical point along the leading edge.

TABLE 7.1 Summary of the Readiness Conditions of the Recognition Stage

When people meet the requirements of the Recognition stage, the following readiness conditions must be satisfied. A critical mass of stakeholders must:

- Have an understanding of the problem that reflects the perspective of people who are close to the problem and are likely to have different views
- Believe that more information is needed to fully understand the problem situation
- Feel the costs of allowing the problem to continue are too high to ignore
- Perceive the benefits of making improvements can be achieved promptly
- Feel that a general plan for solving a problem is feasible
- Believe that people have the ability to do their part of the change process
- Perceive that the organization has the ability to pursue the general approach to change
- Perceive access to a credible resource that can help achieve the solution
- Have a balanced, realistic view of what the change will be like

TABLE 7.2 Summary of Strategies for Prompting the Transition to Recognition

- Ask key stakeholders such as end users, technical experts, and buyers questions to clarify personal and organizational needs and shape a vision of outcomes.
- Arrange testimonials from credible others directly or indirectly from reports and summaries that:
  - Indicate that there is a high-priority problem to solve that will not go away on its own
  - Show how the problem can be solved
  - Show how things will be better once a solution has been implemented
  - Build confidence that the problem is solvable and people have the ability to solve it
  - Illustrate how people will participate in the solution and live with its implementation
  - Demonstrate the competence of the change process and change facilitators
- Arrange dialogue among a critical mass of stakeholders about the five readiness questions and their answers.

Chapter 8

Important Moments in Critical Reflection

> *What can we gain by sailing to the moon if we are not able to cross the abyss that separates us from ourselves? This is the most important of all voyages of discovery, and without it, all the rest are not only useless, but disastrous.*
> —Thomas Merton

The case of Tower Air Flight 41 introduces us to our next critical moment: critical reflection. On a wintry December 20, 1995, Flight 41 pushed back from its gate at JFK en route to Miami. The experienced crew deiced the Boeing 747-100 and headed to the flight line with 468 passengers. When the crew reached the flight line, the flight was 36 minutes late and snow had begun blowing across the runway.

With approval from air traffic control, the captain applied thrust and the plane headed down the runway. As the plane accelerated to 80 knots, it began to slide off the runway. The crew tried valiantly to correct the plane's course, but without success. Failing to correct the course, the crew worked to bring the giant plane to a stop. As the crew struggled with this task, the plane continued to barrel forward; a concrete structure ripped off one engine and contact with rough terrain thrust the nose gear into the cabin. Food carts bounced around as the plane slowed and then came to rest. Twenty-four passengers had sustained slight injuries, and one flight attendant had been seriously injured. To make matters worse, the evacuation of the plane did not proceed smoothly. The flight attendants did not give clear instructions to the passengers following the accident, and disembarking proceeded in an uncoordinated fashion.

For Tower Air, Boeing, and the National Transportation Safety Board, preventing accidents was job one. Yet a serious accident had occurred. What were the root causes of Flight 41's problem? What could be done to solve it? These are the types of questions one asks in the Critical Reflection stage.

While investigating Flight 41, the National Transportation Safety Board (NTSB) examined the physical evidence of the crash site and the damaged plane, listened to recordings of crew communications, and interviewed the crew, flight attendants, and passengers. NTSB staff also reviewed pilot training and simulation procedures. After synthesizing data from multiple sources, they outlined their view of root causes.

First, the crew knew the runway was slippery but not slippery enough to stop the flight. Before the plane reached the runway, airport personnel had completed a test of runway slipperiness. The test showed conditions had worsened. Remarkably, this computation of increased slipperiness or the "runway friction coefficient" was not available in terms that the crew could translate into guidance for operating the 747 differently (e.g., braking will take 20 percent longer). In other words, they had the results of the test, but they didn't understand the results. The crew did not perceive that increased slipperiness was a threat to a safe takeoff.

Second, the crew had relied on the fragile nose wheel rather than the rudder to try to return the plane to the center of the runway. The nose gear provided a high level of directional control at the gate and on the low-speed trip that aircraft take to the runway. As a result, many pilots had developed the habit of steering the plane with the nose gear. Using the rudder control, as operating manuals indicated, is a more effective means of guiding the plane as it accelerates down the runway. While simulator training could have prepared pilots with knowledge of the limits of nose gear control, it did not. In the end, pilot training and experience in the aircraft had encouraged reliance on a weak means of control that would fail on that snowy and slippery day. Third, the flight attendants and flight crew had not worked together to implement an efficient process for getting the passengers off the plane.

As we learn from the experience of Flight 41, clarifying root causes—a primary task of critical reflection—sometimes leads us to unexpected and surprising problem causes. In retrospect, not having an effective means of determining the runway slipperiness, relying on a fragile nose wheel for controlling an accelerating 747, and the absence of a well-rehearsed procedure for disembarking passengers seems remarkable. Practices that were problematic on their own—but were not recognized as such until the circumstances of that day exposed them—produced the accident of Flight 41.

Once we have clarified root causes, critical reflection requires thinking through potential responses. In the case of Flight 41, these responses to the root causes included:

- Criteria for making rapid and accurate decisions about takeoff under slippery conditions
- Training and operating manuals with information about managing slippery conditions
- Modifications of simulator training to accurately reflect the handling of the aircraft in slippery condition
- Better friction measurement and reporting
- Improved safety of food service carts and proper attendant training about ensuring their security
- Better communication procedures between the attendants and the crew
- Better postaccident procedures for attendants to follow when directing passengers

The case of Flight 41 orients us to the basic process of critical reflection. In this chapter, we expand on the mechanics of this stage and how to accomplish its tasks. We begin with a quick reference guide to critical reflection. The guide outlines the outcomes we are striving to achieve at this stage and delineates the activities that achieve critical reflection.

QUICK REFERENCE GUIDE FOR CRITICAL REFLECTION

How do we know that we have been successful at the target outcomes of this stage? People perceive that they:

- Have a deeper, more complete understanding of the problem situation and see it from the point of view of the different functions involved
- Appreciate the root causes of the problem and how they worked together to produce the problem situation

- Recognize that mistakes have been made and see "the" problem as "my and our" problem
- Recognize that there are compelling possibilities for action from which to choose
- See that there are options for action with different costs and benefits
- Believe that there are options for action that are consistent with the company and/or professional identity

Successful implementation of the activities outlined in Table 8.1 promotes critical reflection.

TABLE 8.1 Actions That Promote Critical Reflection

ACTIONS TO PROMOTE TRANSITION THROUGH CRITICAL REFLECTION		HOW THIS TOOL CONTRIBUTES
What are the root causes of the problem?	Situation analysis	Clarifying the strengths, weaknesses, opportunities, and threats helps to focus attention on the broader context of change.
	Historical reconstruction	Constructing the sequence of events that explain how the current problem situation evolved helps us see that "this problem occurred to us given who we are and the circumstances we face."
	Customer surveys	Data from customers helps break through internal biases about what customers think about one's business. Usually, these surveys produce at least a few surprises.
	Benchmarking	Evaluating the performance in relation to comparators helps illuminate opportunities for improvement. Evaluating points where performance exceeds comparators, lags behind comparators, or tracks with comparators helps develop a picture of strengths and weaknesses.
	Climate/ culture survey	The work environment can be a great enabler of (or a drag on) performance. Climate and culture surveys help evaluate the alignment of a work environment with the needs of a business strategy or some other improvement objective.

TABLE 8.1 Actions That Promote Critical Reflection *(continued)*

ACTIONS TO PROMOTE TRANSITION THROUGH CRITICAL REFLECTION		HOW THIS TOOL CONTRIBUTES
	Competency/ skill review	Assessing the competencies and skills in relation to target levels helps to determine the presence of competency and skill gaps. Groups of leaders can be asked to help define target levels or target levels can reflect external benchmarks.
	Analogues and simulations	Working through a simulation that reflects how work is performed today helps people discover the causes of a problem situation. The materials for these exercises work best when they are disguised so that they are not literal depictions of the current reality but capture key dynamics.
	Process mapping and analysis	Outlining the sequence of steps needed to accomplish a major task and evaluating the number of cycles and time a task takes to be completed sheds light on opportunities for improvement.
How do root causes contribute to the problem?	Fishbone analysis	This tool provides a framework for depicting the root causes that contribute to a problem. Root causes can be sorted according to major categories such as people, procedures, materials, etc. This tool helps organize a variety of root causes into a coherent framework.
	Pareto analysis	This tool summarizes a weighting of the relative impact of various root causes on a problem situation. This type of analysis helps clarify which root causes may be having the greatest impact on a problem. Root causes with the largest influence on the problem should receive the most attention.
What can be done to address the root causes?	Generating ideas through brainstorming adapting, borrowing, and combining	Brainstorming involves generating lots of ideas for a problem without evaluating them as they are being developed. Producing many ideas leads to better ideas. The ideas that are developed toward the end of the process tend to be the better ones. Adapting, borrowing, and combining involve using ideas from others to create potential solutions.
	Affinity diagrams	This tool categorizes a large set of ideas into themes or categories. The resulting structure organizes ideas into a coherent set.
	Evaluating trade-offs	Thinking through the trade-offs in positives and drawbacks promotes an informed evaluation of options for action.

For a look at critical reflection in the world of business, we turn to the case of Bob, a vice president in the manufacturing department of a large pharmaceutical company. Bob's organization had committed to dramatic cycle time reductions in product development and commercialization in order to meet an aggressive goal for new over-the-counter product introductions. To achieve this corporate goal Bob would have to work more collaboratively with R&D, marketing, and sales personnel than he had previously. Bob believed he had put forth his best effort. However, the collaborations stalled, and it was brought to Bob's attention that the other departments attributed the collaboration failure to his leadership style. Bob recognized he had a problem. Contemplating root causes and potential solutions was next.

Bob was sent to a leadership program to smooth out some of the "rough edges" inhibiting his effectiveness with his peers in other departments. During the leadership seminar Bob attended, participants were introduced to alternative leadership practices and asked to experiment with them in role-plays with other participants. In the initial sessions, Bob was very active and asked lots of thoughtful questions.

This changed when the seminar turned to exploring what Bob called "warm and fuzzy" leadership alternatives. Bob's enthusiasm and participation in the program exercises diminished. He asked questions about the validity of the concepts. One could just imagine Bob thinking, "I am just not that kind of manager. I can't do this. It just isn't me!" It was clear from Bob's comments that he saw value in the alternatives, but couldn't see a feasible way of implementing the less-familiar ones.

Midway through the seminar, the facilitator invited Bob to lunch. Naturally, the conversation turned to the program's content. Sensing the time was right, the facilitator shared some of his observations. He said, "Bob, you're bright. You size things up rapidly and make decisions quickly. When you disagree with someone and feel the disagreement strongly, you try to be diplomatic. However, my guess is that it's clear to others when you don't like what they're saying. I bet you are sometimes mystified when people react to you negatively despite doing your best to be 'political.'" Sensing some interest, the facilitator continued. "Bob, to increase your effectiveness with your peers you have to figure out how you are going to implement the different strategies we have explored in a way that is natural to you. Devising the best solution to your company's problems on your own and defending it fiercely has not and probably will not work." Bob slowly nodded as the facilitator made his final point. "The question is how are you going to work with your colleagues more proactively to secure their cooperation? How are you going to engage them early enough so that you don't find yourself defending a position with few options and little time?" Bob had no immediate answers to these questions, but during the remainder of the program he picked case studies and exercises in which he could explore answers.

What had broken through Bob's resistance and motivated him to try the alternatives? The answer is twofold. First, Bob knew he had to adjust his style. Management in his organization had made it clear. His future career depended on his learning to accomplish goals with others. Second, Bob's basic management style had been affirmed. He was not being asked to be someone he was not. But he was being asked to flex his style and act more strategically. If Bob had seen his choice as either maintaining a sense of personal continuity or doing things differently, he, like most of us, would have chosen personal continuity and would not have found the motivation to develop new strategies. With a little help, Bob was given a way to think about altering his management practice in a way that preserved his core sense of himself.

Early in the Contemplation stage, change confronts us, as it did Bob, with two critical issues that must be successfully addressed: (1) reconciling being forced to change with a choice to change and (2) preserving self-esteem while embracing the mistakes that were made in the past. The successful resolution of these two issues is the precondition for productive critical reflection, which is the core process of the Contemplation stage.

The preconditions to successful critical reflection are explored in the next section, and the points of this reflection are presented in Table 8.2.

TABLE 8.2 Preconditions to Critical Reflection

THE BASIS OF CRITICAL REFLECTION

PRECONDITIONS	POINTS OF REFLECTION
Reconciling being forced to change with making the choice to change	Am I prepared to act in an empowered way?
	Is there an elephant in the room that I need to deal with?
Admitting mistakes while preserving self-esteem	Is this a problem that needs a solution or a dilemma that needs an agreement?
	What are the options for change?

BEING FORCED TO CHANGE VERSUS MAKING THE CHOICE TO CHANGE

External threats signal that we must change. In effect, we are pressured to change by our environment. Bob's leaders informed him that he had rough edges that needed smoothing. Shifting how one performs one's role is not uncommon when solving problems. The decision Bob's company made to send him to a development program captured his attention. Yet, to make the personal and organizational investment in the process of planning and implementing change external pressure is not enough. Bob, like all of us, needed to see options and choices to progress through the critical reflection.[1]

The tricky question, then, is how do we reconcile being coerced and choosing? Change experts contend that freedom emerges when a person (and in the case of organizational change, a group of people) identifies with the event. Identifying with the event, they argue, generates or creates need for action. Reconciling coercion and choice means helping people in organizations identify with the external forces pressuring them to change. In short, people need to come to view "the problem" as "my problem" or "our problem," which helps them see that this change is happening to us because of who we are and where we fit into the world where we work. Bob came to understand that his management style—his decisiveness and directness—had made him a good candidate for the new role he was promoted to, a new role that oversaw the dramatic increases in speed and efficiency needed to achieve a decisive advantage over competitors. Bob's task was to find a way to add finesse to his strengths.

When organizations provide people assessment tools, they help people work through this process. They provide insight on a model of change that is endorsed by the organization. These models help people answer questions like, "What are we trying to achieve?" and "What is my role in this change?" "What personal goals should I pursue to make this organizational change a reality?" These models expand the way we see ourselves in the context of change our organization is pursuing.

Once a new, more integrated sense of identity develops, people consider which new job behavior or work practice must be adopted to project this identity into the future. As was pointed out earlier, action consistent with identity occurs easily. Actions that are seen as fundamentally contradictory or damaging of personal and/or corporate identity will be difficult to sustain and can only be maintained with force or coercion. When Bob was helped to see change as adding new leadership disciplines to a basically sound management style ("an aggressive, take charge, and get it done leader"), his identity had been affirmed. Bob was then free to engage the process of experimentation. Without such affirmation, Bob would not have modified the way he worked—to the detriment of Bob's career and his organization's interests.

PRESERVING SELF-ESTEEM WHILE ACKNOWLEDGING MISTAKES

A second issue change people face early in Critical Reflection concerns the evaluation of the present state. As was mentioned previously, admitting the existence of a problem means that one must acknowledge that mistakes were made, recognize one's role in the mistake, or acknowledge that one did not correct a mistake made by others. The danger of such admissions is that they can damage self- or organizational esteem. When this happens, people get defensive—discounting the problem situation and/or their role in it and failing to find the motivation to change.

We are helped to acknowledge a problem situation when it results in a temporary but not overwhelming reduction in self-esteem. On an individual basis, this means focusing self-criticism on behaviors and practices that we can control and adjust with moderate effort. In Bob's case, the problem was positioned as "not using the best tools for his new mandate," "not using his strengths in the right way," or "not doing the right kind of planning." The assessment task was not positioned as "uncovering deep personal deficiencies."

In the politically charged context of most organizations, admitting mistakes is a high-stakes and high-risk process. The attack-defend spiral is a constant threat. If this spiral comes to dominate the dialogue between people about the problem situation, the problem-solving process will stall. If the cycle of accusation and denial is contained and energy is not focused on defending oneself but getting to the solution, people can begin to see the problem situation more objectively. They are freer to scrutinize the assumptions, the attitudes, the behaviors, and the practices that generate and maintain the problem.[2] "The problem" is transformed into "my/our problem," and people feel motivated to pursue change.

Facilitators help leaders keep defenses in check by helping people apply models or analytical frameworks that focus the problem definition in a way that limits counterproductive criticism. In a group situation, terms like "role conflict" and "role ambiguity" help team members problem-solve their way to enhanced working relationships and task performance without engaging in personal criticism of another team member. The techniques of business process redesign give people from different work groups a means of collectively defining efficiency problems in a way that spares people the unproductive activity of assigning blame to managers or groups for past errors.

When the issues of coercion, freedom, identity, and self-esteem are successfully resolved, the stage is set for productive critical reflection within organizations about organizational problems. The four questions of successful critical reflection are:

1. Am I prepared to act in an empowered way?
2. Is there an elephant in the room that I need to deal with? (More on undiscussable issues later in this chapter.)
3. Is this a problem that needs a solution or a dilemma that needs an agreement?
4. What are the options for change?

FOCAL POINTS OF SUCCESSFUL CRITICAL REFLECTION

Am I Prepared to Act in an Empowered Way?

When reflecting on underlying beliefs, assumptions, and attitudes, people often come to recognize that they have been making limited, bureaucratic responses to problems they have. Jack Mezirow, author of *Transformative Dimensions of Adult Learning* (1991), describes the bureaucratic response as being characterized by several elements that often unfold in the following way:

- When introducing new ideas, support is sought by trying to convince people. The rationale and evidence for the proposal are found in professional standards or broad goals.

- When attempts to convince others fail, people recognize that politics are at work and try to exchange resources to move ahead. Political leverage and, if need be, coercion, is used to secure support for initiatives. People play their cards close to the vest, and relationships with others are managed cautiously. Power is gained and lost.
- When dealing with authority, compromises are sought to maintain relationships and avoid career risks. Since survival (at all costs) is the primary goal for all involved, individual behaviors that might advance organizational problem solving (e.g., admitting mistakes, confessing uncertainty) is avoided because it may pose a threat to one's security.

When we do effective critical reflection, we expand our view of ourselves in relation to organizational problems. "The problem" is transformed into "my/our problem," and people feel motivated to pursue change. New views of the problem emerge as they are tested and ultimately validated through dialogue with others. Personal change links with organizational change. Through this dialogue, we begin learning our way out of dilemmas associated with organizational concerns. Issues such as overreliance on authority and structure, fear of conflict, and the challenge of reconciling individual and organizational interests are explored.

Psychologists note that people act in an empowered way, they believe:

- I am the originator of my own destiny.
- I need to affirm the future if I am to thrive in it.
- Openness will result in more successful interpersonal relationships.
- I must have the courage of my convictions.
- There are more realities than just one . . . or mine.

Effectively navigating the Critical Reflection stage prepares the way for these insights and thus prepares the way for genuine solutions to problems.

If productive critical reflection is overwhelmed by concerns about personal security, then the bureaucratic response persists and personal empowerment weakens. In such situations, the pressure to conform to the status quo usually dominates a group. The symptoms of conformity pressure include self-censorship, assuming unanimity, pressure on dissenters, and the activity of self-appointed "mind guards" who protect leaders from information that might weaken the leader's confidence in the soundness of his or her decision making.[3] As many of us have learned, these practices protect the status quo and prevent the creation of genuine solutions to problems.

For big problems, the process of breaking through the bureaucratic response and accepting the personal responsibility contained in an entrepreneurial posture can take longer to complete. And, the bigger the problem, the more contemplation about what the causes of a problem are and what is needed to solve it is necessary.[4] Problems that require deep or transformational change, those that involve adjustments in both strategy and culture, are the toughest ones we face.

Is There an Elephant in the Room That I Need to Deal With?

When the preconditions of critical reflection are satisfied, people are empowered to make productive contact with what Chris Argyris, James Bryant Conant Professor Emeritus of Education and Organizational Behavior at Harvard University, called undiscussable issues.[5] Undiscussable issues are often the root cause of blocked organizational problems. These issues involve the way power is allocated, who has prerogative over what, what behavior is rewarded, how it is rewarded and by whom, who can be held accountable for their actions, and so on. In the case of Flight 41, discussed at the start of this chapter, the prerogative of the captain over the control of an airplane would be an example of an undiscussable issue.

Issues become "undiscussable" because people have raised them in the past and have encountered stakeholders who became deeply hurt or uncontrollably angry, or they have received implicit messages from others that this would be the case if the issue was raised.[6] Engaging undiscussable issues evoke strong reactions because the process casts an objective light on the assumptions that bind people together (e.g., power, authority, responsibility). Many of these assumptions protect political interests (especially if left unexamined) at the expense of organizational ones such as productivity or efficiency. Because undiscussable issues are not generally included in the problem-solving process, the solutions people design deal with only a part of the problem situation. The solutions are often ineffective. "Things get different, not better."

We see this process in action in the case of a group of internal HR recruiters of a large pharmaceutical organization tasked with implementing a profound shift in how they performed their role. To meet product development goals, the organization had to dramatically increase both the number and quality of research personnel. The recruiting organization had to transition from a transactional focus to a more strategic role. This meant that they would shift their focus from the administrative tasks of reviewing résumés, screening candidates, arranging interviews, and processing paperwork to consulting line managers on sourcing strategies (such as formulating plans for using the Internet to attract top talent, identifying prospects through networking with professional colleagues, attending professional conferences, and giving presentations at conferences). The recruiting workload was doubling, and simultaneously the organization decided to implement the shift—without adding new recruiters to the payroll. Recruiting management was keen that recruiters implement this shift in a way that enhanced customer satisfaction. There could be no slippage in customer satisfaction ratings as the transition was implemented.

To implement the new service strategy, individual recruiters had to get their internal clients to agree to the withdrawal of administrative support, get client managers to assume responsibility for tasks recruiters formerly performed, and convince clients of the value that a strategic approach to recruiting could bring to them. This was a tall order for a group that had been assailed in the past for a lack of customer responsiveness!

Recruiters and their management were overwhelmed. The new workload exceeded resources. People struggled to implement the new approach. Clients complained. The reputation of the recruiting management team was being sullied. The recruiters and their management became stuck in a cycle of mutual recrimination and blame. To address their problem, the recruiting leadership brought in external consultants.

During the consultants' initial intervention, it became clear that management had not done a good job of creating readiness. The recruiters were not told about larger organizational issues driving the change. Without this information, recruiters perceived that their management had committed to something that was visionary and heroic in scope but completely unrealistic and only adopted to impress senior leadership—at the recruiter's expense.

The company's executive team had tasked recruiting management with implementing the shift, but as there were few models from which to draw practical ideas, the managers were not sure how to implement the change successfully. When recruiters asked for help, their managers simply instructed them to "figure it out." The recruiters felt betrayed. Recruiting management condemned the recruiters as not "strategic" (near a kiss of death in most organizations). Recruiters thought management lacked integrity and competence. Things were at an impasse.

The first task was to outline the rationale for the change in compelling terms. "The problem" had to become "our problem." Consultants asked recruiting management to clarify the rationale for the shift. The managers explained that the executive team had committed the organization to significant improvements in operational efficiency at the same time the shift in recruiting strategy was to be implemented.

The extrapolation of senior management's goals to the recruiting process meant that the organization was no longer able to financially support the more transactional way that recruiters had performed their role in the past. The cost-per-hire of identifying potential candidates in conventional ways (using external headhunters, scanning job boards) was perceived to be too great; the way that managers and recruiters operated had to change.

This information was shared with the recruiting staff. Once the recruiters realized where the pressure was coming from and why the pressure was being created, they became somewhat more responsive. "The problem" was becoming "our problem."

The consultant also looked for an opportunity to deepen contemplation of the personal aspect of this change. This effort began with case study exercises. In these exercises the recruiters tested their ability to renegotiate their role with a disgruntled and dissatisfied client who was resisting the change. The personal skill dimensions of the shift became clear. Recruiters learned that they had a modest ability to resolve the service conflicts that they would continue to face as they implemented the change in service delivery strategy.

This wasn't the whole story, however. Undiscussable issues were involved. In the course of the case study/role-play, recruiters explained that when client managers became dissatisfied with a recruiter's response to them, they would escalate the issue to recruiting management. Recruiting management generally sided with the client manager, did not redirect the client to the recruiters to work out issues, made quick concessions that often included violating the service strategy, and then rebuked the recruiters for poor service. In the process, recruiting management was seen as often retreating from the difficult task of enforcing the change that they were championing when powerful managers complained.

The recruiters asked that a united front be established up and down the recruiting hierarchy. If the shift was to stay on track, management would need to publicly support the recruiters when service conflicts arose.

Recruiting management explained that recruiters would have to improve their capacity to resolve service conflicts successfully. First, recruiters had to sell the change. This meant helping clients understand the change and appreciate its benefits. Simply communicating the change as a management directive was not enough. Recruiters also had to help their clients through implementation challenges. They had to negotiate agreements and do it in such a way that they limited the volume of complaints from dissatisfied clients. In the end, both parties learned that each had their difficult part to play in implementing the shift.

By seeing the problem as "our problem" and exploring undiscussable issues (management's role in the shift; the difficult politics of resolving service conflicts with powerful executives; the need for salesmanship and negotiation), the recruiters and their management developed a more complete understanding of what would be required to implement the change. Both parties approached the point where they were considering the kinds of changes that would accelerate the transition they had to make.

Is This a Problem That Needs a Solution or a Dilemma That Needs an Agreement?

Not all problems are problems. Some problems are dilemmas. A dilemma exists when there is no clear solution—or when choosing any solution comes at the cost of a highly desirable alternative. Choosing between growing revenue or being profitable is an easy example. The obvious answer is that we want both. Another example is pursuing efficiency and having quality. Once again, we want both. Often, solutions become derailed when they are positioned as unacceptable choices between two very important things. Resolving dilemmas often means finding a way to accomplish one priority without sacrificing the other. The starting point is to recognize that our response cannot be either-or. Finding a way to minimally satisfy competing values simultaneously is the answer. This requires dialogue about trade-offs, the conditions under which the values at play can be at least minimally satisfied. The successful completion of this process is an agreement between people concerning how a dilemma will be resolved.

What Are the Options for Change?

Once root causes of problems are developed, the next step is to develop options for what can be done about the root causes. People ask themselves such questions as: "What are the options for action?" "What are potential benefits to be achieved?" "How might my role change?" "How could people be relating to each other differently?" "How might the organization function differently?"

In general, the more time people think through options, costs, and benefits, the less counterproductive anxiety exists as people transition to action. The longer the client resides in the contemplation stage, the less distress there is about the problem. The distress that persists, however, centers on what we will have to give up in order to change.

CRITICAL REFLECTION TOOL KIT

This section outlines contemplation interventions according to the basic steps of the critical reflection process—that is, whether they address the current problem, future possibilities, or alternative responses to the problem.

What Are the Root Causes of the Problem?

A variety of techniques can be used to help clients deepen their grasp of the current state. These techniques vary in their formality and rigor. In general, the more quantitative the data, the more influence it has. The use of quantitative information helps elevate the consideration of the current state from the level of opinion and perception to the consideration of facts. When negotiating through politics of organizational problem solving, a contest about facts leads to better outcomes than a contest about opinions. Interestingly, quantitative rigor is one of the chief values that consultants bring to the change process. They generally have the expertise, resources, and inclination to collect, manage, analyze, and synthesize quantitative information, while clients often do not.

Situation Analysis

Situation analysis is a common strategic planning tool (we have identified it as a tool a couple of times). It focuses people on identifying an organization's or team's strengths and weaknesses and external opportunities and threats in the business environment in which it strives for success.

At the center of these assessments is a clear-eyed view of how well customer needs are being met and what improvements can be made to better meet or exceed customer needs. This information drives the effective learning processes that focus people on innovating effective solutions to the right problems.

- What opportunities are there for us to meet customer needs better than competitors?
- What threats in the business environment challenge our ability to meet or exceed customer needs?
- How do we better leverage our strengths?
- How do we address our weaknesses?

The answers to these questions provide key inputs into personal and organizational learning processes—and these processes, if properly focused, produce effective innovation. Clarity about customer needs is a precondition of effective SWOT analysis of strengths, weaknesses, opportunities, and threats (Table 8.3).

TABLE 8.3 SWOT Situation Analysis

	ORGANIZATION	ENVIRONMENT
Positive	**Strength**	**Opportunity**
Negative	**Weakness**	**Threat**

Historical Reconstruction: The Story of What Has Happened to Us over Time

Constructing the sequence of events that explains how the current problem situation evolved, especially when it emphasizes how identity is reflected in the history, helps people to claim ownership for a problem situation. When people reaffirm their identity in the context of external forces that are pressuring them to change, a problem gets linked to identity. "This change is happening to us because of who we are and where we fit in the business environment." This makes it easier for people to embrace the problem and the needed change.

Customer Audits: What Do Customers Say?

An important source of information about the current state is the customer's view. Here customers include fellow employees and work groups within the organization with whom work is accomplished as well as external customers. The basic methodology for doing customer audits is to (1) establish and/or clarify customer expectations and (2) evaluate gaps between expectations and actual performance as the customer sees it. This work may also include evaluation of how the service of key competitors is perceived by customers as well.[7] There are several formal methods for trapping customer ratings of service satisfaction. For example, the seminal research of Parasuraman, Zeithaml, and Berry (1985) on customer satisfaction has spawned many such tools applied to a variety of contexts. They have isolated several dimensions along which customer ratings predictably fall. These are summarized in Table 8.4. Some 360-degree surveys used in the development of professional skills feature comparisons of self-ratings with ratings of various customers, that is, senior, peer, and junior colleagues.[8] It is not unusual for clients to resist undertaking this analysis. The disconfirmation of one's perception and the anxiety about one's ability to make the necessary adjustments are common sources of resistance.

TABLE 8.4 Customer Service Dimensions

Reliability Consistency of performance and dependability	• Accuracy of billing • Keeping records • Performing service at the designated time
Responsiveness The willingness of employees to provide service	• Calling a customer back quickly • Giving prompt service
Competence Possession of the required skill and knowledge to perform the required service	• Knowledge and skill of the contact personnel • Skill and knowledge of support personnel
Accessibility Approachability and ease of contact	• Waiting time to receive service is not extensive • Convenient hours of operation

TABLE 8.4 Customer Service Dimensions *(continued)*

Courtesy Politeness, respect, consideration, friendliness	• Consideration for the customer's property of contact with service personnel • Clean and neat appearance of service personnel
Communication Keeping the customers informed in language they can understand, and listening to them	• Explaining the service itself • Assuring the customer that a problem will be handled
Credibility Trustworthiness, believability, honesty of service personnel	• Company reputation • Personal characteristics of the service personal
Security Freedom from danger, risk, or doubt	• Physical safety • Financial security
Understanding/knowing the customer Making the effort to understand	• Learning the customer's specific requirements • Providing individualized attention
Tangibles The physical evidence of service	• Physical facilities • Appearance of personnel • Tools or equipment use to provide the service • Physical representation of the service

Benchmarking Current Practice: How Are the Best Performing?

One method for uncovering root causes to a performance gap is benchmarking. Benchmarking is the process of systematically identifying the best examples of any element of the organizational system (strategy, culture, structure, processes, systems, people competencies) as well as its performance (sales growth, market share, program cost per employee, efficiencies) and comparing the client against these to focus problem areas.[9] External references help to challenge the symptoms of "groupthink" and organizational inertia that often stall the critical reflection process.

External references bring a measure of credibility to the process of uncovering root causes. When others have used these ideas to make changes, different results are not just theoretical possibilities but real possibility. If people view consultants as credible, consultant appraisals can be an important clarification of the current state. In fact, one of the consultant's primary values is the evaluative criteria they develop based on their exposure to multiple organizations. As we have said earlier, insight about others can be a quite powerful influence on the way people frame problems they are having and the solutions that they will evaluate for implementation.

Benchmarking also helps people pinpoint weaknesses and identify important improvement areas. One special challenge is picking the comparators that form the basis of benchmarking. People react negatively when they are compared to contexts not like theirs.

Naturally, the quality of measurement is critical in benchmarking. Quantitative benchmarks focus on such questions as:

- How much?
- How fast?
- How good?
- When?
- Where?
- How long?
- What is the size, shape, form, and fit?

There are three types of benchmarking: internal, competitive, and world-class.

- **Internal benchmarking.** Examining the performance of other groups within an organization to determine best practices. Harrington suggests that this type of benchmarking be conducted first since it is the easiest and cheapest to conduct. Internal benchmarking also avoids confidentiality issues.
- **Competitive benchmarking.** This involves collecting information about a competitor's products, services, and processes and analyzing them to identify their competitive advantages.
- **World-class benchmarking.** World-class benchmarking goes beyond one's immediate competitors to organizations in different industries. As Harrington notes, some features of work are generic, such as warehousing, supplier relations, service parts logistics, customer relations, and hiring.

The basic steps of benchmarking are summarized below:

1. Deciding what should be benchmarked
2. Deciding what processes to compare

3. Developing measurements to compare
4. Deciding what type of benchmarking
5. Collecting data
6. Determining performance gaps

Culture/Climate Surveys

These surveys ask people in the organization to record their view of the values, practices, and behaviors of people in the organization or a work team. There are several tools and methods available for facilitating such assessments. Some feature standardized surveys, and others emphasize interviews.

Competency Studies

Competency studies determine the motives, values, aptitudes, skills, and knowledge of the current performers. They identify the current level in relation to some internal standards. For example, a client's management team may be asked to define the competencies that managers in the organization need to achieve strategic goals. Managers then evaluate current management performance against these requirements.

Analogues/Simulations

Analogues or simulations are exercise situations that reflect the main themes involved in the problem situation but not the precise content. The absence of specific content provides some psychological distance from the business problem—enough that people can contemplate the personal dimensions of change with greater security. While no immediate commitments to change are implied in learning from the analogue or simulation, the experience of such events can effectively set the stage for contemplating change in the immediate problem situation.

Process Mapping and Related Organizational Structure and Systems Analysis

Outlining the sequence of steps that are needed to accomplish a major task and evaluating the number of cycles and how much time a task takes to be completed sheds light on opportunities for improvement. Process maps show how different functions interact to accomplish the tasks and the handoffs between functions. Understanding the process can be a large source of improvement.

Plotting Cause and Effect Links
Fishbone/Root Cause Analysis

FIGURE 8.1 Fishbone Analysis

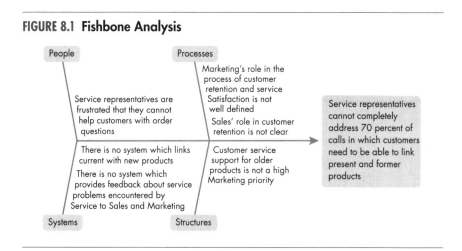

A fishbone analysis (Figure 8.1) is usually conducted with groups of managers and involves developing and depicting the relationships between various causal factors and the problem situation as well as between multiple causal factors and their effect. What results from this analysis is a picture of the network of causes for a problem and their relative role in creating the problem situation.

Pareto Analysis

This tool method provides a structure for considering the relative influence multiple causal factors have on the problem situation. Along one side of a graph are listed the causal factors. For each cause the measurable aspect of the performance problem is outlined. For instance, in Figure 8.2, using the HR recruiting example, the graph shows the causal factors and the measurable aspect of the performance problem (in this case, the percentage of complaints).

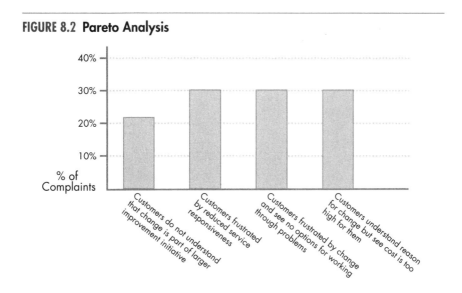

FIGURE 8.2 Pareto Analysis

WHAT CAN BE DONE TO ADDRESS ROOT CAUSES?

There are four main ways of engaging people to efficiently generate options.

Brainstorming

The process of brainstorming usually involves recording ideas on a flipchart. Brainstorming sessions work well when they are guided by a few basic principles:

- Everyone should try to develop as many and different ideas as possible.
- Every idea should be recorded. Even impractical ideas can stimulate creative thinking in someone else.

- Others involved in the session must not critique or evaluate ideas.
- Use ideas of others to stimulate your own thinking.
- Encourage others to brainstorm.
- The ideas that are developed toward the end of the process tend to be the better ones.

Benchmarking information can be a rich source of information to prime the pump for brainstorming.

Borrowing

Borrowing means appropriating from the example of others to create new ideas. Often organizations borrow ideas from the comparators used in benchmarking. The primary benefit of borrowing is that it doesn't require the time and costs of developing and testing an approach from the ground up.

Adapting

In adapting, ideas are collected from unrelated fields, industries, or contexts. The use of this strategy begins by determining the key elements of the problem situation. Then, participants isolate examples of these elements occurring in unrelated industries and/or fields. For instance, the recruiters discussed earlier in this chapter might take a look at how an IT organization successfully implemented complex changes despite political turmoil and adapt some relevant methods to their own situation. These themes are then developed into ideas.

Combining

Combining simply means integrating ideas from several different sources to devise an action plan. There are several ways to combine ideas:

- **Affinity diagrams.** Affinity diagrams organize ideas by themes. They give some structure to ideas developed in brainstorming.
- **Evaluating trade-offs.** Thinking through the trade-offs in positives and drawbacks promotes an informed evaluation of options for action.

CHALLENGES OF CRITICAL REFLECTION

In the Critical Reflection stage, there are a few special challenges that must be managed effectively to keep a business change project on track.

The Impulse to Act Without Adequate Reflection

In many organizations the pressure for immediate action is acute and difficult to redirect. People in organizations tend to be recognized for getting things done and less often for holding out for a better solution. A seasoned project manager once outlined one response to this challenge: "Go slow so you can go fast." The idea that doing adequate reflection and preparation now increases the likelihood of efficient action later is straightforward and is a useful response to the dilemma of speed versus the quality of the result. Trying to do makeup Critical Reflection work in the Commitment phase of the readiness process seriously weakens commitment to act[10] and the quality of the action that will be taken.

A Special Challenge in Organizations: Multiple Stakeholders

In the rush to get to work on a problem, we often skip the step of allowing others to do the same. We develop plans and programs and then delegate implementation to work groups and individuals. Without preparing the environment with activities that stimulate critical reflection, readiness does not develop. Implementation problems like those experienced by the recruiting management team are encountered. When things are off track and in trouble, then people scramble to recover by trying activities that trigger critical reflection. Team-building sessions are scheduled. Training is conducted.

Unfortunately, these "last ditch" measures often cannot get the initiative back on track. The problem owner has already committed itself to specific plans and programs. There is no time or freedom to analyze the problem, question assumptions, or evaluate real options. Thus people do not experience critical reflection nor achieve its benefits. "The problem" does not become "our problem." At best "the problem" becomes "their problem." "And we (the employees) have to solve their problem for them." Plans and programs proceed, but the quality of implementation suffers. Moreover, implementation may occur, but only if management closely and tightly supervises the details, a very expensive undertaking. As Warren Buffet observes, "What the wise do in the beginning, the fools do in the end." Planning how stakeholders will be systematically pulled into the process is an important reflection task when the problem solution will involve others.

SOME DO NOT MAKE THE TRANSITION . . . TODAY

It is a sobering but important fact that some who have engaged in critical reflection decide that the benefits of change are not worth the costs of making it. Some problem owners decide to live with their problem. In fact, Freud taught that the most common outcome of a change attempt is that people learn about themselves but are sadder and wiser. The person understands the problem situation but is unprepared to change it. Unfortunately, many of us do not recognize when a person reaches this point. We push forward with implementation plans, and in the end, produce a low-value work product. When faced with people who are not ready to change, the ideal response is to help them appreciate their situation, assist them in the process of outlining the steps that promote readiness, and facilitate planning for how those steps can be taken.

It is important to emphasize, however, that a decision not to implement change does *not* mean that the process was a failure. As Freud also taught, the client is *wiser*. The client understands the problem situation and recognizes what's needed to achieve the requisite level of readiness required to effect a solution. This awareness is vital to change, though it may not motivate the pursuit of change in the moment.

The reader will recall that research on individual change indicates that people need to build momentum for change over time. Several change attempts are often required before the ultimate follow-through takes place. This means a sense of timing and patience are the virtues of effective change agents, and engineering readiness for change is their overarching goal.

THE TRANSITION FROM CRITICAL REFLECTION

When change initiatives satisfy the conditions of the Critical Reflection, they enter a new phase in the motivational "windup" to action. They have a deeper, more complete understanding of the problem situation, recognize the mistakes that have been made, and see "the" problem as "their" problem. While they feel external pressure to do something about their problem situation, they recognize that they have exciting possibilities from which to choose. These choices are seen as congruent with their core (though perhaps reframed) identity and new in that they contain disciplines that must be added to the work they do or how they do that work. Each choice contains different costs and benefits. These have been considered. At the end of the Contemplation stage, problem owners have embraced an entrepreneurial contract with their organization and are ready to move from critical reflection to building a plan to act.

Chapter 9

Commitment to Initiate

Racing (a yacht) without knowledge of the current is like walking up an escalator that is going down.
—Bob Bavier

This chapter is devoted to describing the currents and signposts of commitment that we can use to stay on course. We enter this stage after defining a problem, determining its root causes, and considering options for solutions and their trade-offs. To support advancing through the commitment stage, we will focus on: (1) what commitment is, (2) how we foster it, and (3) what to do when despite our best efforts the required level of commitment does not develop but we want to stay on track. We begin with a quick reference guide that summarizes the primary points of this chapter. If we do not engage people in accordance with the principles in the following section, we inadvertently find ourselves "walking up an escalator that is going down." Lack of progress, off-track deliverables, budget problems, and missed deadlines are the result.

QUICK REFERENCE GUIDE FOR COMMITMENT TO INITIATE

What outcomes define the successful completion of this stage? People perceive that they:

- Feel pulled to a newly reframed identity—a vision—that creates new opportunities for the organization and its people
- Believe that people have worked together to build a solution to a problem

- See that the points of view people in different disciplines and at different levels have been reflected in the solution
- Believe that good supports have been put in place to overcome the obstacles that may be encountered during implementation of the plan
- See that a climate of safety exists for the trial-and-error process of learning that will be needed to learn to do things differently
- Are committed to pushing through the personal difficulties that they will encounter in making the solution a reality

TABLE 9.1 Ideas for Promoting Commitment

Actions that promote commitment	By granting people enough participation that they (1) "feel ownership" for the solution but (2) have designed it efficiently within the boundaries that define an effective solution; that way we produce a plan with the strongest prospects for success.
STEP 1: BUILD COMMON VISION	
Develop common ground to pull key people together.	When people see that they have common values and priorities, their connections to each other grow and the potential for collective action expands.
Shape shared vision to focus the future efforts of key stakeholders.	Relating shared values and priorities to a set of aspirations about how these will be realized in the future gives focus to future collective action.
STEP 2: BUILD COMMITMENT TO PRIORITIES	
Develop and refine the idea space for developing good ideas.	Draw from the common vision to set boundaries. Asking people to develop ideas within these boundaries (or idea spaces) promotes the development of ideas that support and reflect the broader commitments embodied in the common vision.
Solicit participation of others within the idea space that has been created.	Ask people to brainstorm ideas within boundaries; this helps make what can be a costly process as efficient as possible.
Perform a value-feasibility/ cost-benefit analysis to pick a good idea.	Develop estimates of the cost of a solution and expected benefits. Costs and benefits minimally include financial measures, and work best when they also include other types of costs and benefits— such as ease of use, reliability, and scope of change in work practices and behavior.

TABLE 9.1 Ideas for Promoting Commitment *(continued)*

Complete force field analysis to think through how to best navigate the currents working with you and against you.	Outline the anticipated sources of resistance and support for an idea. This helps focus implementation planning by leveraging features in the situation that will facilitate a solution and containing aspects in the environment that will restrain it.
Do a risk assessment to establish contingencies for the threats that the solution will likely face.	Documenting threats that could impair the implementation of a solution when implementation is under way mobilizes people to think through the contingencies that may be needed to keep implementation on track.
STEP 3: FINALIZE A PLAN	
Develop a focus for effort and resources.	Laying out tasks and subtasks (and the sequencing of both), timing, and accountabilities focuses the efforts of people and teams toward implementation success.
Develop an approach for keeping the project on track.	Setting milestones against which progress can be managed and developing a process for keeping stakeholders alerted to threats to the plan engages people in addressing the factors that push a project off track.
STEP 4: BUILD ENTHUSIASM	
Prepare strategies for maintaining momentum.	Having strategies on hand for a few priority tasks makes it easier to do them than waiting until the implementation plan is under way. Priorities include: • Reinforcing positive expectations • Emphasizing the benefits of change • Reducing feelings of uncertainty Celebrating small wins also builds motivational momentum.

CHALLENGES TO OVERCOME

There are a few challenges to overcome when using participation to build commitment. We outline some important ones in Table 9.2.

TABLE 9.2 Challenges to Overcome in Building Commitment

CHALLENGES	WHAT TO DO
Getting people to participate	To engage fully in a participative process, four conditions must exist. People need to (1) trust the process, (2) view their input as voluntary, (3) experience the process of participating as rewarding, and (4) see their ideas as significantly affecting work products. Meeting these conditions can offset the cynicism that faces many change attempts.
Engineering the right balance between building ownership and being efficient	Create boundaries within which good ideas can be developed and ensure that there is effective facilitation. Ensure that the idea space is broad enough that people feel as though there is sufficient freedom to develop good ideas.
Cascading commitment	Four priorities serve as a focus for cascading commitment: • The direction—both strategy and culture shifts • Developing and installing enabling structures, processes, and systems through which direction is fulfilled • Translating the vision of change given on-the-ground realities; maneuvering the agenda for change in and around obstacles • Motivating frontline staff to implement planned changes
Dealing with readiness gaps	As plans for action are finalized, evaluate whether the readiness needed to proceed with confidence is on hand. If not, build a plan to fill readiness gaps. • Pushing on without sufficient readiness is common but does not usually produce good outcomes. • The readiness assessment tool in the following section helps with this task.

NEEDED LEVEL OF READINESS FOR EFFECTIVE ACTION

Table 9.3 is inspired by Robert Schaffer's perspective on readiness and outlines the conditions that need to be in place for a change attempt to be optimally successful. If sufficient readiness is not on hand, then the initiative should focus on closing the identified readiness gaps, or the change should be scaled to the available level of readiness.

TABLE 9.3 Conditions Needed for an Optimal Change Attempt

CATEGORY		READINESS FACTOR
Organization	Highly perceived need	• People are uncomfortable with the status quo. • The problem to be solved is high priority. • The perspective of leaders, technical experts, and end users shaped the definition of the need or the problem.
	Worth it	• Supporters of the solution will gain more than opponents will lose. • Adequate time, energy, and budget have been allocated to the change project. • Change requires that new practices be added to how work gets done but does not require radical change.
	Clarity of the plan	• The plan for change is simple. • Assignments and schedules are clear. • The changes to work procedures are documented. • A process for evaluating progress and making course corrections based on feedback from customers and people involved in plan implementation is included in the plan.
Solution	Evidence of success	People have seen evidence that the solution has been effective in similar organizations or similar situations.
	Adaptable	The solution can be adjusted and tailored to local needs.
Change process	Credibility	The change agent supporting the change is perceived to be an expert.
	Congruent	The change process is consistent with values of the organization.
	Customer focus	The change agent is focused on meeting the needs of people in the organization.

(continued)

TABLE 9.3 Conditions Needed for an Optimal Change Attempt *(continued)*

CATEGORY	READINESS FACTOR	
People	Understanding of change	People involved in the change project: • Understand the need • Appreciate the benefits of the solution • Understand the success criteria • Understand the plan to implement the solution
	Motivation	• People perceive that change will create significant gain at moderate cost. • The solution will meet some needs of people across the organization—senior management, middle management, and staff. • The plan for change is simple. • People are not fatigued by other recent and large change initiatives.
	Perceptions of support	• People perceive that they have access to key organizational supports (e.g., support of colleagues, training, hands-on technical support, advice, and coaches) that are needed to implement change successfully. • People feel that they can learn and perform against new expectations with tolerance for intelligent and well-intentioned mistakes along the way.
	Change skills	Those involved possess a demonstrated capacity to absorb and exploit new ideas.
	Technical ability	People close to the change are competent to implement its technical aspects.
	Prepared for agility	People see that some thought has been given to events that might push plans off course.

A CLOSER LOOK AT THE COMMITMENT STAGE IN FLIGHT

Let's explore the application of these principles in organizations via the story of how a young leadership team solved a costly safety problem in a large new state-of-the-art distribution system. The leaders of the new facility were relatively young, in their mid-20s and early 30s, and had experienced rapid promotions in the old distribution system. They regarded themselves as very capable and saw their mission as meeting soaring customer demands for tailored and flexible distribution while they worked out the bugs in the facility.

Attempting to meet the challenges of this mission strained the leadership team's capabilities. Work hours increased; supervisors and managers had to problem-solve systems issues and fight to keep the employees focused. The system had to adopt greater distribution flexibility; the company's competitors already had.

Turnover began to spike as employees complained about the hours and about being mistreated by supervisors. Injury rates soared, as did workers' compensation claims. Claims were on track for growing well past $1 million. Union organizers were circling the facility and talking with increasingly more receptive employees. Tensions were also growing between the distribution facility and sales organization. The case for launching the new distribution system had been made by promising that the new system would grant greater flexibility. Sales representatives were promised the ability to tailor product delivery as part of an enhanced customer service model. Whenever deliveries were delayed or incorrect, members of the sales organization complained.

With the assistance of an internal safety consultant, the distribution leadership team chose a set of safety performance goals. The goals were framed as reflecting the organization's broader commitment to being a leader among its peers. The goals were (1) to lower the injury rate at the facility to match the standard established for the distribution industry and (2) to achieve the commensurate level of workers' compensation claims. When the intervention began, safety performance lagged dramatically behind industry benchmarks.

Over several solution development meetings, the team explored the range of solutions used successfully in other organizations. Other organizations, they found, increased safety performance by:

- Using a designated healthcare provider with expertise in work injuries
- Having supervisors accompany injured employees to the hospital
- Establishing an on-site facility for physical therapy
- Providing monthly safety reports up and down the chain of command
- Enabling supervisors to conduct trainings for safe work methods
- Providing incentives for safe performance
- Doing audits of safe job performance

In a series of meetings, ideas were exchanged and reviewed. Some ideas triggered strong negative reactions and were rejected, and others were modified. The final plan agreed to by management included an incentive program, safe work methods training, regular safety audits, and on-site physical therapy. Facility leadership pitched the program to leaders in the corporate office and the program won corporate support.

The new safety disciplines were seen as a needed but inconvenient investment of time and resources in a problem that distracted attention from the team's primary focus: shipping products accurately and on time. At the end of each of the first two months, improvements in injury rates and losses were achieved, and these were noted in management reports that were distributed to senior leaders. These positive achievements were acknowledged in team meetings with "attaboys" from senior leaders.

In the following section, we provide a definition of commitment and a process for developing it.

TOOL KIT: FACILITATING COMMITMENT TO INITIATE ACTION

What Is Commitment?

To begin clarifying how to achieve commitment, we must first define the notion itself. A particularly compelling definition of commitment places emphasis on the behavioral outcomes it creates. Gary Yukl and his colleagues point out that people are committed when they maintain their pursuit of an objective in the face of *significant personal obstacles*. In other words, the disposition to overcome the personal problems and inconveniences one encounters when implementing an idea defines commitment. Since the process of implementing change presents people with a wide variety of such problems and inconveniences (e.g., uncertainty about the right solution, the need to resolve conflicts with colleagues and more senior managers, concerns about accountability), the motivation to persevere despite such difficulties is indispensable to success. To sharpen this definition of commitment and underscore its significance to business change, we will distinguish it from a second motivational outcome change project activities often create: compliance.

Compliance occurs when someone agrees to an objective but will abandon a course of action in the face of significant personal obstacles. Compliance is easier to secure than commitment and, of the two, is the more common response to business change. The problem with compliance is that, while it leads to prompt action, it requires that the change agent and the problem owner invest considerable energy and resources in closely monitoring performance, following up, and reinforcing expectations when performance slips.

Consideration of these two outcomes raises the question, "When is commitment better than compliance?" When the scope of the effort is modest and the change agent and the problem owner have the resources to closely monitor performance, then compliance is an appropriate motivational outcome to pursue. Indeed, much of the successful work done by professional services firms and internal consultants (e.g., accounting, information systems, training, strategy development) is of this type. When viewed on the broad continuum of change efforts from modestly incremental to radically transforming, the efforts of most change agents focus on important but small, though not necessarily easy to accomplish, improvements in the status quo. However, when the scope of the change effort is larger (i.e., the change presents the problem owner with many personal obstacles that must be overcome), and/or the resources needed to closely monitor performance are not available, then compliance will not yield the desired outcomes and commitment is the better course. However, pursuing compliance when commitment is needed often means that plans and agreements are created but long-term follow-through is poor or does not occur.

How Does Commitment Develop?

A manager once described the essence of commitment this way:

> The bottom line of commitment is that you can*not* get people committed to your stuff. People are only committed to their *own* stuff. The key is how you get people to see *their* stuff in *your* stuff.

Build Common Ground

Common ground represents the foundation of commitment. It is made up of priorities, values, fears, and hopes that a group shares in connection to a problem situation. The starting point for building common ground is asking people for their priorities and concerns. The root causes, options for action, and their trade-offs we developed in the Contemplation phase can help jump-start this process. The common ground exercise often surfaces a few surprises that can refine what people think about the perceived common ground that may be in place. Presenting the common ground that people share tightens the connections between them and can be projected into a future.

In the case of the distribution facility, several points of common ground were present:

- Corporate leadership had raised concerns about the facility's subpar safety performance—especially its workers' compensation costs.
- The company had achieved leadership status in several aspects of its operation—leadership was part of the company's identity.
- Previous attempts to solve the problem had not produced much success.
- The management and supervisory team was managing a new state-of-the-art facility that required that they learn new management approaches.
- The organization was willing to make an investment in improving safety performance by funding a consultant and other resources.
- Other local companies had "best practice" safety programs in place that worked with employees that were similar to those who worked in the facility.

As mentioned earlier, building common ground enables people to think of the future. Clarifying this future is the focus of the next stage.

Build Shared Vision

With common ground in place, shaping common vision means synthesizing common vision from personal aspirations or goals for the future. This common vision is a statement of broad goals and broad means. "What is our ultimate aim, and how are we going to achieve it?" In this distribution case, the goal of achieving an industry standard of performance fit the aspiration of the facility management team and corporate leadership for being a leader in its industry. This aspiration translated into the goals of improving injury rate performance and compensation claims experience that met or exceeded industry benchmarks through the implementation of a new safety program.

Propose and Refine Boundaries That Reflect the Vision

Boundaries include goals, requirements, cost constraints, or readiness conditions that exist in a situation. Idea space, or the domain of possible actions, is created by these boundaries. Once the space is defined, then people are asked for ideas that fit within the space. Once the boundaries are developed, then one is able to trigger participation with open-ended questions and active listening. The results from this effort will align with vision.

In the distribution facility example, the idea space was defined by three boundaries:

- Safety performance needed to meet or achieve benchmark levels
- Safety programs needed to reflect components commonly found among industry best practices
- Investments in safety performance improvement could not come at the expense of the team's commitment to leading on-time and accurate product distribution.

Pictures help people flesh out and define boundaries. An example appears in Figure 9.1.

FIGURE 9.1 Idea Space for the Distribution Facility Space

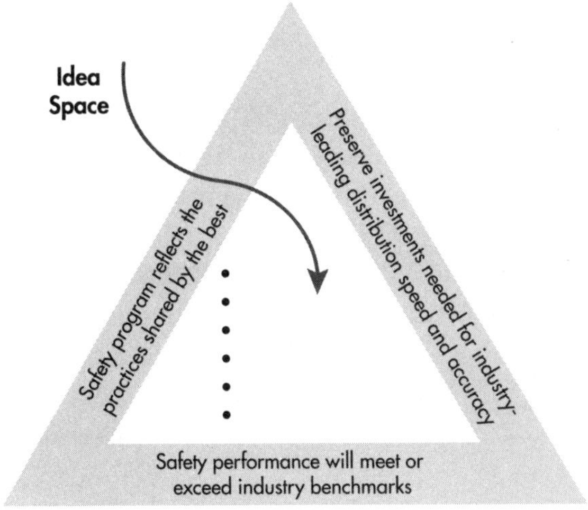

Pull for Ideas

Having established boundaries, the process continues with soliciting ideas. The basic question is: "What ideas fit within these boundaries?" Ultimately, how much input you require is a matter of need and judgment. In the distribution example, managers were given options to consider and select from. These included:

- Using a designated healthcare provider with expertise in work injuries
- Having supervisors accompany injured employees to the hospital
- Establishing an on-site facility for physical therapy
- Providing monthly safety reports up and down the chain of command
- Enabling supervisors to conduct trainings for safe work methods
- Providing incentives for safe performance
- Doing audits of safe job performance

Many of these ideas were selected, and some were rejected. A core concern of the management team was that their investment in safe performance would not compromise their focus on achieving flexible on-time and accurate product deliveries with the new system.

Occasionally, involving others surfaces such conflict. A core task of business problem solving is finding novel ways of reconciling competing interests. A common observation: the inability of powerful stakeholders to resolve such conflicts is at the root of most business change problems.

Identify and Close Persistent Readiness Gaps or Postpone Until Ready

Once the ideas are made actionable though a plan, then the key stakeholders are asked to consider the readiness conditions that are associated with successful implementation of the plan and determine which are present and which are not. Table 9.4 will help with this assessment. When key readiness conditions are not present, two actions are possible: (1) rescoping the task to fit existing readiness conditions and/or (2) delaying the task until missing readiness conditions are filled.

TABLE 9.4 Assessing Readiness Conditions: Focus on Organization and People

CATEGORY	READINESS FACTOR	
Organization	Perceived need	Need for the project is high in the hierarchy of concerns people in the situation have and the perspectives of leaders, technical experts, and end users shape the needs.
	Resource allocation	Adequate time, energy, budget, and systems have been allocated to the change project.
	Compatibility	Change requires flexing but not radically changing the culture.
	Understanding of change	Anyone involved in the change project sees the need and understands the outcomes, and measures of success are guiding the initiative and the plan to implement the solution.
People	Motivation	People perceive that change will create significant gain at moderate cost and feel that everyone involved has the skills and knowledge required to succeed.
	Perceived support	People perceive that they have access to key organizational supports (e.g., support of colleagues, options for training, hands-on technical support, and advice) that are needed to implement change successfully. People feel that they can learn to perform against new expectations with tolerance for intelligent and well-intentioned mistakes along the way.
	Change management skills	Those who are involved have in the past demonstrated the capacity to absorb and exploit new ideas.
	Technical ability	People close to the change are competent to implement its technical aspects
	Contingencies on hand	People see that some thought has been given to events that might push plans off course, and their confidence grows that important change can be achieved.

This second option is rarely witnessed but should occur with greater frequency. If readiness is rarely in sufficient supply, postponing a change attempt is the prudent thing to do. Pushing ahead anyway is common, however. This decision accounts for the relatively low success rate change programs experience. The failure that results leaves teams demoralized and contributes to the cynicism many feel in organizations.

Erin's company was interested in implementing total quality. The company had found a top total quality management (TQM) consulting firm in Japan. Erin and her team went to secure the consultant's support for their firm by pitching to a couple of the members of the TQM consultancy. They politely listened and then, once the presentation was over, said that her team had not done enough homework. Her company wasn't ready.

What? Erin and her colleagues were shocked by the feedback. But, the project was important, and they felt they wanted to prove that they were ready. So they prepared an improved business case and went back to make a second presentation. When they were done, they waited for the go-ahead. It did not happen. The consultants asked where their leadership team was. Erin and her colleagues explained that they had reviewed the document with leaders and that the leadership team was in support of its contents. Once again, the gurus said the company was not ready.

Well, this rejection caught leadership's attention. For the third presentation, Erin, her team, and the leadership committee all attended, and at last the TQM firm agreed to work with them.

Indeed, getting people to postpone a change attempt so that they can prepare can work. This practice is not uncommon in behavior therapy. Setting the dial to "full speed ahead," ready or not, is a common occurrence in business. As the above example shows, sometimes explicitly stating the lack of readiness can galvanize the organization to reach a ready point.

Value-Feasibility Analysis

Value-feasibility analysis means plotting ideas on a chart that makes trade-offs explicit between value, the impact that a particular set of solutions may have, and how doable a solution is—that is, how easy it will be to implement a given solution. The best ideas are those that are high value and implementable. An illustration from the supervisory example appears in Table 9.5. This framework is useful in getting a group of people to do an analysis of options. Once an idea is selected, a cost-benefit analysis quantifies the return for a given investment of organization resources.

TABLE 9.5 Value-Feasibility Analysis

		VALUE	
		LOW	HIGH
FEASIBILITY	LOW	• Supervisors accompany injured employees	• Supervisory safe work methods training
	HIGH	• On-site physical therapy	• Incentives • Safe behavior audits • Safe work methods training • Safety reports • Designated healthcare provider

Cost-Benefit Analysis

This tool involves developing estimates of the cost of a solution and expected benefits. Costs and benefits minimally include financial measures and work best when they also include other types of costs and benefits such as ease of use, reliability, and scope of change in work practices and behavior. A cost-benefit analysis (Table 9.6) can be helpful when driving to final implementation plans. These analyses can be quite detailed

TABLE 9.6 Cost-Benefit Analysis

CONSTITUENCY	DESCRIPTION	HIGH COST	LOW COST	LOW BENEFIT	HIGH BENEFIT	SUM
Customer		-2	-1	+1	+2	
End User		-2	-1	+1	+2	
Sales		-2	-1	+1	+2	
Suppliers		-2	-1	+1	+2	
Manufacturing		-2	-1	+1	+2	
Information Systems		-2	-1	+1	+2	
Finance		-2	-1	+1	+2	
R&DD		-2	-1	+1	+2	
Marketing		-2	-1	+1	+2	
Senior Leadership		-2	-1	+1	+2	
First- line Employees		-2	-1	+1	+2	
Human Resources		-2	-1	+1	+2	
Customer Service		-2	-1	+1	+2	

Sample Cost/Benefit Factors
- Quality
- Operational efficiency impacts
- Work environment changes
- Structural changes
- Service impacts
- Control over resources
- Access to resources
- Work process changes
- System changes
- People changes

Force Field Analysis

As plans are finalized, it is useful to figure out how various factors will contribute to or impair the implementation of a solution. The process involves examining the influences of two categories of factors, restraining and facilitating forces. These are factors at work while pursuing a goal. A group of people can be polled for these factors. These factors are then recorded on a chart. Second, a weight is assigned to each factor. Finally, the sum of the points for restraining and facilitating factors is calculated. When these points are examined, one can then generate ideas for how certain restraining factors can be weakened and how some facilitating factors can be strengthened so that the change is more likely to succeed. Figure 9.2 gives a sample field analysis for a customer service example.

FIGURE 9.2 Field Analysis for a Customer Service Example

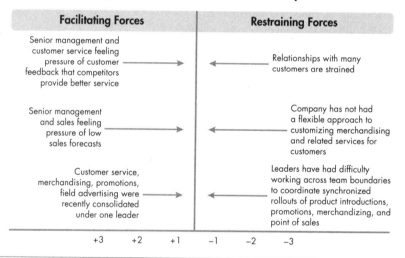

Conducting Small-Scale Pilots

Small-scale pilot programs are limited tests of an idea and its implementation, low-risk experiments in narrower or more circumscribed situations than the one in which the idea will be ultimately implemented. Successful pilots reduce risk, build confidence, and provide credibility to the concept, thus building readiness for larger-scale changes.

Securing Committed Action

After good ideas are developed, then the next step is making them actionable. The question, "Who does what when?" needs to be answered. In short, a project plan is needed. Clarifying action plans often leads to the identification and resolution of resource requirements, timing priorities, and so on. At the distribution facility, a broad plan outlined the main tasks and their timing. Drafts are developed through consultation with others.

Generating Enthusiasm

Prepare communications that promote positive expectations for the benefits of change and reduce feelings of uncertainty by leveraging manager communications about the case for change, its benefits, and updates about successes and opportunities for improvement.

In the distribution facility case, the facility managers and supervisors were convened in a prelaunch meeting in which the facility manager reviewed the program, its outcomes, and its priorities. Facility management knew that monthly reports of progress were going to be distributed to the COO. Performance review goals for the facility reflected the safety improvement goals and provided additional lift.

TRANSLATING COMMITMENTS INTO A PLAN

At the end of the Commitment stage, people have developed commitments to priorities and tasks. These need to be made concrete and public to drive success. The next steps are to build a project plan and project tracking and controlling processes.

Building a Project Plan

A project plan organizes tasks and subtasks, sequences tasks, outlines their timing, and identifies responsible parties. One gets control of the work by organizing it. A project plan template is presented in Table 9.7. This template includes a place to identify readiness outcomes.

TABLE 9.7 Project Plan Template

FIRST LEVEL READINESS OUTCOME	SECOND LEVEL READINESS OUTCOME	DELIVERABLE	TASK/ SUB-TASKS	START DATE	END DATE	RESPONSIBLE PERSON

Keeping the Plan on Track: Tracking and Controlling Disciplines

There are four steps to monitoring the progress of a solution. Establishing commitments to these steps is part of strengthening commitment. These practices establish the feedback loops through which a change initiative is kept on track. The reader may recall some of these concepts from Chapter 2.

Establish Success Criteria

Before a solution is implemented, change agents and problem owners are best serviced by establishing success criteria for each of the main features of the solution. Table 9.8 outlines the typical criteria for each of the project variables at play in the implementation of a problem solution.

TABLE 9.8 Task Variables and Criteria for Success

VARIABLES	CRITERIA
Quality of deliverables	Reliability, maintainability, operability, flexibility, compliance, potency*
Time	On-time completion of project milestones and final project deliverables
Cost	On or under budget performance
Problem owner satisfaction	Extent to which the problem owner is satisfied with the way the change agent works with him or her

*Ability to deliver the desired change

Monitor Performance Against Established Criteria

Once success criteria are established for each of the task variables, then consultants and client managers use both informal and formal monitoring means to determine whether the established criteria are being satisfied and, if not, whether a deviation from the established criteria is critical or not. King (1986) identifies critical deviations as being of strategic relevance, actionable, critical, and urgent. Table 9.9 defines these terms.

TABLE 9.9 What Is a Critical Deviation?

Strategically relevant	The deviation threatens the long-term success of the project. A serious slip or relapse is occurring.
Actionable	The change agent can do something about the deviation.
Critical	A deviation will have a serious negative impact on the deliverable.
Urgent	Something must be done about a deviation immediately.

There are two types of monitoring a change agent and problem owner use to detect critical deviations to the task variables: informal and formal. Informal monitoring involves being alert to evidence of potential threats as one listens to conversations among the people involved on a project or casually observes people working on project activities. The results of informal monitoring are used to identify a potential set of threats; then the task is to confirm the existence of such threats with formal monitoring information.

Formal monitoring means reviewing systematic reporting of project progress. There are five formal types of reports that are in common use.

1. **Time sheets.** Time sheets report the number of hours members of a team spend on the project.
2. **Budget reports.** These reports track progress on the project budget. The best of these reports lay out expected performance and contrast actual with expected performance and feature monthly projections of the total budget. These help the client and the consultant keep projects on track from a resource utilization point of view.
3. **Milestone charts.** A milestone chart lists project milestones and identifies the actual and planned time of completion. A milestone report lists the achievements that represent the milestones, the estimated

date of completion, and actual performance. The comparison of actual with planned date of completion helps identify where special intervention may be necessary to the project on track. A sample milestone chart is presented in Table 9.10.

4. **Status reports.** A status report is a summary of progress since the last report. A status report includes the following elements:
   - Forecasts against the criteria for each variable: outcomes, schedule status, budget status, resource status
   - Upcoming milestones (Table 9.10)
   - Potential threat to achieving the milestones

   Status reports are often the most frequent means of communication between the participants in an implementation project.

TABLE 9.10 Project Milestones

MILESTONE	SCHEDULED COMPLETION	ACTUAL COMPLETION
Senior leadership retreat conducted	2/10	2/17
Middle management planning sessions completed.	3/1	3/1
Leadership review conducted	3/14	3/21

5. **Progress reviews and senior management updates.** These are meetings that are set aside to formally review progress, report threats to project deliverables and timelines, and develop and/or refine corrective measures. These sessions easily devolve into status reports. The point of these two meetings is problem solving. It generally helps to have reviewed some ideas for root causes and their potential remedies with meeting attendees before such meetings to streamline these sessions.

A summary of implementation plan monitoring and control methods is presented in Table 9.11.

TABLE 9.11 Formal Methods for Keeping a Plan on Track

MONITORING	PROBLEM-SOLVING CRITICAL DEVIATIONS
Time sheets	Progress reviews
Budget reports	Senior management updates
Milestone charts	
Status reports	
Satisfaction audits	

SOME TIPS FOR DESIGNING EFFECTIVE PARTICIPATION STRATEGIES

A Question of Balance

The process through which commitment develops involves engaging key stakeholders in the formulation of goals and the means to reach them. Doing this efficiently depends upon finding a balance between two priorities: (1) granting people enough participation that they "feel ownership" on the one hand and (2) controlling creation of the outcome so that a good solution is created efficiently. The data on the business change project success indicates that we often fail to find the right balance between the two within practical constraints present in the situation. Generally, control wins out over participation. Compliance is the motivational outcome, and significant energy and resources are needed to ensure cooperation.

But participation can sometimes be given too great an emphasis. The pursuit of involvement can lead to an endless dialogue about possibilities. Scope creep, delay, and a lack of meaningful outcomes can result. In this section, particular attention will be paid to the steps that can be used to create and maintain a productive balance between participation and control. Throughout this discussion we will be developing what some have called "the art of the possible." This means getting those who are living with a problem and will live with the solution involved in setting improvement goals and creating the means to achieve them within broad but specific boundaries.

Preconditions for Commitment

In general, for this approach to work a number of readiness conditions must exist. Those who are involved must (1) trust the process, (2) view their input as voluntary, (3) experience the process of participating as rewarding, and (4) see their ideas as significantly affecting work products.[1] Often, one or more of these conditions do not exist. Cynicism about being involved can be present in these situations. In such cases, it's our job to engage the relevant stakeholders in the task of addressing these missing preconditions.

Cascading Commitment Between Levels

The question that comes up is: "How do you cascade commitment building up and down an organization efficiently?" Figure 9.3 outlines how to focus participation by levels. It shows the points of participation from vision at the highest level of activity design to the lowest level. From the executive tier to the frontline tier, each level focuses on different points of participation. However, different tiers share design responsibilities. For example, frontline staff have important contributions to make to role and task design.

FIGURE 9.3 How to Focus Participation by Levels

Senior leaders (including executives)	Vision for strategy and culture shifts and development of strategic priorities; design of organization needed to execute the strategy
Mid-level leaders	How strategies are translated into plans; how teams interface within business processes and systems to achieve cross-function goals and design of roles
First level leaders	Design of the team and how hand-offs between other teams and among team members are best achieved
First level staff	How tasks are best executed in way that addresses implementation realities while satisfying customers

COMMON CONCERNS ABOUT PARTICIPATION STRATEGIES

The framework, templates, and tips outlined in this chapter will help efficiently drive people through commitment stage in a way that will produce positive outcomes. Applying these ideas will help contain the concerns that prevent or limit us from commitment.

It Will Take Too Long/the Problem of Patience

While involving others can improve the quality of action plans and deepen the commitment to them, involving others often adds time to the problem-solving process. Time is a precious commodity in organizations, and unfortunate trade-offs are often made in the name of time. The following often-heard complaint captures the experience of many of us: "We never have enough time to do it right, but we have enough time to fix it over and over again."

One powerful antidote to this problem of time is to find a manager or team in the organization that is doing a part of the solution that is likely to develop and use this as the basic building block of the solution. It is quite common that somewhere someone is experimenting with a portion of the likely solution on his or her own. Building upon this previous work reduces the time and the scope of the effort needed to develop a solution.

This Will Be Too Hard

Some problems will demand every ounce of available readiness for change a problem owner possesses. In this region where high levels of exertion are necessary, the expenditure of energy and resources as well as the amount of learning that must occur can come close to overwhelming. Maintaining the confidence of the problem owners and people assigned to the project and bringing problem owners in contact with others who have traversed similar territory are important initiatives that a change agent can help engineer.

Poor Results

People sometimes lack the facilitation skills needed to pull solutions from teams. In a likewise fashion, some organizations lack the institutional support that fosters collaborative problem solving (support of risk taking; trial-and-error process of problem solving). When key skills are missing and/or institutional support is lacking, involving others can yield lots of meetings and decisions—neither of which may be superior to ones generated through more autocratic means. If either the needed skill or support is lacking, then closing these gaps is key. This can mean importing the needed expertise by hiring people or consultants with the requisite skills and process knowledge.

Not Enough Results

Sometimes the process of participation and involvement becomes more important than the outcomes it is intended to promote. Clarity about outcomes and timing (when supported by the project management disciplines of tracking and controlling outlined earlier in this chapter) will limit risk of "not enough results."

Losing Control

When others are involved in the process of problem solving, we surrender some individual control over the ideas we are working on. This surrender can produce anxiety for some people, as the input of others is often unpredictable. A clear problem-solving process with well-established milestones will limit but not erase the fear of losing control. A trade-off we make is the loss of control for improved likelihood of implementation.

Surrendering some control also means relinquishing exclusive authorship over the idea. Since the rewards structure in organizations reinforces individual (not team) performance, the loss of exclusive authorship weakens one's individual claim on rewards. Clearly identifying the teams who will work on problem-solving teams, clarifying roles, ensuring that members have the requisite skills to succeed, and addressing how members will be recognized and rewarded can limit this concern.

Fear of Incompetence
One of the reasons that participation is not embraced is that people sometimes fear that the solution that is developed will require competencies they lack. Once again assurances that people will get the development they need and acknowledgment that there is support for the trial-and-error process of learning will limit this fear.

People Are Unable to Work Together
Ensuring that the people who've been selected for working a change project have the ability to work collaboratively on shared work products is critical. Not all people are well suited to working on teams. Some organizations, such as NASA, spend significant time assessing team capabilities before people are assigned to teams. For while training, expert facilitation, and clear plans can limit the interference a lack of capability may create, they cannot overcome the absence of basic team skills.

PREPARING FOR ACTION: HOW ARE WE GOING TO BUILD MOMENTUM?

Several actions promote the sustained pursuit of the implementation of a solution in addition to applying the principles of effective work/project management. Before the trigger is pulled on the change implementation plan, be sure to outline options for how you will build momentum.

Celebrating Small Wins
Research suggests that early and frequent recognition of success with smaller shorter-term goals builds motivation for the continued effort of implementation. While such wins may appear small in comparison with the ultimate solution, celebrating them in a public way is key. John P. Kotter and Dan S. Cohen, authors of *The Heart of Change: Real-Life Stories of How People Change Their Organizations*, recommend that these wins be unambiguous and visible to management and others in the organization. Celebrating small wins strengthens what psychologists called behavioral momentum.

Encouragement

Support and encouragement, especially early in the change process, can help people overcome self-doubts and implementation difficulties that surface. Encouragements can also reinforce confidence in the plan and the ability to implement the plan that sustains the drive to pursue change goals.

Soliciting Support from the Environment

When a solution involves a change in business practices, we have to secure support from the environment.

Limiting Exposure to Environmental Stressors

When implementers encounter changes in priorities, lose access to resources, or face high levels of resistance, the motivation to sustain their pursuit of goals can deteriorate. Being vigilant about and reducing contact with these stressors will help keep the initiative on track.

COMMITMENT CONDITIONS

Commitment is improved when people:

- Feel pulled to a newly reframed identity—a vision—that creates new opportunities for the organization and its people
- Believe that people have worked together to build a solution to a problem
- See that the points of view of people in different disciplines and at different levels have been reflected in the solution
- Believe that good supports have been put in place to overcome the obstacles that may be encountered during implementation of the plan
- See that a climate of safety exists for the trial-and-error process of learning
- Are committed to pushing through the personal difficulties that they will encounter in making the solution a reality

THE END OF THE COMMITMENT PHASE: ACTION

When the appropriate readiness conditions are satisfied, the commitment to initiate action is achieved and action is the result. The outcome of the Commitment phase is action. Work begins on implementing a solution. A critical task for the problem owner and change agent then is maintaining motivation to pursue action and monitoring potential off-track problems.

CONCLUSION

In the end, forward momentum—supported by the interest and disciplines needed to learn from experience—is the most important goal of business change. As the actions that are reinforcing are the most likely to be sustained, engineering a good fit between readiness and the scope of the solutions that are implemented is vital. Commitment to action requires a clear road map and resolute focus on what is important to the solutions success. In the final analysis, the steps for winning commitment are straightforward. Making them happen in the turbulent waters of organizations is about resourcefulness, relationships, and focus. At the end of the Commitment stage, action has been taken. In the next chapter, we turn to the most critical and overlooked readiness phase of implementing solutions to problems: the Perseverance stage.

Chapter 10

Perseverance

Never for me the lowered banner, never the last endeavor.
—Sir Ernest Shackleton

On August 8, 1914, Sir Ernest Shackleton and an experienced crew boarded the ship the *Endurance* and set out for Antarctica. Their goal was to cross this unconquered polar territory on foot. One hundred miles short of the point from which their on-foot expedition was to begin, an ice pack caught the *Endurance*. The ice pack dragged the ship farther and farther away from its destination and eventually crushed and sank the ship. The crew found themselves stranded on an open ice floe adrift in polar seas.

The efforts of Shackleton and his men to stay alive and return to civilization represent one of the most remarkable feats of human survival.[1] Their tale reveals many of the key elements of perseverance.

For 16 long months, the crew survived with the meager resources they salvaged from the ship as well as food they caught (seal and penguin meat). As food became scarce and the crew's health and morale declined, good fortune smiled on them. The crew's use of navigational aids informed them that the ice floe had drifted close to Elephant Island, and furthermore, a break had developed in the ice. Shackleton ordered his crew into the small open boats that they had managed to save from the *Endurance*, and they made for and reached the island.

While no longer adrift, the crew's situation remained grave. Shackleton gathered five of his best crew members and planned for their best hope of survival: the five of them (along with Shackleton) would set out for a whaling station on South Georgia Island. They would steer a 22-foot boat, the *Caird*, in polar seas to their destination, which was 800 miles and 16 days away. Their task was equivalent to aiming for a needle in a haystack. If Shackleton and his small crew had failed on this voyage, the results would have been tragic: the *Caird* would have been swept out into the open ocean, and the crew on Elephant Island would have been doomed to wait for a rescue that would never come.

Sir Shackleton tasked Frank Worsley, a talented mariner, with guiding the *Caird* to their destination. To succeed, Worsley had to adapt his approach to navigation to the needs of a small craft in turbulent polar seas. He described the procedure like this:

> I peered out from our burrow—precious sextant cuddled under my chest to prevent seas falling on it. Sir Ernest [Shackleton] stood by under the canvas with chronometer, pencil, and book. I shouted "Stand by" and knelt on the thwart—two men holding me up on either side. I brought the sun down to where the horizon ought to be and as the boat leaped frantically upward on the crest of a wave, snapped a good guess at the altitude and yelled, "Stop." Sir Ernest took the time and I worked out the result. . . . My navigation books had to be half opened page by page till the right one was reached, then opened carefully to prevent utter destruction.[2]

The fierce conditions of the South Pole battered the crew and the vessel as they made their way. When the sea kicked up, cold ocean waves splashed over the side and soaked the crew. At a critical juncture, ice formed on every piece of wood, sail, and line on the *Caird*, and the boat began to sink under the weight. The crew had to manually chip the ice away—an especially tricky task when it came to the sail.

Naturally, these extreme conditions took their toll on the crew. Shackleton kept a finger on each man's pulse throughout the journey. "Whenever he noticed that a man seemed extra cold and shivered, he [Shackleton] would immediately order another hot drink of milk for all. He never let a man know that it was on his account lest he become nervous about himself."[3]

Eventually, the appearance of birds and seaweed signaled to the crew that they were close to land. As if the crew had not endured enough, a hurricane blew in to meet them:

> With each blow from the swells, bow planks opened and water filtered in. Caulked with oil paint and seal blood, the Caird strained at every joint. Five men bailed and pumped while one man kept on course. Each man was desperately hungry and thirsty. It had been 48 hours since they had consumed fresh water.[4]

Thanks to Worsley's seamanship, the *Caird* had come within eyeshot of South Georgia Island. On the day they arrived, it was near dusk. This meant that the crew had to postpone their run for the shore until morning. As dawn broke, they saw still another challenge before them. They had to pilot the *Caird* through the jagged reef line, which stretched between them and dry land. In the end, the crew had to mount *five* separate attempts to pilot through the reef before they got through and made landfall.

At last, the crew stood on terra firma. They faced one more daunting challenge: a 36-hour trek across the mountainous terrain of South Georgia Island. The crew prevailed, and a couple of days later (and at the end of their energy), the haggard group finally reached the whaling station. At the end of this tale, 22 problem-rich months after ice ensnared them, the *entire* crew of the *Endurance* was rescued.

LESSONS FROM THE *CAIRD*

We face the business equivalents of fierce winds, ice storms, and treacherous coastlines when driving change in organizations. The process of implementing enduring solutions to problems is often more turbulent than not. Resources can be unexpectedly reduced, the political climate can turn cool to the initiative with little warning, and any tug of status quo can weaken commitment. Though such events rarely threaten life and limb, they can drive solutions off course and rob people of courage and stamina. As was true for Shackleton's story, effective pilots do two things well:

1. Maintain motivation of team members by:
    - Facing setbacks and problems with optimism
    - Mobilizing the morale of the team to adapt and overcome stiff challenges
2. Negotiate responses to off-course events with a:
    - Disciplined adaptation of piloting strategies to difficult and changing conditions
    - Resolute focus on the primary goal
    - Candor about immediate circumstances
    - Dedication to developing resourceful means of getting back on track

When the spirit of learning-based innovation infuses the pursuit of recovery, the process is free of the scapegoating and attack-and-defend spirals that often occur on teams when performance slips behind expectations.

ACTIONS THAT PROMOTE SUCCESSFUL PERSEVERANCE

When we evaluate plan progress and recognize results that are shy of our expectations or do not succeed, we need to adjust our plans to deal with the reality. The question we need to answer is: "Do I need to better execute what I planned?" or "Does my review of results suggest I need to revisit the assumptions that guided my plan and reformulate it?" "Are there triggers in the environment preventing people from getting back on track?" Based on the answers, we plan the appropriate actions.

A Case Study of Perseverance in Action

Let's return to a case example from the previous chapter, where a leadership team solved a costly safety problem amidst the implementation of a new distribution system. The reader might recall that the first couple of months of implementation were stellar, and the mood amongst the team was celebratory. We pick up the story here during the third month of the implementation.

During the third month, the distribution system entered its peak season and faced new demands. Shipping for the busiest season of the year, the "back-to-school" retail season, began. A flurry of unprecedented requests for greater flexibility in shipping created a new level of performance pressure on the team. Customers expected they could request shipping in small units that they could receive at different times. In light of these requests, managers set up and then brought online a small West Coast satellite distribution facility to increase responsiveness to this important market and to experiment with other strategies for increasing flexibility.

Environmental events coupled with the allure of more familiar and higher-profile production problems strained the team's ability to solve people-based safety problems it faced, and momentum stalled. A monthly safety report revealed that the injury rate had jumped up from the low levels recorded in the first couple of months. Attention to safety practices had dropped off, as did the enforcement of on-site physical therapy. Supervisors and the leadership had diverted time formerly given to safety to pressing production problems. Distribution leadership was no longer bringing the same quality of attention to the workers' compensation problem. Injuries and compensation claims were increasing . . . fast.

Three months in, the initiative to improve safety performance now faced the equivalent of an unexpected storm. How could the initiative stay on track given environmental pressures and competing priorities? Abandoning the safety improvement program entirely for the more urgent production problems would be the easy decision. However, the lack of attention to safety would lead to a big spike in workers' compensation losses over the previous year. Moreover, turning attention away from the people factors would worsen other serious people problems. Turnover was also increasing, filling vacant roles was becoming more difficult, and morale was low. Work hours were increasing to keep the pace of work demands.

Then there was this. Giving up on safety would be experienced as a failure, and employee morale would be negatively impacted. Supervisors and managers would infer that employee concerns would be subordinated to business concerns.

During a monthly progress review meeting, the internal consultant shared his observations of what was happening. He outlined the upward trend in injury rates and in claims. Then, the consultant took a chance. He observed that the manager regularly asked supervisors about their progress—but mostly focused his questions and attention on production issues. The leader praised achievement of milestones and urged improvement when performance was slacking. He used independent spot checks to confirm progress. On occasion, he also directly assisted lower-level supervisors in their attempts to resolve tough problems. The consultant concluded that this kind of attention was not being given to the safety problem, and the manager's direct reports had picked up on this.

The internal consultant asked the leader to speculate on why the differences in management practices existed. The manager was a bit startled at first. He said that he did not have the same kinds of management tools with which to address the safety problem as he had for the production problems. To address this concern, the consultant suggested some concrete tools that the manager could use. These included adaptations of safe work methods checklists and safety audits checklists already being utilized by the supervisors. The manager was challenged to use these tools with the same energy and focus that he applied to production. Within a couple of days, the manager tried some of the tools—and invented a few of his own. Employees responded to him favorably as a coach. Supervisors found the clear performance expectations and suggestions for improvement motivating. What was "warm and fuzzy" was now concrete.

Soon progress was restored. The facility team went on to exceed their goals. Injury rates and incurred workers' compensation losses were better than the published benchmarks. The team once more received rewards and recognition for their efforts.

This example illustrates that implementing solutions is a matter of resourceful perseverance through significant personal and organizational turbulence in which success is not a matter of the *quality* of the original plan but how well one negotiates the challenges encountered.

FIGURE 10.1 Process of Recalibrating Plans: Double Loop Learning

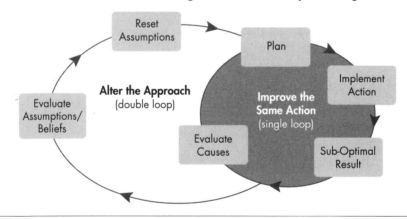

Double learning, developed by Chris Argyris, is an important tool to use for the Perseverance stage. It is comprised of two loops. The first loop in Figure 10.1 demonstrates the common approach to solving problems. In a fairly straightforward fashion, we analyze root causes such that problem solvers can focus solutions on the most potent causes of the problem.

In classic root cause analysis, one asks this question up to seven times to push problem solvers past quickly recognized symptoms to the deeper forces at work. However, the root cause practice is often ignored. In many contexts, doing stuff is more important than taking the time to do the right stuff. Activity addiction—the inclination to cope with the anxiety of getting to clarity by jumping into action—is hard to resist.

The Perseverance stage involves evaluating implementation challenges from the perspective of the second loop of double loop learning. The goal is to look at assumptions and beliefs that influence the performance gaps that people see and resolve. For example, in the distribution example reviewed earlier, some harmful beliefs were (1) that technical issues superseded people issues, and (2) that a leader couldn't influence people to behave differently—"because they are either for you or against you." These assumptions constrained productive problem solving. The gaps were addressed in the story of how the case study we introduced earlier evolved.

ACTIONS IN THE PERSEVERANCE STAGE

- Recover behavioral momentum
- Identify the root cause of critical deviations

This step involves reviewing the main issues that threaten the change project deliverables or timeline—these main issues, the reader might recall, are called critical deviations—and understanding the root causes of these deviations. The majority of off-track factors are people issues, and as such can be difficult to resolve. This step depends on interpersonal sensitivity and acumen to be successful.

The second goal of this stage is to evaluate whether we have to recalibrate our plans. We determine the root causes that pushed us off course (if this happened) and determine how we get back on course. Sometimes we learn that our beliefs and assumptions need to be reset.

In the case of the leader of the distribution system, the evaluation of safety results suggested that there was an opportunity to refocus the original plan and to adjust the approach. In the first case management had diverted its attention to the production challenges that they were facing. The slip in progress triggered them to refocus on the original plan. In the second case, the facility leader's belief that his personal engagement was not necessary was challenged. He reevaluated his role in the project and decided to invest time in personally monitoring safety performance and providing feedback to managers and employees on the distribution floor.

The meeting between the internal consultant and the distribution leader about the loss of traction in safety outcomes was a progress review meeting—it was also the critical moment of the project. The consultant who was working with the leader acknowledged the stiff goals the leader and his team faced. He also disclosed his observation that the facility leader was not showing the same follow-up behavior on safety goals as he did on production goals. Meeting the new production demands was a large task; without modeling from the facility manager about safety management, success was under threat. The good news was that with this modeling success could still be achieved.

DEVELOP THE STRATEGY FOR GETTING BACK ON TRACK

In this step, we confirm final action steps and specify a follow-up. This clarification gives particular emphasis to what the problem owner must do to resolve critical deviations.

Develop Success Criteria

As is true for securing commitment, perseverance demands establishing clear criteria for determining success. As many of the deviations will likely be interpersonal, the success criteria will require some attention by those carrying out and helming the change. Table 10.1 outlines some examples.

Build Enthusiasm for Maintaining the Course

In implementation enthusiasm builds when people learn from their experience how to overcome pesky problems. The "we're breaking through" feeling is quite reinforcing, especially considering that people often experience frustrations with change—so much so that change attempts are often abandoned or things are made only different, not better.

TABLE 10.1 Example of Success Criteria in Solving Deviations

Deviation: Injury rates spiked as managerial attention was diverted by a surge in production demands that strained management's problem-solving process.

ROOT CAUSES	PLAN TO ADDRESS THE CAUSES	SUCCESS CRITERIA
The initiative lost its high priority in the light of other urgent priorities. Early successes had built a sense of overconfidence.	• Clarify people priorities and link to broader business priorities • Ask questions to clarify what was making it difficult to maintain focus • The leader picked a strategy for calling attention to the performance slip and the importance of getting back on track. • The leader outlined his commitment in his leadership team meeting.	• The leader helped design a plan for bringing more personal attention to safety performance. • Physical therapists reported that compliance with visits and treatment programs returned.
The leader did not have a way to model the priority that reflected his status.	• Developed a safe work audit tool that created a summary number that could be recorded and tracked	• Leader conducted periodic safety audits and provided feedback to managers about his observations. • Leader also received audits completed by managers.

THE SPECIAL CHALLENGE OF CHANGING BEHAVIOR

There are two challenges of changing behavior that deserve our focus.

The Organizational and Personal Triggers to Overcome

One of the special challenges of implementing a solution is negotiating the behavior challenges associated with implementation. We introduced Table 10.2 in the chapter on Commitment. It summarizes off-course factors encountered on a set of business process redesign initiatives.

This list parallels factors identified by project management experts like John McManus and others. In the case of Commitment, the table tells us to be on alert. In Perseverance, the table directs our attention to the challenges we need to address once change programs are in flight. The reader may recall from Chapter 2 that a majority of the events that threaten technology, process, or other solutions to organizational problems are people factors. People problems represent 65 percent of off-course events, whereas technical issues represent 35 percent. People factors are often the big problem to solve in getting a change plan back on course.

TABLE 10.2 Off-Track Themes for Consulting Projects of a General Management Consulting Firm

CATEGORY	OFF-TRACK THEMES
Customer Issues (62% of off-track issues)	• Anger about being coerced into project work • Resistance to the implementation plan as too aggressive, too participative, or too analytical • Senior leaders have not assigned project work a high priority • Leaders do not have the needed project management, leadership, or conceptual/analytical skills • Conflicts among leaders slow down the project
Project Team Issues (26% of off-track issues)	• Staff not meeting expectations for their part of the work • Lack of agreement about approach to work slowing down work and threatening timelines • Lack of clear cascaded expectations leading to rework • Ineffective handoffs between staff cycling on and off project, creating slippage on plans

Skillful leaders often anticipate this reality by engaging people in clarifying the types of practice or behavior changes that are needed to support a solution before implementation begins. Still, the importance of making behavioral changes and the difficulties that they can entail are often not fully appreciated—at least, not until we encounter the stubbornness of old practices. As a veteran executive observed, "You often do not really understand an organization until you try to change it."

Common organizational triggers that stall momentum when people are under pressure include the following.

Senior Leader Accountability
Rather than holding others accountable for course correction, leaders take their accountability too far and take over action planning. People tasked with implementation are pressured to assume efforts to keep projects on track. Reinforcing mutual and primary accountabilities for both is an important discipline to emphasize in change.

Personal Accountability
Implementers are often criticized by their direct report managers for bringing problems but not solutions to their leaders. Concerns about the risk of being wrong or scapegoated prompt people to limit their pursuit of solutions. Leaders are triggered to swoop in and try to solve the problem themselves. As we said for the previous trigger, reinforcing accountabilities for leader and implementer is an important discipline to emphasize in change.

Me First, Team Second
Most implementation challenges have their roots in the difficulties of coordinating and collaborating across boundaries. In many cases, multiple teams are needed to achieve a new result. However, working through issues on teams takes more time, which can be at odds with the drive to solve problems quickly. As a result, many abandon the pursuit of team solutions. An African proverb is helpful to remember: "To fast, go alone; to go far, go with others."

Us First, Customer Second
Under pressure, it is easy to become preoccupied with the policies, procedures, and problem-solving routines in one's organization and lose sight of the customer. Involving the customer in the conversation can take time. It also may involve disclosing the problems within your organization that created the customer problem. Disclosing issues appropriately—directly but without weakening customer confidence—is the best, but this can be a difficult action to take.

The Easy Solution Versus a Better One
Problem-solving research suggests that better ideas come later in the brainstorming process. Under pressure, people tend to limit their exploration of options and gravitate to familiar and comfortable solutions. These

solutions tend to not be in line with change objectives. Treating problems as opportunities to develop and applying "lessons learned" in the spirit of continuous improvement drives people to implementing better solutions. Problem-solving agility, addressed earlier in this book, outlines the skills to create better solutions.

People Under Pressure: Personal Styles Under Pressure

When problems occur in implementation, people tend to lean on problem-solving strategies they know; in other words, we stick to what we are good at. The overuse of strengths is a common perseverance challenge we must overcome. Studying a wide range of models of how people operate at work can help people develop insights about these tendencies. We have distilled and simplified personal styles at work in the following list. Calibrating how one engages those with different styles can increase the frequency with which one engages others.

1. **Asserter:** The need to feel as though one is driving to personal goals
2. **Team player:** The need to maintain positive relationships on the team
3. **Innovator:** The need for a solution that will make a difference
4. **Analytical:** The need for careful, well-reasoned action

While each of these motives is present in all of us, one of them tends to drive us more than others. Diagnosing these preferences and tailoring our approach to how we engage others in the Perseverance stage is critical. Under pressure these styles become exaggerated:

1. **Asserter:** "Do it my way!"
2. **Team player:** "Not unless everyone agrees!"
3. **Innovator:** "I have another good idea!"
4. **Analytical:** "Let's do more analysis to pick the solution."

Finding a way to tailor to these needs is one of the big tasks in the Perseverance stage. This is especially important to think about when we are working with people who are different from ourselves.

We highlight a couple of thought starters for addressing each personal style when under pressure. Finding an answer for each of the personal styles listed helps unlock the motivational focus of these styles.

1. **Asserter:** "What action can I take to get this done now?"
2. **Team player:** "How can we develop a critical mass of support for this idea?"
3. **Innovator:** "What idea of yours can we fold into this that will make it effective?"
4. **Analytical:** "What quick piece of analysis will get the needed data?"

The Content of the Change Itself

A second set of behavior issues concerns behavioral change embedded in the solution itself and not just in the process of implementing business change. The shift to a customer-focused organization can illustrate this challenge. This shift is enabled by changes in organizational structures, customer relationship management systems, and reporting systems.[5] Customer-focused organizations also require an adoption of alternate leadership practices. These include:

- Facilitating the coordination between departments
- "Serving others" as a model for service excellence
- Promoting informal communication between people in departments
- Implementing flexible work structures
- Focusing on the well-being of employees
- Empowering employees
- Connecting employee work to actual customer outcomes
- Empowering teams to identify, develop, and implement solutions to recover from service problems

This list emphasizes that when implementing a shift to customer focus, leaders must alter *how* they approach work. However, as we have learned, people tend to underestimate the difficulty of implementing a solution until they try to initiate a change.

Adapting how we engage coworkers, informed by a knowledge of how organizations and people tend to operate under pressure, can help us better manage the challenges of the Perseverance stage.

We conclude with the story of Dame Ellen MacArthur, who broke the record for solo nonstop yachting voyage around the world in 2005, achieving this goal in 71 days, 18 minutes, and 33 seconds, an achievement that earned her the Jules Verne Trophy. This quest tested her with several white-knuckle moments. On her quest she narrowly missed an iceberg that could have ended her voyage and likely her life. She then negotiated 50-foot waves, often with an hour and a half of sleep, while far from any help. At one point she was 2,000 miles away from the closest human—who remarkably enough was sitting in the space station! She changed her main sail eight times, a task that took its physical toll.

Perseverance was key to Dame MacArthur's achievement. One morning she wrote, "I feel like I've been beaten up this morning . . . stiff as hell and moving around with the speed and elegance of an arthritic robot." Yet she continued on to complete her record-breaking voyage.

TARGET OUTCOMES FOR PERSEVERANCE

People perceive that the conditions of the previous readiness stages were met and:
- Are encouraged by early wins
- Feel momentum developing behind the change plan
- Know what the hazards are and how they are to be negotiated
- Have a process for monitoring threats to the implementation of the solution and resolving these threats
- See difficulties—slips and lapses—as natural parts of the change process rather than a fatal flaw
- Come to understand the root causes of the problem and the key factors in the solution more completely
- Feel encouraged to persevere in the face of difficulties or setbacks
- Have a feasible approach for recovering from a slip or relapse situation

TABLE 10.3 Perseverance Actions

ACTIONS	HOW AN ACTION WORKS
Build momentum.	Four practices that maintain momentum: • Reinforcing positive expectations • Emphasizing the benefits of change • Reducing uncertainties • Celebrating small wins
Monitor performance against established success criteria to detect deviations or slips.	Reviewing performance against preestablished success criteria helps us determine whether we are on track and where we are not.
Assess the root causes/triggers of the deviations and slips to focus strategies for getting back on track.	Old attitudes, habits, and practices are resistant to change. When things get difficult, learning how to do things differently becomes harder, and the politics that made issues "undiscussable" assert themselves—which threatens our change efforts. Identifying these off-course factors so we can address them sets the process of recovery in motion.
Develop the strategy for getting back on track.	Building plans to address the factors that push us off course involves crafting solutions to the root causes identified above.
Develop success criteria.	Having clear criteria for determining the solutions to off-course factors' root causes help us evaluate whether we are making progress.
Communicate to build enthusiasm for maintaining the course and implement the plan.	Communicating the slip or deviation in our plan while emphasizing that such slips and lapses can be overcome and outlining the remedies that are being put in place while emphasizing optimism for the success of the plan and outlining commitments to the end goal helps drive people forward.

MOTIVATION CHALLENGES OF PERSEVERANCE

Motivation is a big challenge. There are two motivations on which to keep focused.

Maintaining One's Own Motivation to Persevere

Previously, we made much of maintaining motivation. Yet maintaining motivation is a difficult challenge when you are the change agent. One's esteem as a leader can be threatened when he or she is associated with a slip or relapse. To weather such assaults, some leaders construct peer-coaching networks to help them maintain their focus and solve slips and lapses.

Maintaining the Courage to Engage Others About Their Role in a Slip or Lapse in Commitment

While the slip or relapse is not necessarily a problem owner's fault, the politics of accountability in organizations will lead the problem owner to struggle with accountability and competence. The power difference and accountability dynamics complicate the task of working through a slip or relapse.

In Chapter 1 we detailed the image of the open ocean that greets visitors to the National Maritime Museum in Greenwich, England—a featureless expanse of water with the horizon line far, far off in the distance. The view is simultaneously inspiring and daunting.

The image of an open, landmark-less view serves as an apt analogy for the vast, sometimes intimidating distance between the start of an initiative and the desired outcome with no guarantee of success but faith that people will work together to create something great. But a successful journey is probable with effective navigators and pilots. They not only guide the entire crew safety to the destination regardless of the challenge encountered; they also inspire and maintain the spirit of adventure, learning, and exploration that are vital to sustained organizational high performance.

In the end, leadership matters. Within our nautical metaphor, we have hopefully outlined an effective methodology for optimizing the value of this critical investment in your own leadership resources and ensured that success will be manifested in sailing safely into the ports of your intended destinations.

Notes

INTRODUCTION

1. Davis, J., Frechette, H., & Boswell, E. *Strategic Speed: Mobilize People, Accelerate Execution.* Cambridge, MA: Harvard Business Press, 2010.
2. McKinsey & Company. *The science of organizational transformations.* 2015. www.mckinsey.com.
3. Innosight. *Organizations lack planning and tools to deal with disruptive change.* 2014. www.innosight.com.
4. Lepsinger, R. *Closing the Execution Gap: How Great Leaders and Their Companies Get Their Results.* San Francisco, CA: Jossey Bass: A Wiley Imprint, 2010.
5. PwC. Strategy-execution survey: Key findings. *Strategy&,* 2014.

CHAPTER 1

1. Stringer, B., & Uchencick, J. *Strategy Traps: And How to Avoid Them.* Boston, MA: Lexington Books, 1986.
2. Schaap, J. Toward strategy implementation success: An empirical study of the role of senior level leaders in the Nevada gaming industry, *UNLV Gaming Research & Review Journal, digital scholarship.unlv.com,* 2012.
3. Beshears, J., & Gino, F. Leaders as decision architects. *Harvard Business Review,* May, 2015.
4. Kahneman, D., Lovallo, D., & Sibony, O. Before you make that big decision. *Harvard Business Review,* June, 51-60, 2011.
5. Kesler, G., & Kates, A. *Leading Organization Design: How to Make Organizational Design to Drive the Results You Want.* New York, NY: John Wiley and Sons, 2010.
6. Sull, D., Homkes, R., & Sull, C. Why Strategy Execution Unravels—and what to do about it. *Harvard Video,* 2016.
7. Lepsinger, R. *Closing the Execution Gap: How Great Leaders and Their Companies Get Their Results.* San Francisco, CA: Jossey Bass: A Wiley Imprint, 2010.
8. Guangrong, D., Yang, K., & De Meuse, K. "Leadership competencies across organizational levels: a test of the pipeline model," *Journal of Management Development,* 30, 366-380, 2011.
9. Kouzes, J., & Posner, B. *The Leadership Challenge.* 4th ed. San Francisco, CA: Jossey Bass, 2007.
10. Willis Towers Watson. *How does change affect employee engagement?* 2015.

11. Rose, T. *Creating a Culture of Engagement and Accountability.* AchieveForum Point of View, 2015.
12. Overfield, D., & Kaiser, R. *One of every two managers is terrible at accountability.* Harvard Business School Blogs, November, 2012.
13. Galbraith, J. *Designing the Customer-Focused Organization. A Guide to Strategy, Structure and Process.* New York, NY: John Wiley and Sons, 2005.

CHAPTER 2

1. Heyerdahl, T. *Kon-Tiki.* New York, NY: Simon & Schuster, 190, 1950.
2. Ibid, 192.
3. Ibid, 193.
4. Ibid, 196.
5. Nautical Institute. *Nautical Accidents and Their Causes.* D. Pockett (ed.), 2015.
6. Kite-Powell, H., Jin, D., Patrikalakis, N., Jebsen, J., & Papakonstantinou, V. *Investigation of Potential Risk Factors for Groundings of Commercial Vessels in U.S. Ports.* IJOPE, 1998.
7. Samuelides, M., Ventikos, N., & Gemelos, I. Survey on groundling incidents: Statistical analysis and risk assessment. *Ships and Offshore Structures.* 4, 2009, 55-68.
8. Oakes, G. *Project Review, Assurance and Governance.* Surrey, UK: Gower Publishing, 2008
9. AsianYachting.com
10. De Wit, B., & Meyer, R. *Strategy: Process, Content, Context: An International Perspective*, 4th ed. Andover, UK: South Western: Cengage Learning, 2010.
11. Rothblum, A. Human Error and Marine Safety. *U.S. Coast Guard Research & Development Center*, 2013.
12. Sull, D., Homkes, R., & Sull, C. Why Strategy Execution Unravels—and What to Do About It. *Harvard Video*, 2016.
13. Guttieri, K., Wallace, M., & Suedfeld, P. The Integrative Complexity of American Decision Makers in the Cuban Missile Crisis. *Journal of Conflict Resolution*, 39, 595-621, 1995.
14. Osterman, P. *The Truth About Middle Managers: Who They Are, How They Work, and Why They Matter.* Boston, MA: Harvard University Press, 2009.
15. Brill, J., Bishop, M., & Walker, A. The Competencies and Characteristics Required of an Effective Project Manager: A Web-Based Delphi Study. *Educational Technology Research*, 2006.
16. Kraut, A., Pedigo, P., McKenna, D., & Dunnette, M. The role of manager: What's really important in different management jobs. *Academy of Management Perspectives*, 19, 122-129, 2005.
17. De Meuse, K., Dai, G., Hallenback, G., & Tang, K. Y. Using learning agility to identify high potentials around the world. *Korn/Ferry Institute*, 2009.
18. De Wit, B., & Meyer, R. *Strategy: Process,Content,Context: An International Perspective*, 4th ed. Andover, UK: South Western: Cengage Learning, 2010.
19. Block, P. *The Structure of Belonging.* Oakland, CA: Berrett-Koehler, 2008.

20. Yukl, G., O'Donnell, M., & Tabler, T. Leader behaviors and leader member exchange. *Journal of Managerial Psychology*, 24, 289-299, 2009.
21. Ibid.
22. Rose, T. Creating a culture of engagement and accountability. *AchieveForum Point of View*, 2015.
23. Rose, T. Notes from the Front: Influence patterns in the post-reengineering organization. *National Productivity Review*, Spring, 67-71, 1998.
24. Sull, D., Homkes, R., & Sull, C. Why Strategy Execution Unravels—and What to Do About It. *Harvard Business Review*. March, 2015, 4-10.
25. Ibid.
26. Rothblum, A. Human Error and Marine Safety. *U.S. Coast Guard Research & Development Center*, 2013.

CHAPTER 3

1. Senge, P., Kleiner, A., Roberts, C., Ross, R., & Smith, B. *Fifth Discipline Field Book: Strategies and Tools for Building a Learning Organization*. New York, NY: Doubleday, 1994.

CHAPTER 4

1. Schaffer, R. *High Impact Consulting; Achieving Extraordinary Results*. San Francisco, CA: Jossey-Bass, 2002.
2. Prochaska, J., & DiClemente, C. *The Transtheoretical Approach: Crossing Traditional Boundaries of Therapy*. Malabar, FL: Krieger Publishing, 1984.

CHAPTER 5

1. Lombardo, M., & Eichinger, R. *The Leadership Machine: Architecture to Develop Leaders for the Future*. Korn/Ferry International, 2011.
2. Kahneman D., Lovallo, D., & Sibony, O. Before you make that big decision. *Harvard Business Review*, June, 51-60, 2011.
3. Dorothy, L. Harvard Business School, popularized this idea first expressed by Jerry Hirshberg, founder and president of Nissan Design International (NDI).

CHAPTER 6

1. Kumashiro, M., & Sedikides, C. Taking on board liability-focused information: Close positive relationships as a self–bolstering resource. *Psychological Science*, 16, 732-739, 2005.
2. Kahneman D., Lovallo, D., & Sibony, O. Before you make that big decision. *Harvard Business Review*, June, 51-60, 2011.
3. Cohen, G., & Aronson, J. When Beliefs Yield to Evidence: Reducing Biased Evaluation by Affirming the Self. *Personality and Social Psychology Bulletin*, 26, 1154-1164, 2000.

4. Lord, G., Ross, L., & Lepper, M. Biased assimilation and attitude polarization: The effects of prior theories on subsequently considered evidence, *Journal of Personality and Social Psychology*, 37, 2098-2109, 1979.
5. Ehrlinger, J., Johnson, K., Banner, M., Dunning, D., & Kruger, J. Why the unskilled are unaware: Further explorations of (absent) self-insight among the incompetence. *Organizational Behavior and Human Decision Processes*, 105, 98–121, 2008.
6. Sayles, L. A different perspective on leadership: The working leader. Cited in Kaiser, R, Hogan, R., & Craig, S. (2008). Leadership and the fate of organizations. *American Psychologist*, 63, 2008.
7. Davis, J., Frechette, H., & Boswell, E. *Strategic Speed: Mobilize People, Accelerate Action*. Cambridge, MA: Harvard Business Press, 2010.
8. Rose, T. Creating a culture of engagement and accountability. *AchieveForum Point of View*, 2015.
9. Samuel, M., & Chiche, S. *The Power of Personal Accountability: Achieves What Matters to You*. Katonah, NY: Xephor Press, 2004.

CHAPTER 7

1. Danish Maritime Accident Investigation, Marine Accident Report, Board, December, 2013.
2. Schein, E. *The Corporate Culture Survival Guide*. San Francisco, CA: Jossey-Bass, 1999.
3. Kanfer, F., & Schefft, B. *Guiding the Process of Therapeutic Change*. Champaign, IL: Research Press, 1998.
4. Ibid, 1988.
5. Keystone Associates. A resource for finding your next role, 2011.
6. Miller R., & Heiman, S. *Strategic Selling*. New York, NY: Morrow, 1985.
7. Maister, M., Green, C., and Galford, R. *Trusted Advisor*. New York, NY: Simon and Shuster, 2000.
8. Frame, J. *The New Project Management: Tools for an Age of Rapid Change, Complexity, and Other Business Realities*. San Fransisco, CA: Jossey-Bass, 1994.

CHAPTER 8

1. Prochaska, J., & DiClemente, C. *The Transtheoretical Approach: Crossing Traditional Boundaries of Therapy*. Malabar, FL: Krieger Publishing, 1984.
2. Senge, P., Kleiner, A., Roberts, C., Ross, R., & Smith, B. *Fifth Discipline Field Book: Strategies and Tools for Building a Learning Organization*. New York, NY: Doubleday, 1994.
3. Ibid, 1994.
4. Prochaska, J., & DiClemente, C. *The Transtheoretical Approach: Crossing Traditional Boundaries of Therapy*. Malabar, FL: Krieger Publishing, 1984.
5. Argyris, C. Good communication that blocks learning. *Harvard Business Review*. 77-85, 1994.

6. Quinn, R. *Deep Change: Discovering the Leader Within.* New York, NY: Wiley, 2010.
7. Schneider, B., Goldstein, H., & Smith, H. The ASA framework: An update. *Personnel Psychology,* 48, 747-773, 1995.
8. Rose, T. Notes from the Front: Influence patterns in the post-reengineering organization. *National Productivity Review,* Spring, 67-71, 1998.
9. Harrington, H. *Business Process Improvement: The Breakthrough Strategy for Total Quality, Productivity and Competitiveness.* New York, NY: McGraw-Hill, 1991.
10. Prochaska, J., & DiClemente, C. *The Transtheoretical Approach: Crossing Traditional Boundaries of Therapy.* Malabar, FL: Krieger Publishing, 1984.

CHAPTER 9

1. Hunton, J., and Beeler, J. Effects of user participation in systems development: A longitudinal field experiment. *MIS Quarterly,* 21, 359-388, 1997.

CHAPTER 10

1. Alexander, C. *The Endurance: Shackleton's Legendary Antarctic Expedition.* Knopf: New York, NY, 1998.
2. Ibid, p. 145.
3. Ibid, p. 147.
4. Ibid, p. 151.
5. Galbraith, J. *Designing the Customer-Focused Organization. A Guide to Strategy, Structure and Process.* New York, NY: John Wiley and Sons, 2005

Bibliography

Ahearne, M., Lam, S. K., & Kraus, F. Performance impact of middle manager's adaptive strategy implementation: The role of social capital. *Strategic Management Journal*, 35, 2014, 68–87.

Alexander, C. *The Endurance: Shackleton's Legendary Antarctic Expedition*. New York NY: Knopf, 1999.

Argyris, C. Good communication that blocks learning. *Harvard Business Review*, July–August, 1994, 77–85.

AsianYachting.com

Beshears, J., & Gino, F. Leaders as decision architects. *Harvard Business Review*, May, 2015.

Block, P. *Flawless Consulting*. San Francisco, CA: Jossey-Bass, 1981.

———. *The Structure of Belonging*. Oakland, CA: Berrett-Koehler, 2008.

Bossidy, L., & Charan, R. *Execution: The Discipline of Getting Things Done*. New York, NY: Crown Business, 2002.

Bowditch, N. *The American Practical Navigator*. Washington, DC: United States Hydrographic Office, 1936 ed.

Boyatzis, R. Consequences and rejuvenation of competency-based human resource and organization development. *Research in Organizational Change and Development*, 9, 1996, 101–122.

Brill, J. M., Bishop, M. J., & Walker, A. E. The competencies and characteristics required of an effective project manager: A web-based Delphi study. *Educational Technology Research and Development* 54, 2006, 115–140.

Brockbank, W. *Aligning HR and Business Strategy*. Presentation at the Human Resource Management Group, Boston, MA. 1999.

Cameron, K., & Quinn, R. *Diagnosing and Changing Organizational Culture Based on the Competing Values Framework*. Reading, MA: Addison-Wesley, 1999.

Cleland, D. *Project Management: Strategic Design and Implementation*. New York, NY: McGraw-Hill, 1994.

Cohen, G., Aronson, J., & Steele, C. When beliefs yield to evidence: Reducing biased evaluation by affirming the self. *Personality and Social Psychology Bulletin*, 26, 2002, 1151–1164.

Collins, J. *Good to Great: Why Some Companies Make the Leap and Others Don't*. New York, NY: Harper Business, 2011.

Conners, R., Smith, T., & Hickman, C. *The OZ Principle: Getting Results Through Individual and Organization Accountability*. New York, NY: Penguin Group, 2004.

Cowley, M., & Domb, E. *Beyond Strategic Vision: Effective Corporate Action with Hoshin Planning.* Boston, MA: Butterworth-Heineman, 1997.

Crainer, S. *The 75 Greatest Management Decisions Ever Made . . . and Some of the Worst Business Leaders Talk About the Good and the Bad.* New York, NY: MJF Books, 2002.

Danish Maritime Accident Investigation, Marine Accident Report, Board, December, 2013

Davis, J. R., Frechette, H. M., & Boswell, E. H. *Strategic Speed: Mobilize People, Accelerate Execution.* Boston, MA: Harvard Business School Press, 2010.

De Wit, B., & Meyer, R. *Strategy: Process, Content, Context: An International Perspective,* 4th ed. Andover, UK: South Western: Cengage Learning, 2010.

De Meuse, K., Dai, G., Hallenback, G., & Tang, K. Using learning agility to identify high potentials around the world. *Korn/Ferry Institute,* 2009.

Dormant, D. The ABCDs of Managing Change. In M. Smith (ed.) Introduction to Performance Technology. Washington, DC: The National Society for Performance and Instruction, 1986.

Ehrlinger, J., Johnson, K., Banner, M., Dunning, D., & Kruger, J. Why the unskilled are unaware: Further explorations of (absent) self-insight among the incompetence. *Organizational Behavior and Human Decision Processes,* 105, 98–121, 2008

Frame, D. *The New Project Management. Tools for an Age of Rapid Change, Corporate Reengineering, and Other Business Realities.* San Francisco, CA: Jossey-Bass, 1994.

Galbraith, J. *Designing Organizations: An Executive Guide to Strategy, Structure and Process.* San Francisco, CA: Jossey Bass, 2002.

———. *Designing the Customer-Focused Organization. A Guide to Strategy, Structure and Process.* New York, NY: John Wiley and Sons, 2005

Goldsmith, M. *What Got You Here Won't Get You There.* New York, NY: Hachette Books, 2007.

———. *Triggers: Creating Behavior That Lasts--Becoming the Person You Want to Be.* New York, NY: Crown Business, 2015.

Guangrong, D, Yang, K., & De Meuse, K. "Leadership competencies across organizational levels: a test of the pipeline model," *Journal of Management Development,* 30, 2011, 366-380.

Guttieri, K., Wallace, M., & Suedfeld, P. The Integrative Complexity of American Decision Makers in the Cuban Missile Crisis. *Journal of Conflict Resolution,* 39, 1995. 595-621.

Harrald, J. R. Agility and Discipline: Critical Success Factors for Disaster Response, *Annals of the American Academy of Political and Social Science* 604, Shelter from the Storm: Repairing the National Emergency Management, 2006, 256–272.

Heyerdahl, T. *Kon Tiki.* New York, NY: Simon & Schuster, 1950.

Hunton, J., & Beeler, J. Effects of user participation in systems development: A longitudinal field experiment. *MIS Quarterly,* 21, 359-388, 1997.

Huy, Q. Five Reasons Most Companies Fail at Strategy Execution. http://knowledge.insead.edu/blog. January 4, 2016

Innosight. *Organizations lack planning and tools to deal with disruptive change.* 2014.

Janis, I. *Groupthink: Psychological Studies of Policy Decisions and Fiascoes,* 2nd ed., rev. Boston, MA: Houghton Mifflin, 1993.

Kahneman D., Lovallo, D., & Sibony, O. Before you make that big decision. *Harvard Business Review*, June, 51-60, 2011.

Kaiser, R. B., Hogan, R., & Craig, S. B. Leadership and the fate of organizations. *American Psychologist*, 63, 2008, 96-110, 2008.

Kanfer, F., & Schefft, B. *Guiding the Process of Therapeutic Change*. Champaign, IL: Research Press, 1998.

Kesler, G., & Kates, A. *Leading Organization Design: How to Make Organizational Design to Drive the Results You Want*. New York, NY: John Wiley and Sons, 2010.

Keystone Associates. A resource for finding your next role, 2011.

Kite-Powell, H., Jin, D., Patrikalakis, N., Jebsen, J., & Papakonstantinou. V. *Investigation of potential risk factors for groundings of commercial vessels in U.S. ports*. IJOPE, 1998.

Knutson, J., & Bitz, I. *Project Management: How to Plan and Manage Successful Projects*. New York, NY: ACACOM, 1991

Kotter, J., & Cohen, D. *The Heart of the Change: Real Life Stories of How People Change their Organizations*. Boston, MA: Harvard Business School Press, 2002.

Kottler, J. *Compassionate Therapy: Working with Difficult Clients*. San Francisco, CA: Jossey-Bass, 1992.

Kouzes, J., & Posner, B. *The Leadership Challenge*, 4th edition. San Francisco, CA: Jossey Bass, 2007.

Kraut, A., Pedigo, P., McKenna D., & Dunnette, M. The role of manager: What's really important in different management jobs. *Academy of Management Perspectives*, 19, 122-129, 2005.

Kruger, J., & Dunning, D. (1999). Unskilled and unaware of it: How difficulties in recognizing one's own incompetence lead to inflated self-assessments. *Journal of Personality and Social Psychology*: 77 (6): 1121–1134.

Kumashiro, M., & Sedikides, C. Taking on board liability-focused feedback: Close personal relationships as a self bolstering resource. *Psychological Science*, 16, 2005, 732–739.

Lepsinger, R. *Closing the Execution Gap: How Great Leaders and Their Companies Get Their Results*. San Francisco, CA: Jossey Bass: A Wiley Imprint, 2010.

Lombardo, M., & Eichinger, *The Leadership Machine: Architecture to Develop Leaders for the Future*. Korn/Ferry International, 2011.

Lord, C. G., Ross, L., & Leppers, M. R. Biased assimilation of and attitude polarization: The effects of prior theories on subsequently considered evidence. *Journal of Personality and Social Psychology*, 37, 2098–2109, 1997.

McKinsey & Company. *The Science of Organizational Transformations*. 2015.

McManus, J. *Information Systems Project Management: Metrics, Tools and Techniques*. London, UK: Financial Times Management.

Mezirow, J. (1991). *Transformative Dimensions of Adult Learning*. San Francisco, CA: Jossey Bass, 1991.

Miller, R., & Heiman, S. *Strategic Selling*. New York, NY: Morrow, 1985.

Morris, P. W. Strategic Issues in Project Management, pp 3–26. In J. K. Pinto, *The Project Management Handbook*. San Francisco, CA: Jossey-Bass, 1998.

Nautical Institute. *Nautical accidents and their causes*. D. Pockett (ed.), 2015.

Nutt, P., & Backoff, R. Transforming organizations with second order change. *Research in Organizational Change and Development* 10, 229–274, 1997.

Osterman, P. *The Truth About Middle Managers: Who They Are, How They Work, and Why They Matter.* Boston, MA: Harvard University Press, 2009.

Overfield, D., & Kaiser, R. *One of every two managers is terrible at accountability.* Harvard Business School Blogs, November, 2012.

Prochaska, J., & DiClemente, C. *The Transtheoretical Approach: Crossing Traditional Boundaries of Therapy.* Malabar, FL: Krieger Publishing, 1984.

Puccio, G., Mance, M., & Murdock, M. *Creative Leadership Skills that Drive Change*, 2nd ed. Los Angeles: CA, Sage, 2010.

PwC. Strategy-execution survey: Key findings. *Strategy&*, 2014.

Quinn, R. *Beyond Rational Management: Mastering the Paradoxes and Competing Demands of High Performance.* San Francisco, CA: Jossey-Bass, 1988.

Quinn, R. *Deep Change.* San Fransisco, CA: Jossey-Bass, 1999.

Rose, T. *Creating a Culture of Engagement and Accountability.* AchieveForum Point of View, 2015.

———. Notes from the Front: Influence patterns in the post-reengineering organization. *National Productivity Review*, Spring, 67-71, 1998.

Rothblum, A. Human Error and Marine Safety. *U.S. Coast Guard Research & Development Center*, 2013.

Samuel, M., & Chiche, S. *The Power of Personal Accountability: Achieves What Matters to You.* Katonah, NY: Xephor Press, 2004.

Samuelides, M., Ventikos, N., & Gemelos, I. Survey on groundling incidents: Statistical analysis and risk assessment. *Ships and Offshore Structures* 4, 2009, 55-68.

Sayles, 1993 cited in Kaiser, R., Hogan, R., & Craig, S. Leadership and the fate of organizations. *American Psychologist*, 63, 2008.

Schaap, J. Toward strategy implementation success: An empirical study of the role of senior level leaders in the Nevada gaming industry, *UNLV Gaming Research & Review Journal*, digital scholarship.unlv.com, 2012.

Schaffer, R. H. *High Impact Consulting: How Clients and Consultants Can Leverage Rapid Results into Long Term Gains.* San Francisco, CA: Jossey-Bass, 1997.

Schein, E. *Process Consultation: Volume II.* Reading, MA: Addison-Wesley Publishing, 1987.

———. *The Corporate Culture Survival Guide.* San Francisco, CA: Jossey-Bass, 1999.

Senge, P., Kleiner, A., Roberts, C., Ross, R., & Smith, B. *Fifth Discipline Field Book: Strategies and Tools for Building a Learning Organization.* New York, NY: Doubleday, 1994.

Stringer, B., & Uchencick, J *Strategy Traps: And How to Avoid Them.* Boston, MA: Lexington Books, 1986.

Sull, D., Homkes, R., & Sull, C. Why Strategy Execution Unravels—and What To Do About It. *Harvard Business Review.* March, 2015, 4-10.

Tabak, F., & Barr, S. Innovation attributes and category membership: Explaining intention to adopt technical innovation in strategic decision making contexts. 1998.

The Economist: Intelligence Unit. Why Good Strategies Fail. Lessons for the C Suite. Sponsored by PMI. London, UK: 2013.

Ulrich, D., Zenger, J., & Smallwood, N. *Results-Based Leadership.* Boston, MA: Harvard Business Review Press, 1999.

Werr, A., Syernberg, T., & Doherty, D. The function of methods of change in management consulting. *Journal of Organizational Change Management* 10, 88–307, 1997.

Willis Towers Watson. *How does change affect employee engagement?* 2015.

Index

Accountability:
  and commitment slips, 65
  drivers of, 35–36
  personal, 221
  senior leader, 221
  shared, for piloting and navigating, 107–109, 111
Accountability suppressors, 124, 132–135
Accountable engagement, 34–37
Accountable influence, 49–54
Acknowledging mistakes, 163–164
Action(s):
  challenges to promoting effective, 102–104
  commitment-promoting, 184–185
  committed, 199
  in Critical Reflection stage, 98, 99
  in effective piloting, 66–67
  at end of Commitment stage, 209
  for getting back on course, 62
  and identity, 162–163
  momentum-building, 96–101
  organizing, 83–86
  in Perseverance stage, 217–218, 225
  perseverance-promoting, 214–217, 225
  reflection-promoting, 158–159
  translating strategic plans into, 54–56
  without adequate reflection, 179
Activity addiction, 124, 131–132, 140, 217
Adaptation, of ideas, 178
Affinity diagrams, 178
Agility, mental, 47, 48
Alignment:
  of goals and plans, 137
  of internal capabilities, 22–28
  for shared vision, 29
  stakeholder, 20–21
Ambassador, leader as, 6
Ambiguity, role, 164
Analogues, 175
Analytical (problem-solving style), 222, 223
Analytics, 115
Anson, George, 2, 9
Appreciation, for progress, 56
Argyris, Chris, 166, 216
Awareness blockers, 125–135
  accountability suppressors, 132–135
  activity addiction, 131–132
  courage killers, 128–131
  described, 123–124
  development of, 135–137
  and Johari window, 125–128

Bavier, Bob, 183
Behavioral change, 63–65, 219–224
Behavioral momentum (*see* Momentum)
Behavioral versatility, 47–49
Behaviors, of high-performing leaders, 10–11, 117–118
Benchmarking, 173–175
Berry, L. L., 172
Biases, 114–115, 122–123, 132
Blame, 136–137, 163
Blind spots, 127, 128 (*See also* Change blindness)
Block, Peter, 48
Bolster, Cliff, 129
Borrowing ideas, 178
Bossidy, Larry, 22, 138

238 ❖ Index

Boswell, E., 132
Bowditch, Nathaniel, 7
Brainstorming, 177–178
Bringing people together, 17–18
Browning, Robert, 143
Budget reports, 58, 201
Budget-related success criteria, 57
Buffet, Warren, 180
Bureaucratic response, 164–166
Business environment:
  being forced to change by, 162
  critical moments in, 78–79
  current disruptions in, 5
  navigating at sea and, 16
  navigational aids for shifting, 2–3
  perseverance in, 213–214
  piloting in, 40–41, 213–214
  support from, 208

Caird (boat), 211–213
Cascading commitment, 37–38, 204
Cause and effect links, plotting, 176–177
Celebrating small wins, 207
Centurion (ship), 2, 9
Change(s):
  abandoning, 65
  ability to, 146, 150
  being forced vs. choosing to make, 162–163
  benefits of, 57, 145–146, 148–149
  challenges with implementing, 4–5, 12
  conditions for successful, 1, 26–27, 31–33
  content of, 223–224
  cost-benefit analysis for, 146–147, 150–151
  deciding not to implement, 180
  discomfort with, 101
  documenting, 25
  failed attempts at, 102
  at healthcare services provider, 3–4
  momentum for, 180
  optimal attempts at, 186–188
  options for, 170
  outcome of, 145, 147–148

Change blindness, 121–141
  accountability suppressors as cause of, 132–135
  activities for breaking through, 137–140
  activity addiction as cause of, 131–132
  awareness blockers causing, 123–135
  and biases in perception, 122–123
  courage killers as cause of, 128–131
  development of, 135–137
  in Great Recession, 121
  and Johari window, 125–128
  transition point related to, 96–97
Change Blindness stage, 141
Change readiness:
  assessing conditions for, 195
  building, 30–33, 89
  conditions for, 79–81, 153
  gaps in, 38, 194–196
  misalignment in management on, 88
  for optimal change attempt, 186–188
  piloting organization with lack of, 64–65
  pre-action assessment of, 102
  and resistance, 71
  synchronization across levels of, 102–103
  at transition points, 95–96
Charan, Ram, 22, 138
Cioran, E., 121, 141
Clarification, 45
Climate surveys, 175
Coach, leader as, 6
Coercion, 162
Cohen, Dan S., 207
Collaboration, 26, 206
Collins, Jim, 135
Combining ideas, 178
Commander (problem-solving style), 222, 223
Commander, leader as, 6
Commitment, 183–209
  to action plan, 83
  actions for promoting, 184–185
  building momentum for, 207–208
  cascading, 37–38
  challenges to building, 185–186

concerns that limit, 205–207
conditions favoring, 204, 208
defined, 190–191
developing, 191–199
in distribution system, 188–190
and optimal change attempts, 186–188
and participation strategies, 203–204
to priorities, 184–185
and project plans, 199–203
slips/lapses in, 65, 100, 103–104, 226
of stakeholders, 82
tools for facilitating, 190–199
Commitment stage:
 action at end of, 209
 conditions for, 80
 and pre-action assessments of readiness, 102
 successful outcomes of, 183–184
Commitment to Initiate Action point, 99–100
Committed action, securing, 199
Common ground, building, 191–192
Communication, about change, 26
Competency studies, 175
Competitive benchmarking, 174
Compliance, commitment vs., 190–191
Conductor, leader as, 6
Confidence, 150–151
Conflict, role, 164
Confusion accountability blocker, 134
Connecting, in accountable influence model, 50–51
Conners, Roger, 133, 135
Control, 136–137, 203, 206
Convince (influence strategy), 52
The Corporate Survival Guide (Schein), 144
Cost-benefit analysis, 146–147, 150–151, 197
Courage, 65, 226
Courage killers, 124, 128–131
"Cover your tail" accountability blocker, 134
Crainer, Stuart, 95
Creative abrasion, 115
Credenza buster phenomenon, 77

Critical deviations, 201
 characteristics of, 58
 identifying/addressing root causes of, 60–61, 217–218
 as "people problems," 60–61, 63–64
 success criteria for solving, 218, 219
Critical moments, 78–79
Critical reflection, 155–181
 acknowledging mistakes in, 163–164
 actions promoting, 158–159
 and being forced vs. choosing to change, 162–163
 in "Bob" case example, 160–161
 focal points of, 164–170
 interventions for, 170–177
 and momentum for change, 180
 preconditions to, 161–162
 on root causes of problems, 177–178
 in Tower Air Flight 41 crash, 155–157
Critical Reflection point, 98–99
Critical Reflection stage:
 actions in, 98, 99
 after slips/lapses in commitment, 104
 challenges in, 179–180
 conditions for, 80
 outcomes of, 157–158
 prompting transition to, 153, 154
 transition from, 180–181
Critical Synchronicity, 105–119
 achieving, 119
 and customer-focused innovation, 113–117
 and empowering context, 112–118
 and high-performance leader behaviors, 117–118
 in nautical model of leadership, 106–107
 of navigating and piloting, 107–112
Culture surveys, 175
Customer audits, 172
Customer service, 172–173
Customer-focused execution, 108
Customer-focused innovation, 113–117
Customer-focused organizations, 38, 223
Customer-focused practices, 113–115
Customers, disclosure to, 221

Davis, J., 132
Deliverables, quality of, 57
Demonstrating, in accountable influence model, 51
Detection of problems, 138–140
Deviations (*see* Critical deviations)
DiClemente, Carlo C., 100
Dilemmas, problems vs., 169
Direction, strategic, 24–25
Discretionary effort, 34
Double learning, 216–217
Dunning, David, 128

Economic threats, 144
Efficiency, ownership and, 37
Eisenhower, Dwight D., 45
Emma Maersk emergency, 143–144
Empowering context, 112–118
  and Critical Synchronicity, 106, 107
  customer-focused innovation in, 113–117
  leader behaviors in, 117–118
  in nautical model of leadership, 11, 13
Empowerment, 164–166
Encouragement, 208
Endurance (ship), 211, 213
Engagement, 34–37, 166
Enthusiasm, 62–63, 185, 199, 218
Entitlement, 125, 127
Exchange (influence strategy), 52
Execution (Bossidy & Charan), 22, 138
Exertion, problems demanding high level of, 205, 221–222

Fear of incompetence, 207
Feedforward, 118
Fishbone analysis, 176
Force field analysis, 198
Frechette, H., 132
Freedom, 162

Getting back on track, 62, 218–219
Gibbon, Edmund, 1
Gide, Andre, 15
Goals:
  accountability and, 135–136
  alignment of plans and, 137
  clarity of, 134–135
  converting, into results, 5–6
  identifying, 45
Goldsmith, Marshall, 118, 128
Great Recession, 121
Greed, 131

Henson, Matthew, 39
Heyerdahl, Thor, 39–40
Hickman, Craig, 133, 135
High-performance leadership system:
  Critical Synchronicity in, 106–112
  implementing change in, 12
  in nautical model of leadership, 11, 13
High-performing leaders:
  behaviors of, 10–11, 117–118
  piloting by, 43–44
  practices of, 5–6
High-performing mariners:
  managing of leading edge by, 70–73
  piloting by, 41–42
Historical reconstruction, 171–172

Idea space, boundaries for, 193
Ideas, solicitation of, 194
Identity, 162–163
Include (influence strategy), 52
Incompetence, fear of, 207
Influence, accountable, 49–54
Influencing, 51–53
Ingham, Harry, 127
Innovation, 113–117
Innovator (problem-solving style), 222, 223
Insight, customer, 114–115
Internal benchmarking, 174
Internal capabilities, aligning, 22–28
Internal threats, 144
"It's not my job" accountability blocker, 133

Jobs, Steve, 105
Jobson, Gary, 70–73
Johari window, 124–128

Kon-Tiki expedition, 39–41
Kotter, John P., 207

Kottler, Jeffrey A., 153
Kruger, Justin, 128

Leaders, readiness factors for, 32 (*See also* High-performing leaders; Senior leaders)
Leading edge, 8–9, 69 (*See also* Managing of leading edge; Transition points)
Leading Edge model, 96–101
Learning, double, 216–217
Learning-based innovation, 115–117
Lehman Brothers, 121, 123, 131
Longitude (Sobel), 2
Loring, David, 70–71
Luft, Joe, 127

MacArthur, Ellen, 223–224
Management updates, 59
Managing of leading edge, 69–89
　and Critical Synchronicity, 112
　in "High Top, Inc." case example, 73–75
　by high-performing mariners, 70–73
　in nautical model of leadership, 8
　planning guide for, 104
　and project management, 76–81
　readiness-based approach to, 89
　steps in, 81–89
　work management tools for, 75
Martin, Mike, 70
McManus, John, 64, 220
Mental agility, 47, 48
Merton, Thomas, 155
Mezirow, Jack, 164
Midlevel managers:
　in change implementation, 12, 26–27
　piloting by, 42
　prerogative of, 136–137
Milestone charts, 58–59, 201–202
Mistakes, acknowledging, 163–164
Momentum:
　for change, 180
　for commitment, 207–208
　as goal of change, 209
　maintenance of, 101
　over time, 78

　in piloting, 56–57
　stalled, 219–223
　at transition points, 96–101
Monitoring:
　of impact of change, 87–89
　performance, 57–59, 201–203
　of progress against plan, 200–203
Moral threats, 144
Motivation, 65, 99, 225–226

National Maritime Museum (Greenwich, England), 15, 226
National Transportation Safety Board (NTSB), 156
Nautical model of high-performance leadership, 6–11
　components of, 7–10
　Critical Synchronicity in, 106–107
　current leadership models vs., 6
　overview, 11, 13
　research supporting, 10–11
Navigating, 15–38
　and accountable engagement, 34–37
　bringing people together in, 17–18
　building readiness in, 30–33
　challenges to, 37–38
　at consumer products company, 18–21
　core skills of, 21–22
　creating vision in, 28–30
　maintaining vigilance and aligning internal capabilities in, 22–28
　miscues between piloting and, 110
　in nautical model of leadership, 7–8
　outcomes of successful, 16–17
　piloting vs., 7–8
　process of, 19–20
　at sea and in business environment, 16
　by ship's captains, 1–2
　synchronization of piloting and, 20, 41–42, 107–112
Needs, stakeholders', 149
Negative past experiences, 152
Network of quality relationships, 51
Networking, 148
NTSB (National Transportation Safety Board), 156

Optimal change attempt, 186–188
Organizational change, 150
Organizational navigation (*see* Navigating)
Organizational needs of stakeholders, 149
Organizational piloting (*see* Piloting)
Organizations:
   customer-focused, 38, 223
   design of, 24–25
   readiness factors for, 31
   stalled momentum in, 219–223
Outcome(s):
   of change, 145, 147–148
   clarity about, 206
   of Commitment stage, 183–184
   conceptualizing, 81–83
   of Critical Reflection stage, 157–158
   of Perseverance stage, 224
   of successful navigating, 16–17
   of successful piloting, 43–44
   tasks in support of, 84
Overextended personal finances, 130
Overselling benefits of projects, 152
Ownership, 37, 203
The Oz Principle (Connors, Smith, & Hickman), 135

Parasuraman, A., 172
Pareto analysis, 176–177
Participation:
   concerns about, 205–207
   conditions for, 37
   effective strategies for, 203–204
Patience, 205
"People problems," 60–61, 63–64
Perception, biases in, 122–123
Performance monitoring, 57–59, 201–203
Perseverance, 211–226
   actions promoting, 214–217, 225
   in business environment, 213–214
   challenges to, 219–226
   and getting back on track, 218–219
   in Shackleton expedition, 211–213
Perseverance point, 100–101
Perseverance stage:
   actions in, 217–218, 225
   conditions for, 81
   discomfort in, 101
   target outcomes for, 224
Persistence, 65, 71
Personal accountability, 221
Personal change, 150, 168
Personal finances, 130
Personal needs of stakeholders, 149
Person-job fit, 130–131
Pilot programs, 198
Piloting, 39–67
   actions for effective, 66–67
   challenges to, 63–65
   core skills of, 44
   exerting accountable influence in, 49–54
   focusing teams in, 45–46
   in *Kon-Tiki* expedition, 39–41
   miscues between navigating and, 110
   in nautical model of leadership, 7–8
   navigating vs., 7–8
   outcomes of successful, 43–44
   problem solving in, 47–49
   at sea and in business environment, 40–41, 213–214
   strategic thinking in, 46–47
   synchronization of navigating and, 20, 41–42, 107–112
   tools for implementing, 54–63
Political maneuvering, 125–127
Political threats, 144
Positive expectations, 56
Preparation, by high performers, 70–71
Prerogative, 136–137
Prescribe (influence strategy), 53
Problem recognition (*see* Recognition of problem)
Problem solving:
   in change implementation, 27
   easy vs. better solution from, 221–222
   personal styles of, 222–223
   in piloting, 47–49
   supportive environments for, 138–140
Process mapping, 175–176
Prochaska, James O., 100
Progress reviews, 59, 202

Project management practices, 76–81
Project plans, 199–203
  building, 199–200
  finalizing, 185
  implementing, 88
  keeping, on track, 59
  monitoring progress against, 200–203
  readiness-based, 86
  recalibrating, 61, 216, 217
  reevaluating changes to, 64
  from strategic priorities, 55–56
Pulling up and across, 17–18, 108

Questions, recognition, 145–152

Readiness for change (*see* Change readiness)
Readiness management, 76–81
Readiness-based approach:
  commitment to action plan in, 82, 83
  process and content in, 89
  resolving threat to deliverable in, 85
  work planning in, 87
Recognition of problem, 143–154
  answers to questions for, 147–152
  in *Emma Maersk* emergency, 143–144
  questions for building, 145–147
  setting stage for, 137–138, 141
  and types of work threats, 144
Recognition point, 97
Recognition stage:
  conditions for, 79, 153
  transition from, 153, 154
  transition to, 125, 141
Reflection:
  acting without adequate, 179
  critical (*see* Critical reflection)
Reputation index, 34–35
Resistance:
  actions when encountering, 153
  beliefs inspiring, 91
  and change readiness, 71
  eliciting, 26
  and managing of leading edge, 8–9
Resources, optimizing, 45
Rewards, distribution of, 135

Role conflict (role ambiguity), 164
Root cause analysis, 176, 216–217
Root causes of problems:
  addressing, 60–61, 177–178
  identifying, 60–61, 170–171, 217–218
  and options for change, 170
Rothblum, Anita M., 60–61

Samuel, Mark, 135
Schaffer, Robert, 186
Schein, Edgar H., 144
Scope, project, 32–33
Self-awareness, 127–128
Self-esteem, 163–164
Senior leaders:
  accountability of, 221
  assertions of control by, 136–137
  change implementation by, 12
  collaboration of, 26
  updates for, 59, 202
75 Greatest Management Decisions Ever Made (Crainer), 95
Shackleton, Ernest, 211–213
Sherar, M. G., 105
Simulations, 175
Situation analysis, 170–171
Small-scale pilot programs, 198
Smith, Tom, 133, 135
Sobel, Dava, 2
Stakeholder(s):
  aligning, 20–21
  building relationships with, 49
  commitment of, 82
  critical reflection for multiple, 179–180
  needs/interests of, 148–149
Stakeholder satisfaction, 57
Status reports, 59, 202
Strategic direction, 24–25
Strategic initiatives, 23–24, 70
Strategic priorities, 54–56
Strategic Speed (Davis, Frechette, & Boswell), 132
Strategic thinking, 46–47
Strengths, weaknesses, opportunities, threats (SWOT) analysis, 22–23, 171

Stressors, exposure to, 208
Success criteria:
   establishing, 57, 200, 218, 219
   and getting back on course, 62
   monitoring performance against, 58–59, 201–202
Sully (film), 112
Superordinate purpose of managing leading edge, 76–78
Support, from environment, 208
SWOT (strengths, weaknesses, opportunities, threats) analysis, 22–23, 171
Synchronization:
   of change readiness, 102–103
   in nautical model, 9
   of piloting and navigating, 20, 41–42, 107–112
   (*See also* Critical Synchronicity)
Systems analysis, 175–176
Szabo, George, 71

Task approach, 77, 82, 83, 85
Tasks, in support of outcomes, 84
Team player (problem-solving style), 222, 223
Teams:
   abandoning solutions from, 221
   capability of working on, 207
   focusing, 45–46
   poor results from, 206
Technological threats, 144
Threats, 85, 144
Time, as success criteria, 57
Time sheets, 58, 201
Torrey Canyon (cargo ship), 60–61
Tower Air Flight 41 crash, 155–157, 166
Trade-offs, evaluating, 178
Transition points, 91–104
   actions to build momentum at, 96–101

   in "Joe" case example, 92–95
   and managing of leading edge, 72–73
   optimizing change readiness at, 95–96
   promoting effective action at, 102–104
Transmission belt, leader as, 6
The Transtheoretical Approach (Prochaska and DiClemente), 100
Trust, 115, 146–147, 151–152

Uncertainties, reducing, 57
Undiscussable issues, 166–169
Upward influence, 53

Value-feasibility analysis, 196–197
Vigilance, maintaining, 22–23, 63
Vision:
   boundaries that reflect, 193
   common/shared, 20, 28–30, 184, 192
   helping people to have, 152

"Wait and see" accountability blocker, 133–134
Walker, Stuart H., 69, 91
"Ways of working," 117
Welch, Jack, 22, 26, 116
Work breakdown structure, 54–55, 82
Work environment:
   accountability drivers in, 35–36
   for problem solving, 138–140
Work management tools, 75
Work threats, 144
Work units, hierarchy of, 54–55
World-class benchmarking, 174
Worsley, Frank, 212, 213

Yukl, Gary, 190

Zeithaml, V. A., 172

About the Author

Tom Rose, PhD, is a psychologist with over 25 years of experience as both an outside consultant and an HR leader. Rose's experience equips him with an inside-outside perspective on how organizations implement strategic change and how they best position their leaders to succeed at this challenging but vital activity.

As an executive coach and facilitator, Rose has helped clients develop the agility needed to successfully negotiate the organizational, team, and people issues that confront leaders who do things in a different way to achieve different results.

As an HR leader, Rose has facilitated the implementation of large organizational changes and helped architect people processes that companies have used to implement shifts in strategy and culture.

Currently, Tom leads Innovation and Customer Solutions at AchieveForum, a leading leadership development firm. At AchieveForum, he works with colleagues and clients to build and implement evidence-based leadership development programs that help leaders acquire the insight and skills needed to implement change that sticks.